books by **Lisa Russ Spaar**

Vanitas, Rough
All That Mighty Heart: London Poems
Satin Cash
The Land of Wandering
Blue Venus
Acquainted with the Night: Insomnia Poems
Glass Town
Blind Boy on Skates
Cellar

books by **Drunken Boat Media**

Radha Says: Last Poems by Reetika Vazirani (2010)

Cover art from photograph "Lung" donated and used by permission of Allyson Clay.

Cover Design by Claire Zoghb.

Interior Book Design by Bailey Lewis.

Copyediting and proofreading by David Harrison Horton, Managing Editor, and Ravi Shankar, Executive Director of *Drunken Boat*.

These essays appeared in earlier form in *The Chronicle of Higher Education's* Arts & Academe and Brainstorm blogs. This book's publication and promotion were made possible in part by grants from the University of Virginia, Central Connecticut State University, from our Board of Advisors and from our loyal readers who contributed during our Kickstarter campaign, made possible by Director of Development, Michele Battiste.

For more information on helping sustain the arts online and out in the world, and to interact with the best multigenre work in one of the world's oldest electronic journals of the arts, please visit Drunken Boat at [http://www.drunkenboat.com].

Printed by Book Mobile [Bookmobile.com] and available at [Amazon.com]
Library of Congress Cataloging-in-Publication Data
Spaar, Lisa Russ. "The Hide-and-Seek Muse: Annotations of Contemporary Poetry."
Drunken Boat Media (2013)
ISBN# 978-0-9882416-0-2 (pbk.)
Drunken Boat ISSN #1537-2812

TABLE OF CONTENTS

TABLE OF CONTENTS

TABLE OF CONTENTS

TABLE OF CONTENTS

INTRODUCTION
Nick Flynn, December 2012

This book in your hands—while reading through it for the first time, just now, I very nearly burned the brown rice I was cooking for dinner. I went into the kitchen just now to check on it (the rice)—I must have heard something, or smelled something—a crackle, a burning. Burnt offering, I thought, stirring it. I put the lid on and went back to the world of this book, the book in your hands. I have now lived with it for days, but that first time I got caught up in a poem by Mary Szybist, then a poem by Kazim Ali, then a poem by Joanna Klink. I felt completely alive reading the poems, then reading Lisa Russ Spaar's open and generous and brilliant commentary I felt the world opening. The universe is expanding, inexorably pushing into the void, we know this, but it's not often you get to feel it. We're living in an incredibly rich time for poetry—I tell people that, if asked, and I'm never sure if they believe me, or if they understand. A rich, yet essentially invisible moment, for poetry always lives below the surface. I met the director (& personal hero) Jim Jarmusch once, at a dinner party, I told him I was a poet, and he was, or seemed to be, genuinely interested in finding out about this world, and so I promised I would make him a little packet of poems, but I never did. Or, rather, I made the packet, but never found a way to get it into his hands. I never found his hands again. On the other side of us at that dinner was a woman who played cello for the Houston Opera, Jarmusch knew what type of wood her cello was made of (sycamore maple), and why (tone). He asked me if I listened to DJ Screw, the Houston hiphop star who invented the genre known as "syrup," so named for the codeine cough syrup he ingested (and which eventually killed him) which made his raps languid. Welcome to Houston. Jarmusch is a hero because we're living in a shitty time for Hollywood movies, maybe even for novels from big publishing houses, but poetry (and song) are somehow thriving, thriving in this darkness, like strange beautiful mushrooms. I turned off the flame under the rice pot—it's going to be okay, it will keep cooking in the pot as it cools, it will be perfect. I've also said, recently, that everything, it seems, is a daily practice, or at least everything that matters, at least everything that matters to me. I get the sense that this book in your hands could become part of a daily practice, that these poems, alongside Lisa Russ Spaar's truly thrilling commentary, could be a way to infuse poetry into every moment, or to simply reveal how it is already infused, if we can find the thresholds. I think I'll light some incense, I have a pack of matches in my hand, a black pack of matches with a white mermaid on one side and the word "foc'sle" on the other side. "Foc'sle," I believe, is a window in the hull of a boat. A threshold. I want to write Lisa an email, thank her. I want to eat a bowl of short grain brown rice. My daughter is with the downstairs neighbors, watching a movie—it's movie night. I don't know what movie they are watching, I will ask when she comes back upstairs. I promise if you sit with this book for an hour, or even five minutes, or, even better, play hookie for a day, or stay up later than you should, if you spend some time with this book you will find not what you sought, but something as yet unimagined. Have we been talking all this time? The mermaid matches are still in my hand, my head is in my hand, I keep reading poem after poem, I can smell the sulphur, the incense is waiting, the rice is waiting, they have been waiting all along, as Rilke pointed out in one of the Duino Elegies, how did I forget that? How lucky I am, we are, to have found these hours, these days, these poems, and to have Lisa Russ Spaar as my, as our, Virgil, to lead us through them.

PREFACE & ACKNOWLEDGMENTS

In September 2010, Alexander Kafka, deputy managing editor of the *Chronicle of Higher Education Review*, asked me if I'd be interested in writing as a poetry editor/blogger for a new Arts & Academe on-line poetry feature of the *Review*. On October 4, 2010, we posted the first of what became a regular offering, "Monday's Poem"—a weekly presentation of a new poem by a contemporary American poet, a different poet each week, accompanied by my commentary. Once every month or so from that fall until July 2012, I also wrote a column in which I meditated on some aspect of contemporary poetry. From the start, the venture had no overarching design or program. My only charge was to write about current, compelling poetry for readers who are intelligent and interested in poetry but who might not necessarily be poets. The only other stipulation made by the *Chronicle* was that I consider for presentation poets with some sort of university or other higher education affiliation and/or who publish with a college or university press. We did not know what to expect when we launched the feature, but "Monday's Poem" and the monthly columns attracted a devoted following of readers in and outside of the academy, many of them poets. Although no agenda informed these weekly selections, they almost by necessity came to reflect what Ezra Pound called "the tone of the time." Whether or not the columns and commentaries articulate the Zeitgeist of American poetry at the start of the second decade of the new millennium, the poems I've been privileged to present are aesthetically and culturally diverse, representing fresh work by well-known as well as emerging poets from a wide array of formal, political, and other perspectives, all attuned to issues of originality, influence, debt, and innovation that have ever stalked and emboldened American poetry.

About a year ago, the poet, editor, and publisher Ravi Shankar suggested that we consider collecting some of these *Chronicle* poems, commentaries, and columns into a book, creating a gallery of sorts, a locus, a space in which individual poems and musings might be allowed to resonate with one another and invite the kind of perspective and significance that only deliberate and concerted gatherings allow. An ardent anthologizer, I love the ways in which, when brought into proximity, what is disparate, diverse, and manifold becomes freshly illuminated. What had been for me an almost devotional exercise—to respond to a contemporary poem in the two or three free hours I could devote each week for the task—became something even more as I began to imagine ways of gathering the poems together for a book. The endeavor raised questions: is it possible to characterize American poetry being written in the second decade of the twenty-first century? Who are our ancestors?

Our heirs? What is our future? In what ways are poets responding to and shaping the force of our volatile times? What can bringing these poems into conversation reveal about what engages and animates and provokes American poets working in the present moment, and why should we care?

The work compiled here comes from established, award-winning poets like Charles Wright, Carl Phillips, Carol Muske-Dukes, Claudia Emerson, and Philip Schultz, and also from younger writers such as Kiki Petrosino, Allison Seay, Kazim Ali, Kyle Dargan, Paul Legault, and Jennifer Chang. Some of the poets tend toward more traditional, formal approaches (Mark Jarman, John Poch, Eric Pankey) while others are avant-garde or experimental (Brian Teare, Hank Lazer, Heather McHugh, Srikanth Reddy, Brenda Hillman). Narrative, dramatic, lyric, mashed, crossed, hybrid—the voices represented are repercussively American, and in context and conversation with one another convey a partial sense of an evolving, plural, and kinetic notion of contemporary American poetic attitude and inclination—perhaps even identity. This mesh of influence (Susan Howe: "My precursor attracts me to my future") is felt throughout the collection, as in Debra Allbery's ghazal "Of Evanescence," which culminates in a multi-cultural and pan-temporal conflation of speakers (Allbery, Agha Shahid Ali, Emily Dickinson, and Herman Melville) or as in Paul Legault's Emily Dickinson "translation" project, in which he feistily talks back to Dickinson's gnomic verses, rendering them into aphoristic, provocative, and witty one-liners. In poems like "While Sylvia Plath Studies *The Joy of Cooking* On Her Honeymoon In Benidorm, Spain, Delmore Schwartz Reclines In The Front Seat Of His Buick Roadmaster," Amy Newman attempts to capture chordal glimpses of American poetry itself coming into being.

In curating the work that follows, I settled on the organizational trope of a year, choosing twelve of the monthly columns around which I constellated 52 of the weekly individual poet/poem commentaries in an intuitive way that sometimes had to do with style, at others with theme or innovation or impulse. The monthly columns themselves also mention and include a number of poems by poets not numbered among the 52, including Ron Slate, Philip Schultz, Sarah Schweig, Rachel Hadas, Willie Lin, and David Francis, allowing me both to exploit and transgress any sort of overly programmed approach while at the same time honoring the seasonal and temporal motions that very much informed my ongoing selections and themes each week. Importantly, including poems within my poetry columns sometimes allowed me to feature strong work being done by poets not affiliated with the academy or an academic press. I came to interpret in the most open terms the *Chronicle's* request that I situate the poetry I was presenting in relation to "higher education," with "higher" coming to stand more broadly for inspiration, exhilaration, and intensity. Coleridge called poetry the "best words in their best order." Charles Wright says that poetry is simply language that "sounds better and means more." It is that kind of "higher" and that kind of "education" that I hope these poems reflect.

In *Writing Space: The Computer, Hypertext, and the History of Writing*, Jay David Bolter points out, in relation to Roland Barthes's *S/Z*, that "a commentary is by nature a series of interruptions." Attempting to unpack or offer close readings of a new poem each week sometimes felt, to paraphrase Emily Dickinson, like splitting open the lark in order to find the music. If my remarks on this intrinsically rich work feel to the reader at times like perverse "interruptions" of the poems themselves, I hope that recompensatory flashes of insight nonetheless ensue in the fissures, forays, and interstices the commentaries afford.

Because of the nature of its origins in a weekly blog column of poems intended primarily for the "page" or screen, this collection is not meant to nor could it ever be comprehensive or historical, nor could it begin to represent the many streams and voices and experiments being undertaken now in American poetry, especially in the realm of spoken word and other performative endeavors, or with regard to projects by poets working in visually experimental ways (we quickly learned at the *Chronicle* the limitations of our blogging software when we attempted to present work with unusual formatting). But what assembling these poems in one place does suggest is that American poets are doing what they have always done: restlessly sampling and borrowing and ignoring and trampling the vineyard and forging and foraging and questioning and making things new. It has been said that American poetry can in part be characterized by the difference between the invocatory petitions of Homer's "Sing, O Goddess, the anger of Achilles" or Shakespeare's "O, for a Muse of fire" and Whitman's fiercely individual and independent "I celebrate myself, and sing myself." The process of compiling these essays suggests, however, that early twenty-first-century American poems, like poetry for centuries, continue to defy neat categorizations. And contemporary poets continue to be both fueled and frustrated by the Muses, by Eros and Thanatos. Age-old themes—love, death, memory, art, desire, God-hunger, fear, time, being, politics, beauty, change, truth, mutability, the absurd, language, the pulse of poetry itself—are particularly challenged in our moment by keen awarenesses of the perils, contingencies, nascence, and velocities of technology—linguistic, social, cultural, environmental, political, global—and by urgent political and environmental threats as well as new senses of what constitutes materiality, style, and virtuosity. Even in poems of high lyricism or narrative plain speech, I see a new and renewed, daring interest in excavating, restoring, and breaking with the past; in inter-textuality; in sampling; in collaborative voicing.

In a seminal essay written over thirty years ago, "Pound/Stevens: Whose Era?," Marjorie Perloff explores oppositional aesthetic streams and "mutual distrust" in American poetry in the late twentieth century. The early new millennium poems in *The Hide-and-Seek Muse* suggest to me not so much the question of "whose century is it?" but "whose century isn't it?" With the proliferation of MFA programs in the past three or four decades; the popularity and accessibility of the spoken word surge and a cosmos of cyber-venues; anxiety about who is and is not anthologized into the canon; dramatic changes—philosophical, technological, cultural— in how literature is published, disseminated, and promoted; and the "them what gets, gets" po-biz prize culture, not to mention the fact that there are probably more poets in any one apartment building in Brooklyn than in my entire town, it is important always to refresh and refresh again our awareness of what is being written, and why, and of what in our legacy is therefore being honored, forgotten, transformed, even as new thresholds, new anatomies are being shut down, but also created, made possible. Extension and rupture. Rupture and extension. "Touch the universe anywhere," wrote poet A. R. Ammons, and "you touch it everywhere." Now more than ever this rings true—with regard to American poetry, and in relation to the praxis and theory of writing in general.

As with all anthologies, the great regret is what must, because of constraints of space or for reasons of theme and focus, be omitted from this particular conversation. Every one of the *Chronicle* poems, commentaries, and columns written since the inception of the series is archived at the *Chronicle Review*, and I refer readers interested in exploring the whole menu of included writers to that website, and to the now defunct Arts & Academe and Brainstorm blogs in particular.

I must thank first my discerning, gifted, good-natured *Chronicle* editor, Alex Kafka, for inviting me to undertake this weekly endeavor in the first place. Writing "Monday's Poem" has been an education for me, and working with him each week an enlightening pleasure. That the *Chronicle of Higher Education* allowed Alex and me to bring our passion for poetry into the realm and discourse of the academy in this way for nearly two years is also cause for gratitude.

I am deeply indebted to the intrepid Ravi Shankar for believing that these pieces warranted a more permanent home between the covers of a book, and then offering to publish that book under the imprimatur and auspices of his bold and beautiful Drunken Boat Media enterprise. Ardent thanks to Nick Flynn for offering his fresh, inimitable lens on the project.

Every writer involved in the "Monday's Poem" project has impressed me again and again with his or her unique poetic gifts and great generosity in sharing work with me and with our readers. I think I speak for the poets as well as for myself in thanking the *readers* of the Chronicle offerings, as well. I proffer a special shout-out to the indefatigable and gracious Don Selby and Diane Boller at *Poetry Daily*, who kindly linked the *Chronicle* pieces at their news page every Monday.

Several colleagues—chiefly Stephen Cushman, Jerry McGann, Debra Nystrom, and Jahan Ramazani—have been especially supportive and helpful since the inception of the *Chronicle* series. My poetry students, by their own poetic examples and in our discussions in seminars and workshops, have helped to shape each and every one of these pieces. Special thanks to June Webb for her assistance at every step of the way. Generous support from the John Simon Guggenheim Foundation and from a Carole Weinstein Poetry award afforded deeply welcomed sustenance, emotional and otherwise, during the making of this book. Finally, I am grateful to the University of Virginia and in particular to the Office of the Vice President for Research and the College of Arts and Sciences, whose assistance in the form of an Arts, Humanities, and Social Sciences research award helped invaluably in the completion of this project.

This book is dedicated with love to Jocelyn, Adam, and Suzannah—my Muses, and poets three.

WHITMAN & DICKINSON IN OUR SPACE

WHITMAN & DICKINSON IN OUR SPACE

We live in a time of rampant, mercurial self-portrayal. We can, if we wish, post, profile, tag, chat, friend, transform, lie, project, stalk, date, connect, complicate, simplify, vex, blog, tumble, pin, like, and identify ourselves with dazzling velocity through a protean real-time landscape of social networks, ranging from the ubiquitous Facebook to virtual communities enmeshed by an interest in couch-surfing, opera, anime, and an array of signifying passions whose devotees, virtual and real, are forming and communing and falling apart even as I type.

Poetry—American lyric poetry, in particular—has always engaged in a paradoxical relationship with selfhood, identity, and influence. "I celebrate myself," Walt Whitman pronounced in 1855, revealing later in the same poem a mad, collective desire to be "quiver[ed] to a new identity." Whitman's sister poetic American innovator, Emily Dickinson, wrote "I'm nobody! Who are you?" but could not have been more concerned with the spiritual, emotional, and erotic circumference of the discreet self, what she would call that "Campaign inscrutable / Of the Interior":

> I felt my life with both my hands
> To see if it was there—
> I held my spirit to the Glass,
> To prove it possibler—
>
> I turned my Being round and round
> And paused at every pound
> To ask the Owner's name—
> For doubt, that I should know the sound—.

Their poetic personae were various and contradictory. Whitman could be, by turns, a sensuous speaker of the nation, a vital man, "one of the roughs," or a depraved, broken, street-bound beggar. Dickinson could be coy and childlike, or ferociously masterful ("Title divine, is mine / The Wife without the Sign"), leading Camille Paglia to call her the Madame de Sade of Amherst.

Whitman and Dickinson both composed and copied much of their work on scraps of paper and in small notebooks or hand-stitched booklets. Dickinson wrote at a table the size of a child's desk. How did the exigencies of nineteenth-century life and the technologies of writing culture inform the poems they made—Whitman, the printer, with his choice of an oversized folio for his quicksilver tonal shifts, his relentless lists and cataloging? Or Dickinson's wildly compressed, volatile, arguably Twitterable and hypertextual scribal explosions that often flooded and confounded the page at hand?

How will our rapid-fire technologies—our implacable, virtual networks, tiny screens and keyboards, our busy thumbs—affect the poems we make as we move through the second decade of the twenty-first century? In what ways, if at all, will the writing spaces we inherit and inhabit, and the ways in which we mark them, reflect and create our sense of or unconcern with selfhood in the American lyric poem and how that consciousness is communicated? How will our innovations speak to our influences, literary and extra-literary?

I have students who speak their ideas for poems into their cell phones, which puts me mind of Wordsworth, composing as he walked. Others take up Gertrude Stein and others' avant-garde thread, playing with Flarf, Spoetry, Spamlit, Word salad, and other continually morphing, generative modes that challenge canonical approaches and plunder technologies with intelligence, energy, and subversion—a fresh takes on Hart Crane's "new thresholds, new anatomies."

That poetry continues to explore human consciousness in its slippery, manifest, and veiled complexity binds me to its emerging voices and embodiments. What is the American self inherited and forged in the increasingly multi-cultural and cross-genre American poem? What is the American poem in such a context? I love the ways in which the hybrid autobiographical verses of Kazim Ali's *Bright Felon* or Jennifer Chang's post-pastoral *History of Anonymity*, for example, talk back to both Dickinson and Whitman while exploring cinema, physics, legend, and politics with current attention and savvy. Charles Wright once quipped, "If your backyard is just your backyard, you might as well crack open another Budweiser." In American poems, the turf of the private self will always represent more than itself, formally, linguistically, culturally. That the opposite is also true is also cause to read and make poems.

THE HIDE-AND-SEEK MUSE

THE HIDE-AND-SEEK MUSE

My father, a smart man, believes that poetry is out to trick him, a fact apparent in the deer-in-the-headlights discomfort he exhibits whenever I present him with one of my books or a poem by one of the grandchildren. Coleridge's assertion that poetry is "the best words in their best order" would be a laughable notion to him, a man who prefers to get the news from *The Washington Post* and the *Journal of the American Chemical Society*. And it's not just lay readers who find poetry difficult. Some of my brightest English majors feel this way. The chair of a local high school English Department shared with me that her colleagues are so afraid of poetry that they find ways to avoid teaching it altogether. When faced with the task of coming up with a "definition" of poetry for a state curricular rubric, her group was unable to begin to frame a response, let alone reach a consensus. They finally came up with something like "unusual language that sometimes rhymes and sometimes doesn't."

I'm quite sure I can't come up with a single definition of poetry either. But I suspect that the most resistant or wary readers of verse, even if they can't say what poetry is, have written or received a poem—in a love letter, a diary, a condolence card, a Valentine, a school assignment—a bit of language written under especial duress or frustration or longing or sadness, language forged under pressure, perhaps at a Dickinsonian "White Heat," words that came out not as prose but as something else, something more . . . intense, musical, playful, figurative, compressed. Something urgently expressed, with something at stake in the telling.

The New Jersey poet and physician William Carlos Williams is well known for saying that "It is difficult / to get the news from poems / yet men die miserably every day / for lack / of what is found there." Back when I was directing the Master of Fine Arts in Creative Writing program at the University of Virginia, I used to get at least one telephone call every two or three weeks from citizens seeking a poem recommendation, something appropriate for a funeral, a wedding, an anniversary, a birthday. The calls were especially heavy, as one might imagine, on September 11, 2001, and in the wake of Hurricane Katrina. For emotional, psychic, intellectual sustenance—for inspiration, solace, and a reminder of what it means to be fully human—nothing quite affects us like poetry.

Yet like my high school English teacher friend and her faculty, readers of poetry come to the art with a wide, diverse spectrum of expectations, tastes, predilections, desires. This subjectivity was brought home to me afresh recently in a graduate poetry seminar. We were reading Gertrude Stein's *Tender Buttons*, a text by an author famous for her hermetic poetic experiments, syntactical innovations, and associative linguistic theatrics. A few students had the predictable reaction of wanting, at least initially, to throw the book across the room. Another young woman, who was suffering from a head cold, admitted that she'd begun to appreciate Stein only after she'd consumed some sinus medication and began to rap the poems aloud; this confession inspired an impromptu performance of "Mutton," with a particularly adept classmate providing the bass backbeat soundtrack. Other students in the class, however, a surprising number, found themselves "moved" by the beauty of poems—as language, as music, as testaments of intimacy, eroticism, and love, as in these lines from "A Long Dress":

What is the current that makes machinery, that makes it crackle, what is the current that presents a
long line and a necessary waist. What is this current.

What is the wind, what is it.

Where is the serene length, it is there and a dark place is not a dark place, only a white and red are black, only a yellow and green are blue, a pink is scarlet, a bow is every color. A line distinguishes it. A line just distinguishes it.

Readers, then, with our various "negative capabilities," our distinct temperamental inclinations and varying tolerances for order, for chaos, are drawn, if we're attracted to poetry at all, to different poets and poetic styles. Some of us prefer poems in plain speech, what Heather McHugh has called, in her introduction to *Broken English: Poetry and Partiality*, a "very windexed window," in which "language intends to dissolve in the service of its meaning." Other readers like to get caught in the net of language, Paul Celan's *hindurchgehen*, that going back again through the word-mesh, where the world is not only reflected but created. "That," McHugh writes, "is why poetry is not exposition. It is the place that suffers inscription. It bears the mark or scar of what was seen and what was grasped. . . . It takes upon itself, into itself, what it sees; the song is of insight . . . . it requires you to face the difficulty, the unfathomability, of your life."

In her essay "Invitation and Exclusion," which explores why some poets inspire us as readers and writers while others seem to leave us outside, to shut us down, Louise Glück writes, "The poems from which I feel excluded are not poems from which I can learn. Neither are they poems I can ignore." Some among us will never make reading poetry a practice or habit, despite that closet poem I suspect even my father has squirreled away somewhere. What Glück, McHugh, Stein, and others remind me to do, though, is to make a more active practice of reading (and even writing) poems outside my comfort zone. My own propensity is for the compressed, brocaded, gnomic, and interior lyric. All the more reason, then, for me to delve again into the beauties and gifts of more transparent poems or longer, more narrative pieces, and to challenge and inspire myself, as reader and writer, with aesthetics and sensibilities alien to my own. As Dickinson puts it in a poem from 1861, "A transport one cannot contain / May yet, a transport be—."

EDWARD HIRSCH

To Poetry

Don't desert me
just because I stayed up last night
watching *The Lost Weekend.*

I know I've spent too much time
praising your naked body to strangers
and gossiping about lovers you betrayed.

I've stalked you in foreign cities
and followed your far-flung movements,
pretending I could describe you.

Forgive me for getting jacked on coffee
and obsessing over your features
year after jittery year.

I'm sorry for handing you a line
and typing you on a screen,
but don't let me suffer in silence.

Does anyone still invoke the Muse,
string a wooden lyre for Apollo,
or try to saddle up Pegasus?

Winged horse, heavenly god or goddess,
indifferent entity, secret code, stored magic,
pleasance and half wonder, hell,

I have loved you my entire life
without even knowing what you are
or how—please help me—to find you.

Not a Sunday goes by since its passing out of tabloid insert print format in February 2009 that I do not mourn and miss *The Washington Post Book World,* a fixture of my weekends since I first moved to Virginia in the 1970s. For the better part of a decade in the 1980s, when I lived in Texas, I continued to subscribe to and receive the *Book World* by snail mail. And for a three-year spell, from 2002 – 2005, I looked forward especially to Edward Hirsch's column, "Poet's Choice," a weekly meditation in the *Book World* on some aspect of poetry to which Hirsch would bring his widely read, articulate, capacious, encyclopedic, and ardent discernment. What Hirsch has elsewhere written of Keats—that he "combined . . . associative drift with a startling openheartedness and a ferocious working intellect, the mind of a maker"—might be said of Hirsch as poet and essayist as well.

By the time Hirsch began presenting his Poet's Choice column in the years immediately following the September 11th tragedy, I already knew and admired his poems, which I'd been reading since the early eighties. These Poet's Choice columns—like his poems—always seemed to arrive "on time" for me, rekindling my interest in poetry if the exigencies of my life had dulled its luster for me, introducing me to new poems and poets that provided solace in time's dark patches, confirming and enlarging my own responses to and assumptions about language while challenging me to think in new ways.

Hirsch evinces, in poems and essays, an intimate—and rare—empathy for and with his subjects, which range from high and low culture, from insomnia to Jimi Hendrix, from the resonant mythologies and nostalgias of childhood to the work of under-read poets, many of whom—Charlotte Mew, Pedro Pérez Conde, Jane Mayhall, Alfonsin Storni, Blaga Dimitrova, Lam Rhi My Da, Michael Fried, among others—I encountered for the first time through the generous portal of Hirsch's vision. And at a time when close reading of and forthright enthusiasm for poetry was (and is) often out of fashion, especially in the academy, I have been abidingly grateful for Hirsch's endeavor. The range and depth of such passionate knowledge might be formidable, but he never makes his intelligence an occasion for proselytizing, obfuscation, or showing off, rather inviting, with a Keatsian "inhabitable awe," his readers to share in the protean emotions and complications of being a maker and of engaging with what is possible and mysterious, even joyful, in poetry. I miss his weekly offerings, but turn and return to the printed collection of them, *Poet's Choice*, published by HarcourtBooks in 2006.

In his ode "To Poetry," Hirsch joins a long tradition of poets addressing their muses, especially during fallow, confusing, or distracted periods [in "Too Lazy to Write Poetry," Chu Yün-ming (1461 – 1527) writes, "Spirit of poetry, quickly, come back! / Don't let the spring go by without any poems"]. Hirsch addresses *his* Poetry with a mix of wry humor and plaintive need that confirms a long, deep intimacy with his subject. "Don't desert me," he pleads with characteristically self-directed and mildly mocking deprecation, "just because I stayed up last night / watching *The Lost Weekend*." The meta-nod in the first stanza to the classic 1945 movie pitching a writer against Demon Alcohol, and to the time that writers can waste in all manner of self-indulgent ways, shows us that the speaker already feels a mixture of guilty indictment shot through with an inextinguishable, odds-against-all-odds hope.

The speaker goes on to confess all of the ways he's betrayed his lover/muse over the years, talking too publically about her "naked body to strangers" and "gossiping about lovers you betrayed" and stalking her "in foreign cities / . . . / pretending I could describe you." Hirsch's narrator is clearly speaking here as both a writer *of* and writer *about* poetry, and I admire his chutzpah. The admission that to try to decipher poems, to interpret them, even to "pretend" to understand their meanings involves a violation or impossibility is a brave and uncommon gesture, especially from someone who has devoted much of his life to doing so. Hirsch's narrator follows his confession with a dazzling, swift pitch of deft moves: a plea for forgiveness, an apology (whose punning cannot disguise pain the speaker feels—separation from his beloved at the same time that it betrays a belief that he just might win her over if he's clever enough, if he can just find the right words to do so), and a rhetorical question in which the narrator pulls his last trick—divine invocation—seemingly out of the core of his very being:

> I'm sorry for handing you a line
> and typing you on a screen,
> but don't let me suffer in silence.
>
> Does anyone still invoke the Muse,
> string a wooden lyre for Apollo,
> or try to saddle up Pegasus?
>
> Winged horse, heavenly god or goddess,
> indifferent entity, secret code, stored magic,
> pleasance and half wonder, hell,
>
> I have loved you my entire life
> without even knowing what you are
> or how—please help me—to find you.

In an interview in *The Nashville Review*, Hirsch states that "The muse, the beloved, and duende are three ways of thinking of what is the source of poetry, and all three seem to me different names or different ways to think about something that is not entirely reasonable, not entirely subject to the will, not entirely rational." Poetry—whether mythic divinity, oblivious force, whether encoded or magical, "pleasance and half wonder" or "hell"—is a conflation of muse, lover, and Lorca's beautiful, unappeasable sadness. "To Poetry" is Hirsch's homage to his version of his beloved Keats's "demon Poesy." Just as Hirsch describes Keats's odes, his own poem represents "the claiming of an obligation, an inner feeling rising up to meet an outer occasion, something owed." Ode. Owed. This kind of love, that takes us by life force and commands us beyond our capacity to understand, might be seen as a state of grace. Its force accounts, I believe, for the seemingly inexhaustible and continually refreshed power of Edward Hirsch's sojourn in the vale of soul-making.

DAVID BAKER

Swift

1.

into flight, the name as velocity,
a swift is one of two or three hundred
swirling over the post office smokestack.
First they rise come dusk to the high sky,

flying from the ivy walls of the bank
a few at a time, up from graveyard oaks
and back yards, then more, tightening to orbit
in a block-wide whirl above the village.

2.

Now they are a flock. Now we're holding hands.
We're talking in whispers to our kind, who
stroll in couples from the ice cream shop
or bike here in small groups to see the birds.

A voice in awe turns inward; as looking
down into a canyon, the self grows small.
The smaller swifts are larger for their singing,
the spatter and high *cheeep*, the shrill of it.

3.

And their quick bat-like alternating wings.
And the soft pewter sky sets off the black
checkmark bodies of the birds as they skitter
like water toward a drain. Now one veers,

dives, as if wing-shot or worse out of the sky
over the maw of the chimney. Flailing—
but then pulling out, as another dips
and the flock reverses its circling.

They seem like leaves spinning in a storm,
blown wild around us, and we are their witness.
Witness the way they finish. The first one
simply drops into the flue. Then four,

five, in as many seconds, pulling out of
the swirl, sweep down. So swiftly, we're alone.
The sky is clear of everything but night.
We are standing, at a loss, within it.

David Baker's autumnal "Swift" recounts a community's gathering to witness a primal and instinctual motion of the *other*, of the animal world, a flock of homing swifts in ecstatic murmuration. The poem evokes and conjures them first as singular, as bird, as word, allowing the eponymous title to enjamb with the first line of the poem: "Swift // into flight, the name as velocity." And as the birds exponentially, almost magically, unfathomably multiply ("a swift is one of two or three hundred / swirling over the post office smokestack . . . // flying from the ivy walls of the bank / a few at a time, up from graveyard oaks / and back yards, then more, tightening to orbit / in a block-wide whirl above the village"), the townspeople themselves form a flock, clustering below, "holding hands" and "talking in whispers to our kind."

"Swift" embodies what Baker himself, in *Radiant Lyre: Essays on Lyric Poetry*, has said so eloquently of the lyric poem and the "problem of people"—how the privacy of the lyric's intense, transient, "swift" interiority is also "a vital feature of cultural identity, even perhaps of collective survival." In shared ecstasy, the self rediscovers itself as both part and whole : "A voice in awe turns inward; as looking / down into a canyon, the self grows small," and then the birds, our words, our selves transform: "leaves spinning in a storm, / blown wild around us, and we are their witness."

In *Varieties of Religious Experience*, William James says that for an experience to be visionary or ecstatic it must be passive (that is, it must happen to us—it cannot be induced); it must, perforce, be transient, fleet, swift; it must be noetic (that is, it must inspire a sense of new or profound knowing); and it must be ineffable, beyond the reach of words. "Swift" is both a description and embodiment of ecstatic experience. By richly figuring the word "swift" itself (as bird, as velocity, as metonymic stand-in for Time, Connection, Love, Life, Mortality), Baker manages to articulate an ineffable truth about beauty, the sublime, and the way the self forms in the wake of an unlooked for and newly recognized desire. "We are their witness," the poet tells us before the poem shifts into the imperative:

> Witness the way they finish. The first one
> Simply drops into the flue. Then four,
>
> Five, in as many seconds, pulling out of
> The swirl, sweep down. So swiftly, we're alone.
> The sky is clear of everything but night.
> We are standing, at a loss, within it.

In this way, the reader, too, becomes privy to and part of the lyric poem's predicament, its "we" moment of deep and essential privacy.

BRENDA HILLMAN

In High Desert Under the Drones

We are western creatures; we can stand for hours in the sun. We read
poetry near an Air Force base. Is poetry pointless? Maybe its points
are moving, as in a fire. The enlisted men can't hear. Practice drones fly over-head
to photograph our signs; they look like hornets [*Vespula*] with dangly legs dipping in
rose circles with life grains. They photograph shadows of the hills where coyotes'
eyes have stars. They could make clouds of white writing, cilia, knitting, soul
weaving, spine without nerves, dentures of the west, volcano experiments, geometry
weather breath & salt. Young airmen entering the base stare from their Hondas;
they are *lucky to have a job in an economy like this*. The letters of this poem are also lucky
to have a job for they are insects & addicts & thieves. Volcanic basalt recalls its rock
star father. Creosote & sage, stubby taupe leaves greet the rain. We hold our signs
up. We're all doing our jobs. Trucks bring concrete for the landing strip they've just
begun.

      A cliff   stands out   in winter
      Twin ravens drop fire   from its eyes

My inner life is not so inner & maintains the vascular system of a desert plant. I'm
grateful to Samuel Beckett & to my high school boyfriend whose drunk father yelled
when we closed the door & read *The Unnamable* during the Tet offensive. A sense of
the absurd can always help. Outside the base we see borax mines in the distance—
the colors of flesh, brown, black, peach, pink, bronze. We stand there as the young
airmen settle into their routine. The Gnostics noted it is difficult to travel between
spheres, you've had to memorize the secret names & the un-namable haunts every
aspect of your routine. The names grow heavier as you carry them between the
spheres.

(Photo credit: Janet Weil, image of Robert Hass)

Brenda Hillman, over the course of her daring career, has always understood that a poem itself, as language, as act of resistance, is a complex personal, environmental, spiritual, cultural, and political system, an ecology, what Christopher Arigo has called "a microcosmic ecosystem in which itself dwells." Risk and sanctuary, beauty and horror, growth and decay coexist. "In High Desert Under the Drones" is a *haibun*, a Japanese literary composition comprised of prose and haiku, often focusing on landscape and travel. The backstory of Hillman's poem involves a trip she and her husband, the poet Robert Hass (pictured in the poem's photograph), took with two friends to Creech Airforce Base in the desert outside Las Vegas. In a note to me about the poem, Hillman writes, "[Creech] is the place from which the drones (unmanned aircraft) are sent for surveillance—and bombing—to Afghanistan. Because we couldn't manage to time our protest with those of other groups, we drove to Creech on our own, just the four of us; we did a protest for two days, holding signs and reading poetry—off the highway—as the service personnel entered and left the base. 'Practice' drones flew over our heads while we did our action. It is extremely eerie and creepy, not to mention horrifying. The pilots sit in Nevada and 'fly' the aircraft which are actually flown from sites nearer to Afghanistan and Pakistan. The drones are responsible for the deaths of many innocents and are extremely costly."

On the page, Hillman's *haibun*, two prose passages pivoting around a photograph/ haiku cluster, creates a space for negotiating its subversive vision. The opening prose field offers up the central public questions of the poem: "Is poetry pointless?," for instance, or are "its points . . . moving, as in a fire," a query that reminds us that words can be weapons, too. What does it mean that these drones of destruction "could [instead] make clouds of white writing, cilia, knitting, soul weaving, spine without nerves, dentures of the west, volcano experiments, geometry weather breath & salt" or that the young airmen feel "*lucky to have a job in an economy like this*." Perhaps most radically, Hillman invites the reader to wonder what to make of the statement that "[t]he letters of this poem are also lucky to have a job for they are insects & addicts & thieves"?

The opening prose passage culminates, "We hold our signs up. We're all doing our jobs. Trucks bring concrete for the landing strip they've just begun," and then, about mid-way through the *haibun*, this first field of prose concludes and falls into white space in which the reader encounters an embedded photograph, visual grammar depicting a slant-shot view of Hass holding up a protest sign before a stark scene of sage and highway. Lineated around the photograph is a roughly 15-syllable haiku—"A cliff stands out in winter / Twin ravens drop fire from its eyes"—that helps us to see the torsos of the protesters as themselves kinds of cliffs, pitched against the winter landscape, with poetry, words, like black birds deploying "fire"—ire, anger, protest, life force—from their kept vigil.

From the poem's start—"We are western creatures; we can stand for hours in the sun"—Hillman lets us know that her vision is neither simplistic nor isolated. That "we" forces the reader to locate herself or himself in relation to the voice, a "we" that is "western"—as in Occidental, as in not Eastern, as in American, as in left coast, as in mortal, heading the way the sun does. "We" are implicated in the very machinations of the Western world the plural narrator protests. It should be no surprise, then, that Hillman moves, after her haiku, from the collective voice of the opening passage to a first-person speaker who forthrightly and with wry, self-conscious accountability and humor confesses, "My inner life is not so inner & maintains the vascular system of a desert plant. I'm grateful to Samuel Beckett & to my high school boyfriend whose drunk father yelled when we closed the door & read *The Unnamable* during the Tet offensive. A sense of the absurd can always help."

Hillman honors the absurdity of the poem's predicament and the paradoxes inherent everywhere—in the gorgeous palette of the borax mines, the work ethic of the young airmen at their deadly task, the resorting to and ignoring of words in time of spiritual and political difficulty—perhaps most powerfully at the poem's conclusion, when, as "[w]e stand there [and] the young airmen settle into their routine," Hillman reminds us of the belief in certain early Gnostic texts that the soul must pass through several spheres on its way to heaven, offering secret names as passwords to cross thresholds along the way. Those names—the naming of things, the noticing of things to be named—may "grow heavier as you carry them between the spheres," but Hillman's poem testifies to the crucial importance of speaking one's understanding of the truth despite futility, boundaries, irony, and crises that might otherwise overwhelm us into silence.

STEPHEN CUSHMAN

List List

Wine list, wish list,

to do list, top ten list,

grocery list, Christmas list,

price list, packing list,

bestseller list, mailing list,

back list, short list,

passenger list, casualty list,

guest list, shit list,

black list, hit list.

Time Management

Oil change: every three thousand;
tire rotation: every five thousand;
dental check-up: every six months;
annual physical: figure it out;
paint the house: one side a summer;
service the furnace: every October;
mow the grass: once a fortnight,
except in drought, if one's informal;
rake the leaves: easier to mow them;
turn over new leaf: every January;
shave the face: every other day
makes the shave closer;
brush the teeth: morning and evening;
floss the teeth: when stuff gets caught;

read the Bible: morning and evening;
reread Walden: in phases of crisis;
hug somebody: eleven times a day
for emotional health according to an article;
rejoice in being so bourgeois: once in a while
but only as needed; honor eros:
could be frequently, at least in theory;
serve eros: could be less frequently,
at least in practice; pray without ceasing:
figure it out; pump out the septic:
three to five years, easy to remember
with elections for president.

Stephen Cushman is a poet obsessed with the calendar. His poems mark time. Personal and historic anniversaries and other landmark passages (weddings, deaths, births, diurnal and nocturnal motions, the months—his collection *Heart Island*, for instance, takes as its backbone twelve poems apostrophizing each of the months of the zodiac—the seasons, "sacred" thresholds of all sorts) provide occasion for poetic musings that, though they may begin with noting or honoring a pattern in nature or human behavior, always move the reader into unexpected and provocative territory. As Stanley Kunitz once said of the poetry of Robert Hass, reading Cushman is like stepping into water that is the same temperature as the air. Before the reader knows it, he or she is plumbing transformative depths of a new element belied by the approachable, even amiable accessibility of diction and tone the reader may have encountered back on terra firma, at the poem's start.

While many of us choose as a New Year commences to take stock, to make an accounting of the past twelve months, to draw up pro and con lists or to make pledges of resolution regarding behaviors, rehabilitations, and goals for the 365 days to come, one senses that every day is new year's day for this poet. Any experience is plunderable for what it might reveal about how to live one's life, what questions to ask, what is worthy of letting go, of keeping, of noticing and remembering and of using as a catalyst for new understanding or change. There's nothing self-righteous about this undertaking, however. Cushman is a poet eager to understand, but he doesn't use his curiosity and intelligence against himself or his reader. He's got some ideas about what's going down, but never presumes to intuit all the answers, to give the game away, or, worse, hoard illumination, to keep it hidden and arcane. This is a poet who believes that his reader is at least as sharp as he, and so the revelations of his poems always finally belong as much to the reader as to the poet—there is that kind of generosity about them.

In "List List," a *meta* poem if there ever was one, the word "list" appears 20 times in ten lines (including the title, where it appears, obviously, twice). Compelled to consider what constitutes a "list," the reader is reminded that, in addition to the obvious cataloging, the simple mnemonic or descriptive series the word most familiarly denotes, "list" can also be an intransitive verb meaning to wish or choose, deriving from the Old English *lystan*, lust—to desire, to lust. *List* can also connote a remnant, a selvage, as in the Old High German *lista*, edge; similarly, with the same etymology, it can be a verb meaning to deviate from the vertical, to tilt.

Bearing these meanings in mind, the reader moves through the list that is the poem. The title alerts us to a complexity of meanings, but the poem opens fairly straightforwardly, with a catalog of seasonal, celebratory lists: wine, wish, to do, top ten, grocery, Christmas, price, packing, bestseller, mailing. Subtly, swiftly, however, the poem deepens into the darker side of consumerism and accrual, so that by line six the speaker reminds us that at the very same time something is back-listed, put out of circulation, made unavailable (perhaps because of unpopularity, but also perhaps because of failure or mishandling) other things are being "short-listed"—both in the sense of their being culled and promoted as finalists for special recognition or award, but also in terms of having one's list cut short, for whatever reason—death, shortfalls, scarcity.

Similarly, a "passenger list" for a trip might well become a "casualty list" (and again, the context here is cultural as well as personal—while some travel for pleasure, others are dying in wars). As the poem culminates, it makes clear that implicit in any "guest list" are the uninvited, the cursed, the black-balled, the marked. By the poem's conclusion, we are no longer in the cheery world of wine and wishes, but we have not negated these desires, either; in this brief, incrementally repetitions, and rhythmic poem, all meanings of "list" remain with us acoustically, metonymically, figuratively; joys are brought into the realm of the bereft, the done for. "List List," we see, is a tautology, an *ars poetica*. One reads the last line, "black list, hit list," with the sense that any *desideratum* that does not include this kind of range is not fully human, or fully realized.

"Time Management," two sentences organized by colons and semi-colons and trellised over 26 lines (same number as the letters of the English alphabet: coincidence?), is also a list. The poem begins with various tasks to which one must attend, followed by a sense of how often these duties should be performed:

Oil change: every three thousand;
Tire rotation: every five thousand;
Dental check-up: every six months;
Annual physical: figure it out . . . .

In the fifth line, Cushman shifts into a nominal imperative ("paint the house: one side a summer; / service the furnace: every October; / mow the grass: once a fortnight, / except in drought, if one's informal"), and as his list of tasks and the timetable/calendar/justification of responsibility for each proceeds, the reasons for accomplishing the deeds become increasingly conditional. In line ten, he brings his first sentence to a light close with a play on the world "leave": "rake the leaves: easier to mow them; / turn over new leaf: every January." At this point, we realize that the expectations set up by the opening lines have already been tested and transformed. We're not on shore anymore, with our "build Rome in a day" "to-do" list affixed to the refrigerator. We are in a new zone, where the stakes are more consequential.

The next sentence of the poem begins in lower case, and conditions intensify, with the tasks and reasons for them breaking more and more often out of the "equations" of "task colon reason semi-colon line break" that began the poem. We do things not only by rote, the poet suggests, but also when things "[get] caught" and "in phases of crisis." All the elements of Cushman's calendrical poetics are here—numbers, months, seasons, days, nights—but we come to see that time is "managed" as much in terms of our inner weather (crisis, Eros, theory, practice) as it is in terms of the dictates of automobile maintenance manuals, the medical establishment, and the natural world. By the time the speaker admonishes "pray without ceasing: / figure it out," the repeated phrase "figure it out" calls us to see, if we have not already, the *figurative* in all of this numerical and time-haunted figuring.

Yet lest we think that "emotional health," an honoring of Eros, getting enough hugs, and reading and rereading important texts, for example, is all that is at stake, the speaker concludes with, again, lines that move the poem into yet a more consequential place: "pump out the septic: / three to five years, easy to remember / with elections for president." Here the quotidian, household purging of the septic tank is compared to the ritual by which, in a nation, presidents are elected every four years, intimating that we negotiate the time we are given by a complex of psycho-historical, personal, and natural imperatives, and that the upshot of enacting these rituals reaches both deeply into and far beyond ourselves.

Both of Cushman's poems recall us to our own human propensity to make lists, to catalog, to record. But each suggests that it is not enough to merely list, to enumerate, and then relax because it's January 2nd and Miller Time. The quality and thoughtfulness of our lists, and our attention and devotion to them over time and in the context of our culture and our responsibilities, is a measure of who we are and what we might, or must, become.

MARY SZYBIST

Happy Ideas

> I had the happy idea to fasten a bicycle wheel to a kitchen stool
> and watch it turn.
>> Duchamp

I had the happy idea to suspend some blue globes in the air

and watch them pop.

I had the happy idea to put my little copper horse on the shelf so we could stare at
each other all evening.

I had the happy idea to create a void in myself.

Then to call it natural.

Then to call it supernatural.

I had the happy idea to wrap a blue scarf around my head and spin.

I had the happy idea that somewhere a child was being born who was nothing like
Helen or Jesus except in the sense of changing everything.

I had the happy idea that someday I would find both pleasure and punishment, that
I would know them and feel them,

and that, until I did, it would be almost as good to pretend.

I had the happy idea to string blue lights from a tree and watch them glow.

I had the happy idea to call myself happy.

I had the happy idea that the dog digging a hole in the yard in the twilight had his
nose deep in mold-life.

I had the happy idea that what I do not understand is more real than what I do

and then the happier idea to buckle myself into two blue velvet shoes.

I had the happy idea to polish the reflecting glass and say

hello to my own blue soul. *Hello, blue soul. Hello.*

It was my happiest idea.

Mary Szybist's anaphoric litany, "Happy Ideas," resounds with a note of whimsy and the kind of resolution one entertains at the start of a new year or at the end of an old one, that liminal spell of days between the winter holidays and the Janus-blade of the new year. For some of us, this spate of out-of-time hours, often disordered by changes in routine, can be a welcome reprieve from quotidian demands, providing more than usual time for reflection, taking stock, and anticipation of a fresh start. For others, the week can be a toilet flush, a slough of despond, a time of unmet expectations, of feeling out of synchronicity with the celebratory acoustics of the season.

Szybist's playful catalogue—threaded through with tempered accruals and incremental repetitions of the word "blue" that intensify the emotional stakes of the poem as it proceeds— takes its title from and opens through the lens of an epigraph from the Dada artist Marcel Duchamp: "I had the happy idea to fasten a bicycle wheel to a kitchen stool and watch it turn." About his sculpture *Bicycle Wheel* (1913) Duchamp said in an interview, "The *Bicycle Wheel* is my first Readymade, so much so that at first it wasn't called a Readymade. It still had little to do with the idea of the Readymade. Rather it had more to do with the idea of *chance*. In a way, it was simply letting things go by themselves and having a sort of created atmosphere in a studio, an apartment where you live. . . . To set the wheel turning was very soothing, very comforting, a sort of opening of avenues on other things than material life of every day."

Szybist appropriates Duchamp's notion of "Readymades" (objects manufactured for another use—snow shovels, urinals—and presented as works of art) to her own poetic purposes. Note how her understanding of what can constitute a found object becomes more and more metaphysical as the she makes her list:

I had the happy idea to suspend some blue globes in the air

and watch them pop.

I had the happy idea to put my little copper horse on the shelf so we could stare at each other all evening.

I had the happy idea to create a void in myself.

Then to call it natural.

Then to call it supernatural.

I had the happy idea to wrap a blue scarf around my head and spin.

With each spin, with each line's revolution, Szybist creates for herself some of the comfort of which Duchamp speaks in his interview, the repeated motions of turning the wheel allowing the artist both to transcend and accept the mire of the everyday. Eschewing sentimentality and quick fixes, Szybist takes (and offers) as much pleasure in broaching existential, wide-reaching historical ideas ("I had the happy idea that somewhere a child was being born who was nothing like Helen or Jesus except in the sense of changing everything") as she does in conveying notions decidedly domestic and intimate ("I had the happy idea to string blue lights from a tree and watch them glow. / I had the happy idea to call myself happy"). Both the philosophical and the grounded give pleasure, as these rhymed lines that come near the poem's conclusion demonstrate: "I had the happy idea that what I do not understand is more real than what I do / and then the happier idea to buckle myself into two blue velvet shoes."

In his gorgeous, irreverent *On Being Blue,* a book-length philosophical essay on blueness in all its resonances and contexts, William Gass writes, "Being without Being is blue." As "Happy Ideas" concludes, Szybist's speaker embraces her blue soles, the intrinsic blueness, the full menu range of her emotional being: "I had the happy idea to polish the reflecting glass and say / hello to my own blue soul. *Hello, blue soul. Hello.* / It was my happiest idea." Szybist's poem is a call to accept if not celebrate the full menu of our "being"—blue-shod and dancing.

SPRING & ALL:
POETRY & THE SEASONS

SPRING & ALL: POETRY & THE SEASONS

The Roman calendar marked the new year, and spring, as commencing at the start of March. In early spring on the central East coast, as gritty snow piles at the local shopping center shrink and snowdrops and crocuses tremble at the foot of tree trunks, it isn't premature at least to begin to turn one's thoughts, if not to love, then to shedding heavy coats and ordering rose canes for the garden and anticipating mornings unshackled by the scraping of ice off the windshield for the privilege of driving in to work.

In its broadest usage, a "season" can be any period of time characterized by a particular activity, phenomenon, or circumstance—hunting season, for instance, or football season, trout season, flu season, theater season, tick season, conference season, mating season. The word "season" comes from the Latin *sation* - , *satio*, from *serere*, to sow. Perhaps most commonly, then, *season* refers to a specific division of the earthly year, determined by changes in weather and the tilt of the planet's axis in relation to its revolution around the sun. And although meteorological and astronomical seasons are reckoned in a myriad of ways in different parts of the globe, ever since the Societas Meteorologica Palatina defined the seasons in 1780 as groupings of three months, the northern hemisphere has marked four of them— spring, summer, autumn, and winter.

Poets and poetry have ever been attuned to the seasons, to the stirrings they engender, the possibilities they present or refute. In his journal, Henry David Thoreau wrote, "Each season….gives a tone and hue to my thought. Each annual phenomenon is a reminiscence and prompting. Our thoughts and sentiments answer to the revolution of the seasons, as two cog-wheels fit into each other….A year is made up of a certain series and number of sensations and thoughts which have their language in nature. Now I am ice, now I am sorrel."

Emily Dickinson uses the word some 20 times in her verses, and she seemed to be especially fond of spring, calling it "the Period / Express from God." And who does not know the poetry of the King James translation of Ecclesiastes 3:1: "To every [thing there is] a season, and a time to every purpose under the heaven" or Shakespeare's plays and poems, which are full of songs and references to these turnings of the year:

The seasons alter: hoary-headed frosts
Fall in the fresh lap of the crimson rose,

And on old Hiems' thin and icy crown
An odorous chaplet of sweet summer buds
Is, as in mockery, set. The spring, the summer,
The childing autumn, angry winter, change
Their wonted liveries, and the mazed world,
By their increase, now knows not which is which.

(*A Midsummer Night's Dream*, 2.1.112-119)

Chinese poetry has always been especially beholden to the seasons, as in this poem
by Su Ting (670 – 727):

The year is ended, and it only adds to my age
Spring has come, but I must take leave of my home.
Alas, that the trees in this eastern garden,
Without me, will still bear flowers.

 Across cultures and time, then, poetries connect with and at times depend upon
the transformations signaled by seasonal changes to articulate all sorts of emotional
and psychological conditions. The phenomenologist Gaston Bachelard called
the seasons "the fundamental mark of memories," going on to assign them "soul
values." In a poem called "The Human Seasons," John Keats writes, "Four seasons
fill the measure of the year; / There are four seasons in the mind of man." After
extolling the beauties of spring, summer, and autumn, Keats concludes: "He has
his Winter too of pale misfeature, / Or else he would forego his mortal nature."
Wallace Stevens presses this point in "The Snow Man." "One must have a mind of
winter," he claims, in order to behold the "Nothing that is not there and the nothing
that is."

Yet anyone remembering even a few of this past decade's dramatic seasonal weather
events knows that the seasons as we know or understand them are changing.
Wikipedia reports that "ecologists are increasingly using a six-season model for
temperate climate regions that includes *pre-spring (prevernal)* and *late summer (seritonal)*
as distinct seasons along with the traditional four." And although we know that
changes always are occurring, that change is the norm, and that most "climate
forcings," as the experts call them, happen at a glacial pace, over millennia, each
generation must feel itself, at some point, to be the one poised to witness first-
hand, in real time, these inevitable eonic disruptions, a conspiracy—ecological,
climatological, environmental, political, human—that certainly must eventually alter
everything about the earth as we know it.

And so it's hard for a certain kind of naïve mind at a restless, awakening time of year not to wonder, for example, what a seasonless world might mean for poets, for poems. Shall I compare thee to a weirdly hot, dry purgatorial spell of days broken by torrential spates of relentless rain whose climactic aberrations may be caused by ozone depletion? Or to the aftermath of Cyclone Yasi wreaking havoc in Western Australia? To devastating eruptions of the earth in New Zealand? Well, maybe yes. Because poetry is about nothing if it's not about transformation. Never mind that the kind of apocalyptic changes that could occur may make the writing of poems moot. That the seasons have confirmed and perhaps even created human understanding of life's mutability for poets is undeniable. Here are the last lines from the end of Stanley Kunitz's beautiful poem "The Layers":

Though I lack the art
to decipher it,
no doubt the next chapter
in my book of transformations
is already written.
I am not done with my changes.

Clearly we have our interior weathers, our human seasons, too.

CAROL MUSKE-DUKES

To a Soldier

Imagine it: a world away, Autumn.
Leaves scattering but not in fiery
Effusion, like the red/gold sentinels
Of the Smokies or north of Boston.
A world away: not enough Fall to
Make a cliché, the one we love about
The season's redemptive powers, its
Dazzling imitation of death, the gold & blood—
Colors. In the desert, in the cities of armaments—
You tell me leaves die without turning—
Without color, they die. Without a sign
Of how it ended, the season, how it was lost to us.

To ask what is the role of the poet in a time of war might be to ask what is the
place of the poet in the world at all. Armed strife and violent conflict between and
among people are as old as human experience itself, older perhaps than singing, and
certainly predating the writing of verse. Awareness of wars near and far, inner and
outer, must always be a subtext of the examined life, even of the most private and
interior sensibility, and can be a source of empowerment, despair, and anxiety for
those wielding pens instead of swords.

W. H. Auden stated that "poetry makes nothing happen," but poets have always
made wars—their heroes, victims, consequences—the subject of a myriad of
poems. "Sing, Goddess, the wrath of Achilles" begins the *Iliad*, attributed to Homer
at about the 8th century BC, and in a translation by Sam Hamill, the Chinese poet
Tu Fu (712 – 770 AD) writes, "Sleepless, memories of war betray me: / I am
powerless against the world." One thinks, too, of Thomas Hardy's "The Man He
Killed" or Sappho's bold statement that what one loves is worth more poetry than
any legion of horsemen or warriors.

Carol Muske-Dukes's "To a Soldier" is an epistle of sorts, an imperative, a call to
a soldier in "a world away" to imagine autumn happening back home, in subdued
"red/gold sentinels," while in the desert, where the soldier lives, "in the cities of
armaments – // …the leaves die without turning – / Without color, they die."
So much happens in these four tercets! A far cry from a "wish you were here"

postcard, the poem indicts any poetic act that fails in such a context to push beyond consoling tropes and the familiar poetic recourses to myths such as the fall, "the one we love about / The season's redemptive powers, its / Dazzling imitation of death."

In a surprising and powerful volta at the poem's conclusion, the poet turns the missive on herself, on the reader, on "us." It is *we* who are being called to imagine that other world, where soldiers, like leaves, die: "without a sign / Of how it ended, the season, how it was lost to us"—and where a lost season—lost time, lost life—is as crucial and significant as a lost battle.

We must waken, Muske-Dukes admonishes, to our need to empathize, to overcome our great human tendency to forget, to distance, to protect ourselves from the conditions of others, to things happening elsewhere, something that is perhaps most dangerously possible in language. This poem is an act of passionate imagination— of the ability to empathize—without which, William Blake and others have challenged, social and cultural and political transformations are impossible. Wallace Stevens, who lived and wrote through two world wars, said that "the role of the writer in war remains the fundamental role of the writer intensified and concentrated." Disarmingly simple and clear, Muske-Dukes's lapidary, ardent poem recalls us to our losses, our selves, a responsibility that extends "to a soldier"—to a man, to a woman.

LAURA KASISCHKE

March

It's the murderer
who got away with it
sitting on a park bench
thinking about snow

and how it's over. Little
flower-faces peeking
out of dirt
to shriek hello. While

the babies wheel
by, absurdly bright. The old
men in amber. The light
on the steeples served up
in cones of white.

But something here
is not quite right:

Old lady
in a little girl's bonnet.
Ugly dog
with a child's wide smile.

Always, in spring
you'll find
someone with regrets
she's allowed herself
to forget:

Eye at the keyhole.
Milk in the saucepan.
Strange wet kiss that went

on and on and on.

In the northern hemisphere, the month of March, marking as it does the pivotal vernal equinox, is often a period of flux, belonging both to established but waning winter and incipient spring. It is an interlude of muddy ruts, birds, stalwart shoots, late snows. It is also a month whose name, in English, like "May," is rife with several meanings. No wonder poets are captivated by its messy thrall. To Linda Pastan ("March Snow") it is "no more / than another promise, soon to be broken." For Ted Hughes it is the month when "the earth, invalid, dropsied, bruised [is] wheeled / Out into the sun." Dickinson refers 21 times to the word in her oeuvre, calling March "the Month of Expectation."

From the pronominal ambiguity of its opening quatrain, Laura Kasischke's "March" signals a sense of a season awry. "It," March, the speaker says, is "the murderer" who got away with "it" (the murder)—the month is both criminal and crime, perpetrator and victim. The poem, with its fairly tidy initial three-stressed lines that are quickly undercut by tipsy breakings out of meter, exaggerated and unpredictably situated, ambushing rhymes, and eerie, David Lynch-like imagery ("flower-faces peeking / out of dirt / to shriek hello"), indicates an uneasiness and unpredictable volatility. The murderer must know that he's not scot-free. Winter is not over. "Something here," as the poet puts it, "is not quite right." What?

"Riddle" and definition poems like this suggest a movement from a stated or implied question to an answer, a revelation. Kasischke is an adept at manipulating rhetoric in a way that uses peripheral details (as Donald Hall suggests, "Peripheral vision is where the symbols are") to create those unteachable states of "internal difference —," as Dickinson puts it, "Where the Meanings, are —." And so, after presenting us with several cinematic shots of a weirdly warped "cheery" spectacle of spring in a park ("absurdly bright" babies wheeling by, old men cast in "amber," "the light / on the steeples served up / in cones of white"), which reaches a particularly distorted moment in stanza five:

Old lady
in a little girl's bonnet.
Ugly dog
with a child's wide smile,

Kasischke makes a shift in the penultimate stanza from an outwardly viewed scene of description, and into another, closer-to-the-bone point of view. Although bearing the sweep of a general, imperative address ("Always, in spring / you'll find"), the pronoun shifts (you, she) here suggest a far more personal, particular culpability and extremity than the guilt of murdering March thinking it's gotten away with something, the crime of winter erased by snow that's now safely a thing of the past. The vicissitudes, the ambivalent uncertainties of March awaken in a certain kind of mind or temperament (the speaker's?) "regrets / she's allowed herself / to forget":

Eye at the keyhole.
Milk in the saucepan.
Strange wet kiss that went

on and on and on.

These last lines, in particular, reveal Kasischke's lyric gift. A whole spectrum of guilt and repining, reinforced by insistent rhythmic stresses (*eye* and *key*, *milk* and *sauce*, the protracted, spondaic "Strange wet kiss" and relentless "*on* and *on* and *on*") are suggested by this catalog—spying, voyeurism, secrets, forgetfulness, carelessness, lust. Perhaps this is the answer to what's "not quite right" about March; it is *we* who are never completely quite right. Rather, we, like this month, must belong both to our winter and our spring weathers. Our transgressions, from the minor—accidentally scalded milk—to the more strangely erotic (that covert kiss), are never something that can be completely put away. "It" is never over, and the flux of awakening to a renewed spring brings it psychological stirrings as well, including those "regrets" we might choose to bury or forget.

L. S. KLATT

Hearsay

The mailman sent piecemeal a rare donkey
to the city of waters; to the city of waters
a rare donkey was sent, swaddled
in blueprint.

And it came to pass that the waters
were troubled. Woe
in the great city.

Nothing is more beautiful than to admit
the truth, or more difficult.

The head & tail & all that is in between.

When piecemeal the beast was sent,
the engineers knew their place.

For if disassembled like a boat
the rare donkey could be
put together.

But to separate the members of a living
thing, to cast dispersions on it,
this is to create a question
unanswerable.

First Frost on Windshield

Perfect stitches suture the glass, & if patient enough
watch them disappear.

Like the dead dog in the middle of the road, the invisible
dog that an ice cream truck hit & the rest of us
skirted. Was the last thing tasted
the last thing?

It whimpers, the muzzle of the dog head; the hackles
become rimed with diamante. I say:
here are lucent things.

When frost arrives, it has the soul of famine,
but also catatonic the headlights as the crow flies.

What Helen Vendler called, in relation to John Keats and Wallace Stevens, "the
taming of mind to the season," is something poets often do, and November—the
tail end of autumn, the harbinger of winter—has a particular way of taking ahold
of and a hold in poets. Merwin called November a "debt." Plath considered it her
"property" ("Two times a day / I pace it, sniffing / The barbarous holly with its
viridian / Scallops, pure iron, // And the wall of old corpses"). Stevens named it a
region ("It is like a critic of God, the world // And human nature, pensively seated
/ On the waste throne of his own wilderness" from "The Region November"),
Williams a design:

 Let confusion be the design
and all my thoughts go,
swallowed by desire: recess
from promises in
the November of your arms.

(from "Design for November")

Though not specifically about November, two recent poems by L.S. Klatt, in
their different ways, seem to grow out of what Stevens has elsewhere called the
"exhilaration of changes." "Hearsay" (which in its fabular imaginings, disturbed
logic, and philosophical figuration reminds me very much of Stevens and his
notion of "the malady of the quotidian") possesses what poet and critic Ron
Slate has called Klatt's "domesticated wildness." It relays a tale that feels like a
parable, mixing ordinary details (the mailman, the engineers) with Biblical syntax
("And it came to pass") and a cryptic, aphoristic, philosophically charged sense
of mastery/mystery ("Nothing is more beautiful than to admit / the truth, or
more difficult"). It's clear that Klatt means us to read his poem as more than
just "hearsay." Everything about the poem is charged with symbolic resonance.
Perhaps we're meant to read the poem as a definition of "Hearsay" or rumor, and
to feel the consequences of what happens when something rare is taken apart
and disseminated and then partially or inaccurately reassembled in a way that is
dissembling and "unanswerable."

It is hard for me not to read "Hearsay" as a political poem, a comment on what can happen to something, say, like the democratic party (with its donkey mascot) if, "piecemeal," it is sent in shards ("The head & tail & all that is in between") to "the great city." The poem gives us much to contemplate in any season, but especially in a presidential election year. When the donkey was in pieces, the speaker tells us, "the engineers knew their place. // For if disassembled like a boat / the rare donkey could be / put together." There are clear echoes here of another provocatively riddling poem, Humpty Dumpty, which can be read, on the one hand, nonsensically, but which also suggests political interpretations, as well. What happens, Klatt's poem warns, when "the members of a living / thing" are separated and cast with dispersions? Can such a broken body ever be reassembled? Restored to meaning? Is there an answer to such a riddle?

If "Hearsay" seems a nod to the "region November" of the body politic, "First Frost on Windshield" is more forthright in its engagement with the changing season. But there is nothing immediately transparent about this poem, which, like "Hearsay," is concerned with things (like a country, a body, a year) that are broken and must be "sutured," reassembled in the mind of the reader. With characteristic word-play (the way "patient," for example, works with a kind of implied imperative—"If you are patient enough you can watch the stitches of frost disappear"—as well as evoking the body of a patient requiring repair), rhetorical elision, and disjunction, Klatt moves with an undiscursive, figurative forcefulness from his initial image of a frosted window glass to what Harold Bloom, again in relation to Stevens (and Dickinson), calls an antithetical image "that disrupt[s] the realm of bodily eye":

Like the dead dog in the middle of the road, the invisible
dog that an ice cream truck hit & the rest of us
skirted. Was the last thing tasted
the last thing?

A "dead dog"? What? And not one most likely struck, say, yesterday, but a while back, in the season of ice cream trucks. And an invisible dog, a dog no one saw. And a dog which, perhaps because "skirted," continues to haunt, whimpering still (not the whole dog, mind you, but just its muzzle, part of its head)? Through the lenses of memory, guilt, and remorse, the hackles of the dog, the speaker says, "become rimed with diamante," with the first frost of conscience, the consciousness of cowardice, of avoidance, of avoidance of death. Klatt concludes his lyric, again, with a vatic, aphoristic statement that, with its elided, unstable syntax, is not entirely decipherable, at least not through dialectic or ordinary logic or syllogism:

I say:

here are lucent things.

When frost arrives, it has the soul of famine,
but also catatonic the headlights as the crow flies.

This kind of language has an almost nonsensical feel on first reading, but if
we allow its juxtaposed figures ("[frost] has the soul of famine") and idiomatic
phrases ("as the crow flies") to conflate (the experience of doing so is akin to
looking at Magic Eye® images), we emerge from the poem with a new sense of
the interconnectedness of the fierce, implacable motions of the natural world,
the seasons, and the human capacity either to be numb or alive to these truths.
"Surprise," Bloom writes, "is the American poetic stance." Just as November takes
us aback, with its inklings, frosts, shearings, and beheaded blooms, Klatt's poems
startle us with their imaginative negative capabilities, their choice of lucent vision
over any form of personal, political, or artistic numbness.

JENNIFER ATKINSON

Lemon Tree
after Agnes Martin

Tilled snow

Plucked arpeggios

Of revery rungs

Laddered for zero

The inverse of music

Undelirious lines

Correggio's

Unchecked hand

Minus the background

Noise of content

The aftereffect of citrus

Scent and the curious

Dryness left

On your hands

When you pare

The fruit opens

The eidetic lyricism of Jennifer Atkinson's poetry owes in no small part to her limned verbal restraint and passionate sparseness. An almost sacred silence blooms among the lenten boughs of her elegant phrases, allowing the perfumed mystery of what can never be fully known to palpably ghost the natural world that is often the occasion for her spiritual, political, aesthetic, and erotic meditations.

Wonderful, then, and not surprising to find that Atkinson's poem "Lemon Tree," the epigraph tells us, is in part modeled upon and inspired by the work of painter Agnes Martin, and perhaps specifically by Martin's painting also entitled "Lemon Tree." Martin (1912 – 2004) is best known for the austere, exquisite text/ile-haunted screens of her six-foot-square canvases, described by art historian Anna C. Chave as covered with hand-rendered, "thinly lined grids (composed purposely, unlike graph paper, of rectangles and not squares)." Martin's work, Chave tells us, concerns states of "innocence, happiness, beauty, and exaltation. Those states [Martin] saw as inextricably linked with experiences of nature, and her titles often feature natural images, such as in *The Islands*, or *Night Sea*, *Leaves*, and *Lemon Tree*. As to how Martin found her 'vision,' she explained: 'When I first made a grid I happened to be thinking of the innocence of trees and then this grid came into my mind and I thought it represented innocence, and I still do.'" Martin's moving canvases are so faintly etched and opaquely luminous that Nicolas Calas referred to her project as an "art of invisibility."

Floating over and into Atkinson's hibernal pagescape of "tilled snow" and "rungs / laddered for zero / The inverse of music," the "lemon tree" of the title insinuates its attar, its inkling of warmer climes, of hope itself. In a poetic essay on Jean Valentine, *writing a word / changing it,* published by Albion Books, 2011 (Valentine being another deft poet of "strange and irreducible lines like an antenna broken off of a radio, like a caduceus"), the poet C. D. Wright says that Agnes Martin (like Atkinson, I would add) was interested not so much in painting grey geese descending as "the emotions we feel when we see grey geese descending." The sensibility here is of

Undelirious lines

Coreggio's

Unchecked hand

Minus the background

Noise of content.

This poem offers not, then, an aesthetic of tropical, lavish embellishment or of Keatsian fine excess (or of Correggio's lavish, fully fleshed opulence, for instance), but rather a pure, spare lyric, with its "story" conveyed not by the dramatic static of content but by the suggestion of emotional movement, an implication of a whole life sketched in the residue of its "aftereffect . . . / Scent and the curious / Dryness left / On your hands."

The closing lines give us the heart of Atkinson's ekphrasis and express the formal poetics Atkinson shares with Martin: "When you pare," she writes, "The fruit opens." Mallarmé, Char, Cage, Celan—joining these and other poets with voices at once urgent and reticent, Atkinson, in "Lemon Tree," makes the reader feel what Celan called "the word won by silence." The poem offers its message like the charged eidolon an opened orange makes, pared by hands somewhere in a dimmed, dusty train car at night, perhaps, triggering a score of memories and associations, transforming every destination, altering everything.

WORDS IN LOVE

WORDS IN LOVE

Human courtship rituals, across centuries and cultures, can be highly formalized, involving elaborate family negotiations and a series of prescribed tasks, exchanges, and behaviors, including internet and speed-dating protocols, or they can be casual—an impromptu game of beer pong in the frat house, say, or a hook-up phone text message sent from a parking lot. From ancient times to the present, however, poetry—in addition to the sharing of meals and spectacles, acquiring of matching tattoos or rings, and of swapping gifts, personal histories, phone calls, letters, photos, or CD mixes—has been part of the process of erotic wooing.

Three-thousand-year-old papyruses from ancient Egypt, for instance, such as those housed at the Chester Beatty Library, recount the courtship rituals of love-struck couples and their matchmakers ("He knows not my wish to embrace him, / or he would write to my mother"). In the Japanese court culture of the Heian period (794 – 1193 AD), poetry writing played a crucial role in all aspects of society, and especially in mating, with poems of specific syllable count going back and forth at key romantic junctures, on specific subjects (dewy blooms were popular) and on certain kinds of paper, scrutinized by all parties involved for calligraphic beauty and poetic skill, booty hanging in the balance. Any Renaissance person at court worth his or her salt knew the value of being able to write a decent love sonnet, and one thinks of Francesco Petrarch (1304 – 1374 AD), who wrote some 366 "scattered rhymes" to a married woman named Laura (who may or may not, finally, have been partly a projection) with whom he was passionately in love despite having little or no contact with her during her lifetime, and about whom he continued to write poems after her death. And who can forget Bill Clinton's gift to Monica Lewinsky of a copy of Walt Whitman's *Leaves of Grass*—never mind that Bill also gave Hillary a copy of the same book during their courtship? In rituals of love and mating, we tend to deploy what we hope will work.

But what if we don't achieve our aims? Some would argue that it is not the act of winning but of petitioning the *unattainable* that is the real source and abiding electrical current of Eros. In *Eros the Bittersweet*, poet, classicist, and philosopher Anne Carson writes, "The Greek word *eros* denotes 'want,' 'lack,' 'desire for that which is missing.' The lover wants what he does not have. It is by definition impossible for him to have what he wants if, as soon as it is had, it is no longer wanting. This is more than wordplay." Yet the triangulation Carson speaks of— lover, the beloved, and whatever comes between them—can be felt palpably in many of the most powerful love poems: Sappho's fragment 31 (see Anne Carson's translation, "He seems to me equal to gods that man / who opposite you / sits and listens close / to your sweet speaking . . . " in *If Not, Winter: Fragments of Sappho*), the anonymous lyric "Western Wind," Keats's anguished blank verse fragment "This living hand" ("now warm and capable / Of earnest grasping, would, if it were cold / And in the icy silence of the tomb, / So haunt thy days and chill thy dreaming nights / That thou would wish thine own heart dry of blood / So in my veins red life might stream again, / And thou be conscience-calmed . . . "), Emily Dickinson's heart-wrenching, ardent documents we know as her *Master Letters* ("'Tell you of the want' – you know what a leech is, don't you – [remember that] Daisy's arm is small – and you have felt the horizon hav'nt you – and did the sea – never come so close as to make you dance?" [Letter 233, ed. Johnson]), and so many more—Kevin Young's tail-chasing love poems in *Jelly Roll*. John Donne. Andrew Marvell. Elizabeth Bishop. Dorianne Laux. Constantine Cavafy. Pablo Neruda. Rumi. Mirabai. The redactor of the *Song of Songs*. . .

Whatever the aim and outcome of love poetry—success, frustration, a condition of being in love with the idea of love—the endeavor speaks to the limits and reaches of language. "To try to write love," writes Roland Barthes in *A Lover's Discourse*, "is to confront the *muck* of language: that region of hysteria where language is both *too much* and *too little*, excessive (by the limitless expansion of the ego, by emotive submersion) and impoverished (by the codes on which love diminishes and levels it)." And whether or not, when we are touched by love, we respond to it in poetry, the experience becomes crucial to our narratives of self. Carson puts it this way: "As Sokrates tells it, your story begins the moment Eros enters you. That incursion is the biggest risk of your life. How you handle it is an index of the quality, wisdom and decorum of the things inside you. As you handle it you come into contact with what is inside you, in a sudden and startling way . . . . It is a glance down into time, at realities you once knew, as staggeringly beautiful as the glance of your beloved."

A challenge and a tall order to consider for those of us scanning the aisles of Wal-Mart for heart-shaped boxes of candy, perusing who's who on Faceparty, opting for a solitary night with a good novel, or daring to put our desire for our beloved, for desire itself, into words.

JENNIFER CHANG

Love after Love

I   understand   he

called   it   a   bird

because   he   was

unhappy the sky has

no faith but I gather

leaf-fall the dried-out

catalpa   pods   and

once loved him the

mountain orchard the

honeylight   the   last

lowing   of   wind

before dusk I tell you

he was a mistake but

you do not believe in

mistakes and I agree

and let us sleep until

our skin burns with

thoughtless thought I

wake to show you the

last pink streak in the

sky why are we
always looking at the
sky why was he a
mistake soon the
fields will give us
nothing to gather not
even the dark we
love autumn because
nothing has died yet I
kiss the heat out of
your neck you speak
odd tender before
you open your eyes
and I'm calm because
I know the other way
the world ends bring
the sky closer don't
look

In his elegy for Yeats, W. H. Auden says that any poet, finally, "[becomes] his admirers // . . . scattered among a hundred cities." Chang's love poem plays self-consciously with the texts of other poets she clearly esteems. Her title, for instance, owes directly to Derek Walcott's "Love after Love": "You will love again the stranger who was yourself. / . . . . the stranger who has loved you // all your life, whom you ignored / for another, who knows you by heart." Chang's poem—with its simple diction, and rich, unpunctuated, expertly enjambed, fluid, and resonantly ambiguous syntax, all fully justified in a columnar field of language pressed to the left margin of the page—is haunted, too, by Frost, Williams, Glück, Ashbery, and others, but perhaps most strikingly defines itself, formally and thematically, in relation to the imperatives of Walcott's strophic lyric.

Walcott's speaker addresses, self-reflexively, a "you" (with whom the speaker might well be conflated), urging that subject to gaze into "your own mirror," to love again the self that was subsumed for a time by a shadowy "another," and to "[f]east on your life." Chang's poem is also triangulated, as poems about Eros must be, and she clearly shares Walcott's desire to find or believe in the possibility of love after love has ended. In Chang, however, the "you" and "I" are distinct, and there is a "he," as well—the former lover, perhaps. Meditating repeatedly upon whether or not this "he was a mistake" is one engine of the speaker's meditation. But we learn that the *you* of the poem (a new lover, God, the self?—all possibilities are there) "[does] not believe in mistakes"—and soon the pronominal mesh (I, he, you, us, we) and Chang's agile syntactical gestures serve to honor the complexities of the situation and at the same time clarify them. This passage, for instance—"why are we always / looking at the sky why / was he a mistake soon / the fields will give us / nothing to gather not / even the dark we love / autumn because nothing / has died yet I kiss the / heat out of your neck"—offers up an array of possible readings, turning the poem's subjects and objects into one another everywhere, depending upon where the reader locates the volatile nouns, the verbs: Was he a mistake the fields will give us? Or will the fields give us nothing to gather, not even the dark we love? Perhaps we love autumn because nothing has yet died? Or because nothing has yet died yet I kiss the heat out of your neck? Again, all of these readings are contiguous and present and valid, informing one another emotionally.

It is as though Chang has taken the anguished folds of an intricate origami and opened them up to reveal the secrets in the convoluted pleatings of relationship (one thinks of Gilles Deleuze, whose wonderful treatment of "the fold"—Le Plis—in his *Fold: Leibniz and the Baroque*, poses notions of interiority and exteriority that have been taken up in architectural and other theoretical contexts). Chang's love poem (her field, her long scroll, her unfolded space) is both contained and yet invites room on the page for an else, for more, an otherwise, an unknowable. In the space of this poem, figure and ground, past and present, I, You, and He blur as the economies among these entities dilate, increase, opening continuously to new possibilities.

In the wake of lost love and our hunger for renewed/new love, should we turn our questions obsessively outward? Or should we, because we "know the other / way the world ends bring / the sky closer [and] look" not out, but rather within, for answers, for sustenance? *Both*, the poem seems not only to suggest but, in its linguistic embodiment, to achieve. Perhaps love, Chang puts forward, like the ongoing lives of poems and poets, resides not in a linear arc, but in a dynamic space and ever evolving continuum.

RANDALL COUCH

Pressed

A leaf in a letter.

Beauty depends on circumstance.
For instance,
black as the tents of Kedar
            was apt once for a bride.

The leaf, on the other hand, is not black.
Green heart, yellow ring, red star.
Here on the dry plains,
rare as a rasta tam.
Pressed, from damp woods where you are,
like a fresh shirt.

Your envelope marked *urgent fragile*
wraps spring inflamed
            by low sun, long nights.

Beauty is only a promise we return to redeem.

Come look again
            though I'm afraid of changing.
Good bones and late fire will tell,
            an echo in the mirror.

I was alarmed a few years ago when a colleague off-handedly mentioned at the
mailboxes in the faculty lounge that beauty was beginning to come back into fashion
in literary and cultural theory.vvI was not concerned about beauty's alleged return to
critical favor. Rather, I was a little unnerved that I hadn't realized, perhaps because I
spend a lot of time reading poetry and taking walks, that beauty's currency had ever
dropped.

What is clear, whether one reads Nietzsche, Plato, Carson, Kant, Scarry, Nehamas,
Eco, Keats, or a host of others, is that notions of beauty and the beautiful (in
poems and theory as in life—think of the wildly divergent responses people
have to phenomena like Björk, velvet paintings, Tarantino, shad roe, and Bauhaus

architecture) are as contradictory and various as those who meditate upon them. Kant, for instance, considered beauty to be a subjective experience while Adorno claimed that "All beauty reveals itself to persistent analysis." Wallace Stevens called death "the mother of beauty." Centuries ago, Sappho (translated here by Stanley Lombardo) wrote:

Some say an army on horseback,
some say on foot, and some say ships
are the most beautiful things
on this black earth,
    but I say
it is whatever you love.

Randall Couch's "Pressed"—its title evoking not only something flattened or preserved (like "a leaf in a letter," as we learn in line one) but also a sense of being assailed, harangued, importuned, urged—moves forthrightly into the theatre of the beauty meditations:

A leaf in a letter.

Beauty depends on circumstance.
For instance,
black as the tents of Kedar
        was apt once for a bride.

Who is speaking in these lines? Although it will be another stanza before a "you," the sender of the leaf, enters the poem, and not until the last strophe that our narrator appears in the first-person, the allusion to the *Song of Solomon* (1:5) and to those goat-hair tents once thought to be a fitting trope for the swarthy beauty of the beloved, signals that what is at stake in this poem concerning what is beautiful and "apt for a bride" is complicated by intimacy, distance, and an especially keen awareness of the winged chariot of time. There is a poly-vocality in these first couple of stanzas that is not unlike the dialogic motions of the *Song of Songs*, and this ventriloquism only serves to heighten the erotics of beauty with which the poem is engaged.

These lovers are geographically separated. Thus, in an envelope "marked *urgent fragile*," one has sent the other an autumn leaf: "Green heart, yellow ring, red star," the recipient says, "Here on the dry plains, / rare as a rasta tam. / Pressed, from damp woods where you are, / like a fresh shirt." That sonically lovely and ingenious phrase "rare as a rasta tam" has the power of what Roland Barthes calls, in his *Camera Lucida*, the *punctum*—that detail in a photograph that "pierces the viewer" with its riveting personal truth. Not only does the rasta tam simile vividly conjure for the reader the tri-colored leaf ("spring inflamed / by low sun, long nights") but it also suggests the closeness, sensibility, and wry humor these two people share.

And so when Couch follows his "*urgent, fragile*" stanza (itself an envelope recalling an inflamed spring, "low sun, long nights") with another statement about beauty—"Beauty is only a promise we return to redeem"—the reader is alerted to a deepened "reading" of this leaf, this vernal epistle, this poem. It is a *memento mori*, addressed to the sender as much as to the recipient. Beauty is only a vow that we must return *to* (and *return*—that is, give back) in order to "redeem"—to be valued, to be received, to be saved. Any beauty to be found in leaves, in love, in faces, the poem posits, depends upon our willingness to reciprocate, to "return" its promise by gazing back despite fear, vanity, and inevitable loss, and despite, too, the risks involved in sending such a symbolically charged gift at all—are the sender and recipient, for example, making "art" of their love? of their life and death, together or apart?

In *On Beauty and Being Just*, Elaine Scarry says that beauty "seems to incite, even to require, the act of replication." And so the narrator, in the last stanza, invites the leaf-sender to return, to gaze again, to redeem what beauty might be found in one another despite forces at work in the fallen leaf, the aging or the sick body—forces which for this couple would appear to be especially "urgent" and "inflamed":

Come look again
      though I'm afraid of changing.
Good bones and late fire will tell,
      an echo in the mirror.

I love the forthrightness of the speaker's confession: "I'm afraid of changing." Beauty may be only a promise. But it is a promise, a vow inseparable from the lovers' desire ("[g]ood bones and late fire") echoed in the mirror. As Alexander Nehamas says in *Only a Promise of Happiness: The Place of Beauty in a World of Art*, "the value of beauty lies no further than itself; it is its own reward . . . . And only the promise of happiness is happiness itself." That beauty, yearning, and love can, despite the certainty of death, be redeemed, even through ruin, by the avowal of beauty, yearning, and love, is at the green heart of this poem.

CATE MARVIN

Let the Day Perish

I was meaner than a flimsy dollar the change machine refuses.
I was duplicitous as a Canadian dime.
I slid through your town only to announce my prejudices.
And only to slip my tongue into the slot of your mouth.

Bade you come over. Covered your hand with mine.
Bade you lay down. Stroked your neck, allowed your story.
Bade you pull my body down. Bore me half to death.
This is where the what and when happens. Two

people on a couch, liquored up and lousy at the mouth.
I dislike everything in your refrigerator.
I criticize your cupboards, suggest you replace
your glassware. I pick up a broom when you're not

looking (yet you were looking) and sweep your whole
house out. I make a comment about your teeth.
(Mine are very fine and straight.) I complain about
the cotton/poly sheets. (They make me sweat.)

There was a light from your window that bore
right through me. I wanted nothing more than
to put my tongue to your teeth. I'd have licked
your whole house clean, bought you a crystal set

of glassware, laid down the dinner table with new
plates. I'd scrub your tub, your toilet. But perhaps
you did not understand my critique as servitude.
I was merely asking to be put into your employ.

I happen to like your mud-wash eyes. The mean
bags beneath your eyes. The jitter your hand does.
I don't actually care about anything but that.
Everything's been lousy since I left. Someone

smashed my car window just for the hell of it.
I am constantly harassed by thoughts of you.
I have made a poor investment in real estate.
When you took me out into your back yard

and showed me the koi pond you'd filled with
cement, it made me sad.
      Then you said you could bring it back.

Cate Marvin's "Let the Day Perish" situates itself, from the speaker's first boastful
line ("I was meaner than a flimsy dollar the change machine refuses"), in the
centuries-old tradition of seduction ballads, and her ambiguously gendered narrator
plays with stereotypes of the bad stranger, the reckless itinerant, the rogue passing
through, the rake.

That third word, "meaner," announces from the get-go the poem's two principle
economies—literal and emotional impoverishment, fecklessness and cruelty.
But this poem means to be more than a stock tale of a seduction gone predictably
wrong (the "perish" of the title derives from the Latin *perire: per*—detrimentally,
ire—to go; that is, to go badly). The luring and deed are over in the second and the
third quatrains. Addressing the "you," the speaker says that I

Bade you come over. Covered your hand with mine.
Bade you lay down. Stroked your neck, allowed your story.
Bade you pull my body down. Bore me half to death.
This is where the what and when happens. Two

people on a couch, liquored up and lousy at the mouth.

In the stanzas that follow, however, the seducer seems unable to cleanly extricate
from the victim. Shifting tenses and mood, the narrator mixes up condescending,
ruthless dissing (the "you" is criticized for everything from cheap cotton/poly
sheets to bad teeth) with a passive/aggressive cruelty that sometimes poses as what
may or may not be mock servility:

I wanted nothing more than
to put my tongue to your teeth. I'd have licked
our whole house clean, bought you a crystal set

of glassware . . .
        . . . .perhaps
you did not understand my critique as servitude.
I was merely asking to be put into your employ.

It is these sado-masochistic tendencies that complicate this psychological portrait.

Our "duplicitous" aggressor/narrator flirts at times with various victim poses; after listing all of the things about the "you" that are despised, the speaker admits that "I happen to like your mud-wash eyes. The mean / bags beneath your eyes. The jitter your hand does. / I don't actually care about anything but that." When the narrator confesses that "There was a light from your window that bore / right through me," Marvin's second use of "bore"—to tire, to invade—suggests that a kind of spiritual or psychic *ennui* may be at the root of this speaker's vexing, almost Iago-like motiveless malignancy and of the terrible torpor and paralysis of this closet drama, which seems not to be as much about relationship as it is about the speaker's own rootless swervings between brutality and a troubled, helpless futility.

The conflation of victim and aggressor intensifies: "Everything's been lousy since I left," the speaker complains, using "I" where the reader would expect to see "you," and one gets the strong feeling that the narrator could well be in conversation with him or herself at this point. But the poem's final image—anti-Romantic, too fresh to be the figment of a patent fantasy— reminds us that this poem is more than a moralistic or cautionary tale (the poem's title echoes the well known phrase "perish the thought"—an admonition to guard against mistakes or misbegotten attempts), but is an account of emotional circumstances between an I and a you that are all too genuinely fraught with shame, power-play, hurt, and sadness:

When you took me out into your back yard

And showed me the koi pond you'd filled with
Cement, it made me sad.
        Then you said you could bring it back.

In old ballads like "The Blacksmith" (19th-century), the wronged ingénue, when she confronts her fickle lover about his betrayal, is taunted by the rake to "bring your witness, Love, and I'll not deny you." Who or what is witness to this psychologically dark, astute "story"—to the complex, murky "what and when" of it? Obviously it must be the reader. The title suggests, too, that the eye of day (the gaze boring through the window) is also what brings these dark passages to light. In January, when the days seem to extinguish early, it is also paradoxically true that day light, like the unlikely but looked for restoration of the koi pond at the poem's end, is on the comeback. It would be a misreading of this poem to suggest a happy ending for its players. But that Marvin grants the "you" of the poem, in the privileged last line, a wish for restoration, if not the actual means to pull it off, is also undeniable.

SUZANNE BUFFAM

Happy Hour

I'll have an Icecap.
Make it a double.

Bring me a Fog on the River,
A Niagara Falls on the rocks,

And a Tempest with a chaser of Hail.
I don't want to be rescued.

I want to crawl through a honeycomb
Of sub-glacial passageways,

Shove my head under God's faucet
And keep chugging until I pass out.

I want thirst to drink me.
I want to come back as a bucket of blood.

If I were going to sidle up to the bar at, say, Cocteau's *Café des Poètes*, and order
a Suzanne Buffam cocktail, it would, judging from the intrepid work in her first
two prize-winning collections, include a generous, bracing double-shot of Yankee
sensuality, a "ripple of [ecological and/or human] extinction," and a mixer of
metaphysical musing. In another poem, "Vanishing," for instance, she writes,
"When I think about the fact // I am not thinking about you / It is a new way
of thinking about you." I'd also get a kicky dash of aphoristic brilliance; one of
Buffam's short poems, "On Last Lines," reads: "The last line should strike like a
lover's complaint. / You should never see it coming. / And you should never hear
the end of it." Another contains the lines "Experience taught me / That nothing
worth doing is worth doing / For the sake of experience alone." Pass a scintillating
capful of forthrightness over a shaker brimming with ice created from an eon's
worth of tears, intensity, time, rue, and humor, and I'd be served up an elixir meant
for the mouth, that elemental palate and portal for the unquenchable thirst of the
soul.

In "Happy Hour," Buffam appropriates the lingo of the cocktail hour, the language
of intoxication. Her tone is on the one hand ludic ("I'll have an Icecap. / Make it a

double"), playing self-consciously with inebriation, its slang and syntax—nightcaps, pub crawls, chasers, rocks. But this is not social drinking. What this speaker is having, and notice she's not asking, is the world itself, both poles and everything in between. In fact the poem quickly moves from the indicative to the imperative: "Make it a double. // Bring me a Fog on the River, / A Niagara Falls on the rocks, // And a Tempest with a chaser of Hail." Our narrator wants the whole, dramatic menu—sublime, high-volume, and straight up.

"I don't want to be rescued," the speaker tells us, lest the reader feel inclined to stall the headlong crash course of this increasingly accelerating bender of a poem. At this point the language moves from a fabular, ballsy, hyperbolic braggadocio into the precincts of ecstasy, shot through with the dark romance of oblivion, the apophatic allure of the via negativa. This speaker wants to be brought to her hands and knees in a "sub-glacial" maze that is, in a Petrarchan frisson, both freezing and lusciously honeycombed. With a syntactical and verbal insistence that defies impediment, the speaker's desideratum turns forceful, even sexual, and undeniable: "I want . . . // [to] shove my head under God's faucet / And keep chugging until I pass out." This is no fluffy blender drink she's after, no glass of house white. The intoxication this speaker demands (intoxication < ML *intoxicatare*, "to poison") is spiritual, cosmic, almost lethal, and speaks of a desire to take in the world and its mysteries that is so profound that the speaker, like a dervish mendicant drunk on God-lust and the enormity of her own capacity for desire, is brought to the very edge of her being and then beyond: "I want my thirst to drink me."

The last line is a killer. Allusions to the 1959 eponymous comic horror film aside, Buffam bellies up to the "blood bucket," Western slang term for an especially raucous saloon, taking her vision as far as she can. Consumed by her own immense thirst, the speaker wants to come back transformed by the entirety of what has transpired—melting polar caps, all manner of ferocious forces, not the least of which is her own passion. That "bucket of blood" reminds the reader of the six quarts of blood that comprise the human body—enough to fill a bucket—and we see that this is not just a poem about being wildly on fire for experience and the protean and manifold reaches of desire. The poem reminds us that this is who we are—we are polar caps, ice melt, seawater. We are what we love. As for the ending of this poem, I did not see it coming. And I want never to hear the end of it.

MONICA FERRELL

The Date

This time we'll come gloved & blind-
folded, we'll arrive on time.

With bees in our hair,
with an escort of expiring swans.

We'll appear to out-of-date & out-of-tune
violin music, we'll lie on our side.

Wearing rotting lotus behind our ears,
musk between our thighs.

This time we'll be tied down.
We'll cry out.

We'll only smoke if surprised
by tragedy's approach, as it noses closer.

This time we'll fall in love
with the blood color

of the sunset as we're walking home
over the bridge that takes us

between here & there.
This time we'll forget

how ancient Sarmatian lions go on
bearing marble messages for no one

who can understand their sarcophagus language,
forget sloths who climb so slow

they die before mating.
We'll grow improvident & stop believing

there was ever such a thing
as alone, such a hard

nail in the coffin
for one.

"I like a look of Agony," Emily Dickinson once wrote, "Because I know it's true— / Men do not sham Convulsion, / Nor simulate, a Throe—." I think of these lines, betraying my own mild agony, I suppose, as I trawl the greeting card aisle of a local drugstore, looking for Valentine cards (there has to be something between the saccharine puppies and the thong-clad cupids draped suggestively over cases of beer) to send to my grown children and my nieces and nephews. The fluorescent-lit, dropped ceiling above is hung with pre-cut hearts and the row itself, tucked between aisles of cold remedies and foot treatments, is festooned with red crepe-paper ribbons and flanked by a wincingly pink and red display of cards, whose messages of affection are dross. Where is the Valentine that rings true?

I find myself fantasizing about another kind of missive printed with real love poetry—poems that confront what is difficult, transgressive, jealous, obsessive, and unconventional in matters of the heart. Imagine, for instance, opening a folded piece of cardstock and finding inside this homoerotic excerpt from Cavafy's "The Bandaged Shoulder" (translated by Don Paterson):

. . . to be honest—I liked looking at the blood.
That blood. It was all part of my love.

When he left, I found a strip torn from the bandage
under his chair, a rag I should have thrown
straight in the trash—but I picked up and raised it to my lips,
and kept there a long while:
his blood on my lips, O my love, my love's blood.

Or this passage from Dickinson's "If I may have it, when it's dead," with its dark whiff of necrophilia and wild possessiveness:

Think of it Lover! I and Thee
Permitted—face to face to be—
After a Life—a Death—we'll say—
For Death was That—
And This—is Thee—.

There's an appeal to the ungenerous love poem, one which doesn't let its addressee off the hook, perhaps because, as Dickinson says, such expression rings true. When Keats writes

This living hand, now warm and capable
Of earnest grasping, would, if it were cold
And in the icy silence of the tomb,
So haunt thy days and chill thy dreaming nights
That thou would[st] wish thine own heart dry of blood
So in my veins red life might stream again,
And thou be conscience-calmed—see here it is—
I hold it towards you,

we believe that he means what he says: if I were dead, he asserts, you would feel so bad that you didn't love me while you could. So love me. Now.

Monica Ferrell's "The Date" is such a love poem, playing naughtily, at least at first, in a decadent kind of Djuna Barnes-meets-Cindy Sherman way, with the patent expectations and artifice of dating/mating rituals and the fetishizing of coupledom. Her couplets, smartly enjambed, and her use of a conflated present/future tense keep any notion of a credible fairy tale romance/happy ending precarious even as she indulges in arrestingly gothic, extravagant scenarios:

This time we'll come gloved & blind-
folded, we'll arrive on time.

With bees in our hair,
with an escort of expiring swans.

We'll appear to out-of-date & out-of-tune
violin music, we'll lie on our side.

Wearing rotting lotus behind our ears,
musk between our thighs.

Just as the speaker urges a kind of abandonment to hedonistic desire, with hints of bondage as freedom,

This time we'll be tied down.
We'll cry out.

A sense of foreboding is also present in this erotic tableaux, so that even the expected post-coital cigarette ("We'll only smoke if surprised / by tragedy's approach, as it noses closer") must be confronted both as cliché and as the inevitable heeding of a certain impending demise. "This time we'll fall in love," the speaker says, a sentiment Ferrell immediately, expertly enjambs and complicates "with the blood color // of the sunset as we're walking home / over the bridge that takes us // between here & there."

Although she knows where things are heading, Ferrell's speaker can't help but linger a moment on the bridge, and with "This time we'll forget" she moves into a Keatsian "More happy love! more happy, happy love!" passage, in which "ancient Sarmatian lions go on / bearing marble messages for no one" and "sloths . . . climb so slow / they die before mating." As the lines telescope and abbreviate, however, the reader senses the dissolution of the artificial coupling of "the date" and the contraction of the poem's indulgences until the poem brings us to a line of monometer and the ultimate solitude that is the real truth of the poem:

We'll grow improvident & stop believing

there was ever such a thing
as *alone*, such a hard

nail in the coffin
for one.

Ferrell's "The Date," then, is deliberately "out-of-date"—with its readers' expectations of romance, with its own story. Obsessed with time ("this time," "on time"), the poem insists on the significance of "date" in all of its implications—a particular day, a special occasion, an anniversary of a beginning or an ending, something we come to blind or with hyper-awareness, even date as fruit, with its attendant connotations of first fruits, carnal knowledge, and the fall from paradise. And the poem does so even as it "stops believing" in its own fiction of its lavish, improvident belief "that there was ever such a thing / as alone." Now that's a different kind of valentine.

VERSE'S RICH WEB PORTALS

VERSE'S RICH WEB PORTALS

Like many who live in a university or college burg, I am keenly aware, despite lots of town/gown collaboration and mixing in restaurants, coffee houses, private homes and apartments, art galleries, places of worship, music halls, bookstores, apple orchards, yoga studios, streets, food banks, the aisles of supermarkets, and the classroom, of the fact that our community is comprised of the members of an institution of higher learning and everyone else. A weathered sign on the roof of a now defunct local pancake shop still reads "Where Students, Tourists, and Townspeople Meet." One bar, also closed, advertised its watering hole as a gathering place for "Mountain Men and Debutantes." Though I'm not exactly sure how the distinctions play out in this last slogan, it would be disingenuous to think that some vestigial sense of "the university" in relation to the rest of the city does not endure and affect our identities and interactions.

The culture of poets in the academy can be afflicted by similar demarcations. Those "inside" tend to be acutely conscious of poets teaching at other institutions, many of whom were our former teachers, classmates, or students. We teach one another's books, invite each other to give readings, and await one another's new publications with an interconnected anxiety and eagerness. Our professional publications and conferences feature, print, and advertise the work being published by university presses and by colleagues in the nation's plethora of writing programs.

All the more reason to be grateful, then, for the protean community of writers both in and outside of the halls of higher education made manifest and widely accessible—and in a genuine way created—by the manifold, diverse internet websites, blogs, and other cyber-interactive spaces available to poets and readers of poetry. On an afternoon in mid-2011, for instance, a Google search of "poetry websites" yields some 4,710,000 results. "Poetry blogs" turns up 7,950,000. Some of these links will, in turn, offer their assessment of the best (and worst) of these sites. Clearly, a boundary-obliterating, ever evolving legion of readers and writers of poems burgeons.

Poet Ron Silliman, who maintains one of the most respected and longest running poetry-related sites in the blogosphere (http://ronsilliman.blogspot.com), comments that one consequence of their being "some 3,000 MFAs per year and fewer than 70 jobs available...is that the academy is becoming a much smaller part of the picture than it ever was before. I still think that the big story about writing in my lifetime lies in the demographics, from a few hundred poets to tens of thousands. The meaning of poetry in the aggregate is changing, and I don't think any of us has a very good handle as yet about what that really means."

A colleague of mine recently commented that he'd know it was time to retire when he grew weary of keeping up with the technologies involved. And that says something, given how universities and colleges are often playing catch-up in this regard. My friend was speaking in frustrated response, I think, to our university's implementation of a new Sisyphean student information system, but he has a point. Though there are many within the halls of higher education, even in creative writing, who are on the cutting edge of the most current technologies, there are others, like myself, who hold steadfastly to e-mail and who do not do Facebook or Tweet or otherwise—and not out of any Luddite bully pride but because, in my case at least, I feel lucky to get my hair washed each busy week, let alone keep up with all those friends. Still, I want to stay connected, especially with new and intrepid work being done by people I do not know or of whom I've not yet heard, which makes me all the more appreciative of those sites which reach out in various ways to people not inclined to spend a lot of time on-line.

Of these, I'd like to mention two in particular, though there are many.

Poetry Daily (http://poems.com) was founded in the mid-1990s by Diane Boller, Don Selby, and Rob Anderson. At the time, all three were working at a law publishing company, exploring how the Internet could be used to sell law books. Boller and Selby continue to maintain this popular poetry site (depending upon the time of year, *PD* gets slightly over 10,000 unique visitors on popular days, and well over 12,000 email addresses are listed as subscribers to their weekly newsletter), which offers, in a kind of clearinghouse, a new poem a day, accompanied by a featured book, press, or journal, along with a list of recently received books, a weekly updated news page of current reviews, essays, and awards, a list of contests, and a splendid archive of poems. Boller writes that when she and her colleagues started the site, "the Internet was brand new…and seemed an exciting way for niche print publishers to make their work more widely known. We're poetry readers, not poets, and did not have an academic institution as an anchor, so it was difficult for us to find out what poets were publishing where (in which journals), or even sometimes to find books by poets whose work we had already discovered and admired. We started *Poetry Daily*, inviting publishers to send us their publications, so that we could introduce representative poems to our readers, one a day. We were surprised and pleased to discover that there was a large audience of poetry readers who were, like us, trying to figure out which poets they enjoyed reading, and where to find their poetry." On a Tuesday evening in November 2010, for example, a reader can find at the *PD* site four new poems by London freelance journalist and critic Alan Brownjohn, a note about his new book, a smart essay by Carol Moldaw about whether writing poetry is a "luxury or necessity," reprinted from *AGNI*, and a host of recently arrived titles and poetry news-related pieces. For those potential readers not inclined to browse the Internet on their own, Boller and Selby send out a weekly e-mail newsletter missive alerting readers to features of the week ahead.

I have never met the poet and critic Ron Slate, but I know something of the quality of his mind thanks to the periodic e-mails he sends out, alerting readers not regularly browsing the Internet or receiving pokes and tweets to his website, *On the Seawall* (http://www.ronslate.com). The site serves as a homepage for Slate, but is devoted primarily to his discerning, elegant, forthright reviews of new work by others. His far-reaching and aesthetically diverse tastes have acquainted me with many poets, fiction writers, artists, and critics I would not have otherwise encountered. He periodically invites other writers to recommend new books in a kind of round-up, and in this way creates a space that feels generative and full of dialogue.

On the Seawall was launched in August 2007, on Slate's 57th birthday. Slate tells me that he intended at first "to blog in the stricter sense — that is, to post comments regularly and generate conversation. But I discovered that I had little to say and no desire to obligate myself to say it every day. Writing about books, however, gives me enough space and time to understand the shape of my response. A book of poems (or any artwork) tries to create a place for experience. My job is to discover the place and describe the source of my pleasure as specifically as I can. William Meredith said, 'One cannot review a bad book without showing off.' A writer should be wary of conforming to his own tastes, so I cover a range of poetry (and other genres). I'm not interested in devoting energy to work that fails to stimulate or provoke me just to tweak someone's nose. *The Seawall* is an American poets' site—but its impulse is cross-genre and global. To admire is tantamount to being influenced—and since I take much out of my fiction and non-fiction reading, I assume other poets do, too. In sum: I maintain *The Seawall* to keep in touch with people, to enjoy our communal literary life, to bring accomplished writing to the attention of my following, and to elevate my pulse."

It's not surprising that many of these poetry-related sites are maintained by poets: Ron Silliman, Jerome Rothenberg, Don Share, Slate, and countless others. Perhaps what's most exciting about these sites that blur distinctions between writers in and outside of academic settings is the way they encourage us to read. Long ago, when I graduated from college, I thought: At last I can read, really read, the way I want to read, and not just what's assigned to me, but in a way that allows the authors I encounter to lead me to new texts. If Ai read Plath, I would read Plath. Plath read Dickinson: I would read her; Dickinson read Emily Brontë, and so I'd read her next. And this might bring me round to Agha Shahid Ali, Claudia Rankine, Anne Carson, Susan Howe, Rae Armantrout, and so forth, backwards and forward in time, across sensibilities and cultures. I am grateful for the ways these virtual sites invite this kind of exchange by providing a wider, more various, vital, world and mind-opening lens into poetry and poetics than I might be able to find on my own. Since so many of these steadfast, stalwart stewards of the poetry of others rarely tout their own work at their own sites, I offer below a poem by Ron Slate, which offers a richly restrained account of the death of Erik Satie, the experimental, minimalist composer and avant-garde writer. Slate's poem considers Satie's literal demise, of course, but also explores his death in terms of the parallel decay of certain sensibilities, or the perception of them, in one's milieu. It's rich to think of Slate's account of Satie in the context of the rapidly changing landscape by which American poems make their way into the world. Following the poem is a short list of some of the sites Slate is currently visiting, a catalogue that includes *Silliman's Blog* and *Poetry Daily*.

Here is Ron Slate's poem:

The Death of Erik Satie

The arches aspire to a point
in the church of childhood,
a single note here and here and here.
Drafty gothic undertones, the grandiose
obscurity of the modern mind.

Cirrhosis, then pleurisy.
Hours waiting in stillness,
as in an empty cabaret.

A bell tinkles in the corridor, the viaticum
drifts toward the dying man next door.
Something long ago made the world
hostile. So of course one mocks
a style no longer exploitable.

Conversation with the nuns --
You understand, the Creator
commits technical errors, he keeps us
at arm's length, his soiled cuff
fills us with medieval joy.
The patient rebuffs Poulenc and Ravel –

but admits Braque, Brancusi, Stravinsky,
stand there and there and there.
There is nothing left to renounce.

Choirs, music hall songs, then through the war
anyone could witness the decline.
Curses for the idiots -- Mon Cher Directeur,
you are brutal, inhospitable, you are under arrest.
The Pope is excommunicated! *Monsieur et cher ami,*
vous n'êtes qu'un cul, mais un cul
sans musique. One must reject the obvious.

Final years, cognac and beer,
then home to a dusty room with a depleted piano,
desolate possessions, scores inscribed
affectionately by Debussy, before the feud.

Franc notes poke from the pages
of books, advance payment for final music.
The rolled umbrella clutched more tightly.

A filament of notes,
each one intended. Something long ago
created this secret sorrow. Erik Satie dies
at the Hôpital Saint-Joseph.

and Slate's recommended sites:

Poetry Daily, http://poems.com/
Silliman's Blog, http://www.ronsilliman.blogspot.com/
How A Poem Happens, http://www.howapoemhappens.blogspot.com/
Poems and Poetics, http://www.poemsandpoetics.blogspot.com/
Squandermania, http://donshare.blogspot.com/
Poets at Work, http://poetsatwork.tripod.com/

MICHAEL RUTHERGLEN

Went Viral

It was for you
alone I wrote the song
I sang into the screen and sent
to you alone, that someone else
then saw and sent among
their friends, their friends among
still others still beyond
me, omphalos node
of a lopsided system—
new lines of transmission
bloomed askew from spreading hubs—forgotten, though
each watched me sing as if to him or her

of you, your *amor fati*, face
across an asymptotic gap
in time awaiting our arriving late
by planes delayed by planes delayed,
your glance's axis glancing off of mine
across the gate, above computers closed,
exhausted from all we'd watched thereon—
crashes, water drops and bullets shot
at ten thousand frames per second,

feats of song in blurred
exurban bedrooms—overloaded
glance that turned
to gaze to blazons
sung into my screen and seen
and seen through countless eyes alike aglaze
with blazing frames of video-memes,
through minds aswarm with same,
like ours that sudden once, our addled
pleasure centers blazing gray
and out before we saw each other,
numb to wonder
among ever-doubling wonders.

Cursor on a Chinese Poem

Steady liquid
crystal ictus.
Exiguous

calligrapher.
Beacon in the branching.
Interstitial

to glyphs
in a winter epistle,
serifed dædal

shadow-tracks
on a snowfield's face.
You trace-

lessly retraverse
or erase—
There are no birds.

Snowblind under
summits, a hermit,
I drift

awaiting—what?
You blink in place.

Stone, fingers, charcoal, wax, blood, ink, spray paint, bridge girders, vellum, quills, clay tablets, sticks, wolf hair, rice paper, papyrus, styluses, lipstick, mirrors, indelible markers, thighs, printing presses, typewriters, mimeograph machines, keyboards, cartridges, pixilated screens—writers require some sort of space/surface on which to make their markings and a means by which to make them. In the way that sipping gin from a glass martini saucer is a different experience from enjoying it out of a red plastic cup, the technologies with and by which we write alter the nature of our relationship with those processes and with manifest text. Writing is itself, of course, a technology (<Gk *techniká*, of art and craft). And just as literacy, the ability to make language visible, radically changed everything (Anne Carson writes that "Oral cultures and literate cultures do not think, perceive or fall in love in the same way"), the computer and related technologies have rapidly, radically affected

the *techne* of writing—not only the means by which we write, but also how we internalize, interact with, and relate to the materials and processes of language. Michael Rutherglen's "Went Viral" and "Cursor on a Chinese Poem" concern themselves with these economies in a way that exposes and enacts some of their attendant risks, possibilities, and power. "Went Viral" recounts how, by cyber-accident, something presumably private, written for and then sung "into the screen" by the speaker "to you / alone" (the "song" may have been an actual musical composition or it may refer to a poem; "sang" may be literal as well—the speaker may have recorded himself on video speaking or actually singing on camera before sending the video off electronically—or he may have simply sent off the text), is picked up and sent widely and indiscriminately about in the phenomenon, often courted deliberately by marketers and other intentional promoters, known as "going viral." The quietly relentless velocity of Rutherglen's telegraphed and flashing lines—which take up and repeat whole words and parts of words (*gaze, blazon, aglaze, blazing*)—mimics the self-replicating and infectious motions by which viruses are spread: "It was for you / alone I wrote the song / I sang into the screen and sent / to you alone, that someone else / then saw and sent among / their friends, their friends among / still others still beyond / me, omphalos node / of a lopsided system." As this intimate, troubadour chanson "bloom[s] askew from spreading hubs" (could computer technologies be closer to oral than to page-bound culture?), the speaker/author finds himself somatically effaced ("forgotten") by all the song's burgeoning host-cell, public readership, despite the fact that each stranger "watched me sing as if to him or her // of you."

In some ways, of course, this is what happens with all love poems, even the most personal, once they make their way to readers. "Shall I compare thee to a summer's day?" Shakespeare asks, and we think he is speaking to us. Rutherglen, however, is interested in pressing beyond this obvious ruse and into the ways in which the promiscuous privacy of cyber dissemination can affect our capacity for intimate speech and intimate listening. Interestingly, he withholds the original song—the one meant for the "you" and seen by everyone else—from this poem. Nonetheless, he is determined that the intent of his *blason* (part anti-Petrarchan love poem, part complaint) not be lost. Whatever romantic ardor may have inspired the original, private poem, its meaning has been irrevocably changed by the fact of its being now "seen / and seen through countless eyes alike aglaze / with glazing frames of video-memes, / through minds aswarm with same." Do our cultural "feats of song in blurred / exurban bedrooms" (infiltrating our most private space through television, news reports, YouTube, iPhones, even radio, all of our communications) overload us, making "real" face-to-face meetings asymptotically impossible by interfering technologies, "your glance's axis glancing off of mine / across the gate, above computers closed, / exhausted from all we'd watched thereon— / crashes, water drops and bullets shot / at ten thousand frames per second"? Lest we too easily read in this an indictment of the forces of technology, however, Rutherglen brings us back, at the conclusion, to the romantic passion that began the poem, to that "sudden once" of ecstasy that may have been the initial inspiration for the poem that "went viral": "our addled / pleasure centers blazing gray / and out before we saw each other." Perhaps, the poem puts forward, the risks of truly becoming one with another person are, finally, transient if not impossible. Private ecstasy, like communal ecstasy, might prove fatal if sustained without dilution, leaving us "numb to wonder / among ever-doubling wonders"—ever the paradox of Eros, in body, in text.

"Cursor on a Chinese Poem" possesses, visually, the intricate exactitude and syllabic artfulness of an ideogram. Several layers of text and meaning shimmer from the vertically reticulated, scroll-like strokes/strophes, as Rutherglen shows us a computer cursor (<L *cursor* runner) moving over the text of a Chinese poem (presumably translated and printed from a poem that may have once been inked on rice paper) that floats now on a computer screen, the framed text of which is in turn depicted within the printed page of Rutherglen's poem (and further reproduced here). Through the poem's kinetic valences, we see the cursor as an agent ("Steady liquid / crystal ictus. / Exiguous // calligrapher"), integral to the poem over which it pulses ("Beacon in the branching. / Interstitial / to glyphs / in a winter epistle, / serifed daedal // shadow-tracks / on a snowfield's face").

At this point the cursor is making meaning in the poem; it has become part of the text, with the unique capacity not only to trace (like the brush-strokes, like the eye, like the strokes of syllables) across snow of the screen/page, but to "trace- / lessly retraverse / or erase," as well. By the time the poem gives us the lines of the Chinese poem—"*There are no birds. // Snowblind under / summits, a hermit, / I drift / awaiting*—what?"—the reader, too, like the speaker/hermit, is lost in the snow of the page, the poem. With "You blink in place," Rutherglen reassembles the reader/writer/translator/text contract, but not without leaving us, too, blinking in wonder, transformed by the thrilling transgressions and textual/temporal crossings and liaisons made possible by the poem's many ghosted incarnations and by its summoned, foregrounded electronic technologies.

KYLE DARGAN

Note Blue or Poem for Eighties Babies
(also for T.P., 1950-2010)

If it's Teddy singing it—*don't leave me*
this way—it's not that version of the song
your parents spun themselves through, becoming
one of those strobe-lit dervishes. Listen
as it pounds. Think of them not dancing but stilled
in a corner, buttressed by their own sweat
and clairvoyant uncertainty. Every plea
and atonement that reaches
sweet and hard from Teddy's vocal folds
is ambivalent towards their present's
travails—the night humid and reduced to tissue
paper's fragility. It's June, 1976, years before
code like *mother* and *father*—before either
is prepared to admit they could never imagine
the uphill slope of love after disco
wore its vinyl tongue unfurrowed
and the babies—babies that began
as mere exchanges
of pheromones on a dance floor—
began falling into their young laps.
It isn't your fault. You did not stop the music.
Or if you did, it was Thelma Houston's cover,
not this bearded prayer of negative capability—
the *pleaseplease* under each footstep your parents took
beyond the cusp realizing that nothing so good
could stay that good so long.

Kyle Dargan has been praised, in the *New York Times* and elsewhere, as a poet with
a hip, original take on the ways in which musical textures stalk the language and
culture of poems. This particularly rich, nostalgic, forgiving poem—part address to
the speaker's brother and sister children of the 1980s, part portrait of the unwitting
disco-gen parents who created them, part elegy to the magnificent drummer and
vocalist Teddy Pendergrass, who passed in 2010—reveals another of Dargan's
poetic gifts: a kinetic stereoscopy that allows, in any one poem, a provocative
conflation of personal and public histories, of past and present situations ("If it's

Teddy singing it—*don't leave me / this way*—it's not that version of the song / your parents spun themselves through, becoming / one of those strobe-lit dervishes"... but rather "Thelma Houston's cover" that by the mid-70s defined the disco craze). In this way, Dargan manages to conjure vividly the parents both *before* they were parents—in strobe-lit, pheromone-driven dance floor heat—and *later*, on "the uphill slope of love after disco" into parenthood and responsibility. The poem also invites the reader—implicated, in part, in the "you" of "Eighties Babies" the poem addresses—to attend to the vulnerability tissued within the syncopated clubglitz soundtrack of that earlier parental generation, and to find there origins of mutual, cross-generational desire, disillusionment, and need for absolution ("It isn't your fault").

All generations do the best they can with what they inherit, and I love how the poem enacts a kind of (un)"covering" as it moves among its players, Pendergrass and Houston included. Because of Dargan's pop-cultural breadth and savvy, I rarely read one of his poems without subsequently seeking out a book, a historical figure, a song he's mentioned. If you can locate your Harold Melvin & the Blue Notes *Wake Up Everybody* LP (or check it out on YouTube), with Pendergrass on vocals, "Don't Leave Me This Way" is worth a spin. There's so much poetry even in the humming with which Pendergrass starts off and in the rap with which he concludes the song. I confess having had to interrupt the writing of this commentary several times in order to get up and dance to the "bearded prayer of negative capability" that saturates the yearning bridge of that song, Dargan's poem, perhaps all art.

KATE DANIELS

Disjunction

On my knees in my office,
leaning over the metal can
of waste, I squeeze my breasts
to express the milk that's accrued
in my graduate seminar on postmodern
poetry. Six hours since the last feed
and only eight weeks postpartum,
the pressure's enough to kill a cow.
Talking head reduced by hormones
to a pitiful creature on bended knee,
weeping and milking her own hot tits.
It's thin and blue, this milk intended
for my daughter's mouth. Instead,
it's spurting coolly on my ink-stained hands,
dribbling in a painful start, then flowing
unencumbered on the paper detritus
of my chosen work – the dean's agenda
for the faculty meeting, a debatable
policy on sexual harassment,
the first draft of some idiot's
poem on fraternity love: unprotected
rutting on a bed of crushed empties.
                    —Life is so unutterably
weird, isn't it? Organizing my thoughts
on the cultural disjunctions of the end
of the century, and how they break their way into
our literature and art, and how bizarre
is the era that has stranded me here
wastefully wringing the milk from my breasts
in the same office where I scheme to procure
permanent tenure.

Landing a decent job, or any job, keeping that job, proceeding to promotion, securing tenure—these hurdles are always on the minds of academics. Kate Daniels's "Disjunction" first appeared over a decade ago, at the *fin de siècle*, but the ironies and anxieties it addresses remain strikingly relevant. The on-line Merriam-Webster defines "disjunction" (a 14th-century word, <L. *disjunctionem*, separation) as

"a sharp cleavage between theory and practice," and as Daniels's speaker describes herself expressing "the breast milk that's accrued / in my graduate seminar on postmodern / poetry" into a waste basket in her office ("Six hours since the last feed / and only eight weeks postpartum, / the pressure's enough to kill a cow"), the reader can't help but pick up on the dark humor of the various resonances of "cleavage" in this context. And while the circumstances being described in the poem are arresting in their ironies,

Talking head reduced by hormones
to a pitiful creature on bended knee,
weeping and milking her own hot tits.
It's thin and blue, this milk...
...spurting coolly on my ink-stained hands,
dribbling in a painful start, then flowing
unencumbered on the paper detritus
of my chosen work—the dean's agenda
for the faculty meeting, a debatable
policy on sexual harassment,
the first draft of some idiot's
poem on fraternity love: unprotected
rutting on a bed of crushed empties,

Daniels resists over-simplifying this situation. The era that has "stranded" her speaker, "wastefully wringing milk from my breasts / in the same office where I scheme to procure / permanent tenure," is one shaped not just by university and broader socio-economic systems that exact certain priorities and sacrifices in the workplace (and not just in the academy and not only by women), but also, one presumes, by personal issues: career goals, ambition, the exigencies of making a living, and a desire to have children despite the demands of one's job. The "disjunction"—the break between theory and practice—that has brought a lactating woman to her knees (in ironic worship? sheer exhaustion? anger? self-directed dark humor? all of the above?) in her own office after conducting a seminar on post-modern poetries (where, among other things, she's tried to organize her "thoughts / on the cultural disjunctions of the end / of the century, and how they break their way into / our literature and art") does raise questions about how and why, for instance, a woman seeking tenure might not openly breastfeed in class, but Daniels is careful not to place easy blames. It could well be that toting her infant along to class is something the speaker herself would prefer not to do. And it also appears that this speaker has, for whatever array of unnamed reasons, made the decision to have a child and breastfeed it while continuing to work and receive the respect and security she deserves for doing so, and in a context that for one reason or another compels her to express herself (and Daniels must certainly be thinking of the pun here) in this way.

Just as Daniels eschews what in the broader arena of the university might be an easier route—to make the system solely culpable for her speaker's predicament—she also takes a playful shot at the very "post-modernism" that is the subject of her "work," her spent graduate seminar for which she is making certain sacrifices. Is, for example, there an "author," or is he or she merely a frottaged, shifting theoretical construct of socio-economic, cultural, ecological, biological, and personal forces? Well, maybe yes, maybe no. But certainly someone who might be an author, *the* author (those "ink-stained hands"), finds herself, in the text that is Daniels's poem, defined by such forces, w(h)etting the "paper detritus / of [her] chosen work" with her own body's generative fluids in a very palpable, identified, value-charged, and human moment.

JENNIFER KEY

Delay at Washington National

The flags these days are always at half-mast.
Enlisted men and women grown fatigued
in uniforms the shade of sand and mortar, wars
no one can win, supposedly are mustering

or, rather, sit and stare inside the terminal
of Reagan National. Our flight is stalled as well
by silver screens of rain that cordon off
our coast. Wet weather in the heartland holds

us here. No shadow falls except the Monument's,
a sundial ticking down the hours until dark.
Who knows how long our narrow rows must wait.
The child a row ahead repeats her endless whys,

And sunlight, firing in flashes, ricochets
across the river's tongue that forks this spit
of jetty and the Capitol – America's
own Pantheon, its marble layers stacked

like cake for congressmen to slice and serve.
The fathers of our country can't be found;
instead, the boys in cufflinks play at war,
their sandbox half the way across the world.

Lords of pork, lapel pins, legislation;
Pater Familias to beltway wives
swanning in suits the color of lipstick;
well-heeled progenitors of rustbelt states

and sons in seersucker who do not kneel
but prep under St. Alban's cross upon the Mount,
this season swathed in sweet wisteria
that weeps alone for those unblessed by birth, the rest

who shall not harden here on velvet playing fields
but once deployed grow wiser in the awful grace
of God (who, it's said, must be on our side).
At last the engines rumble, gunned to life:

the flight attendant's cue to take the stage
and pantomime procedures for takeoff.
Any moment now we'll rise above entrenched moats
of Metro churning underground or Zoo,

where moms with strollers watch orangutans.
The stewardess, Tippi Hedren honey-blond
and alabaster cool, rehearses her escape.
She pirouettes in navy pumps; we see

her up-do's swirl, a cyclone pinned in place.
How casual survival when in flight!
Even her navy ascot's earned its wings.
She flashes us her smile, which disappears

beneath a yellow mask. To start the flow
Of oxygen inhale. But I'm already slouched
against the window's plastic curve to watch
spring-green Virginia crenellate before

I number every sail boat on the Bay
that writes the wind onto the waves in wakes,
a trail of V's chalked white and soon erased.
The stewardess strolls our rows to demonstrate

the proper way to clutch a cushion just in case.
In case of water landing (in which case we won't
Be landing) *for your safety we're equipped*—
The child begins to bang her sippy cup.

Attention please for just a minute, folks!
She wants to show us how to save ourselves,
but we've been belted in for so damned long,
the lot of us just stares, too tired to look up.

Although often reported to be among the safest modes of getting from one place
to another, airplane travel, in the words of a colleague who does a lot of flying, can
feel like a whoosh down a big commode. Tragic accidents aside, who does not have
a minor horror story—a night or two spent sprawled over four hard bucket seats in
a 24/7 wash of greenish neon light, the entire airport shut down by fog or blizzard
or security alert, or that sequence of delayed, missed, and protracted connections

that finds the traveler, counter-intuitively, back at the very same airport she left nearly a day before? How about those hours burning fuel inexplicably on the tarmac, one passenger in a cramped row of disgruntled fellow sojourners, every one of them wanting to scream like the toddler in the back, and one person in particular, the one seated next to you, taking off her shoes just when you thought the pong of perspiration and frustration couldn't get worse?

That same friend, the frequent flyer, likes to remind me that travel derives from the Anglo-French *travailler, travail*: to torment, labor, suffer, strive. And while it's true that air travel can be difficult, the limbo of airports can also provide for the laid-over, grounded, or simply waiting wayfarer a kind of limbo space—a climate-controlled realm that, despite Wi-Fi and cell-phone outlet poles designed to accommodate an international array of chargers, can also provide unaccustomed time for reading *The New Yorker* or *Saveur* cover to cover, putting in that long-put-off phone call to an estranged friend, or even, for someone unused to daytime drinking, making one's way to the nearest Vino Volo (it's 5 o'clock somewhere in the world, yes?).

Air travel has become even more complicated since recent wars, the attacks of September 11th, and other terrorist threats and incidents have heightened sometimes controversial security measures. Such is the world in which the speaker of Jennifer Key's "Delay at Washington National," stranded on the runway by bad weather elsewhere ("silver screens of rain that cordon off / our coast"), finds herself:

The flags these days are always at half-mast.
Enlisted men and women grown fatigued
in uniforms the shade of sand and mortar, wars
no one can win, supposedly are mustering

or, rather, sit and stare inside the terminal
of Reagan National.

The website of the Metropolitan Washington Airport Authorities reports that the Ronald Reagan National Airport (formerly Washington National airport, renamed in 1998 by Bill Clinton to honor the Gipper) is located just across the Potomac from the nation's capital and "features an unequaled view of Washington D.C. and key monuments." Key's speaker uses her purgatorial stalled time in the idling cabin to meditate on just that view, on the Monument, "a sundial ticking down the hours until dark" and on the sunlight that,

...firing in flashes, ricochets
across the river's tongue that forks this spit
of jetty and the Capitol – America's
own Pantheon, its marble layers stacked

like cake for congressmen to slice and serve.

Laid out like a national tableau before her, this iconic American scene contrasts
strikingly with the psychic "wet weather in the heartland" of our narrator, who,
with a wry mix of sadness and ire despairs that "the fathers of our country can't be
found" even as "boys in cufflinks play at war, / their sandbox half the way across
the world," a vision that extends to despair at the "beltway wives / swanning in suits
the color of lipstick" and at the privileged "sons in seersucker who do not kneel /
but prep under St.Alban's cross upon the Mount."

Key's use of a roughly pentameter, 10-syllable line in quatrains lends an elegiac,
almost Wordsworthian ("Milton! Thou should'st be living at this hour") aspect to
her national lament, which moves beyond the scene before her and into meditation
on the "season" of war itself, wherein wisteria "weeps alone for those unblessed
by birth"—for those who, "once deployed grow wiser in the awful grace / of God
(who, it's said, must be on our side)."

Issues of risk and danger take a new focus once the plane engines "[gun] to life,"
and a flight attendant "[takes] the stage." Key's tone changes slightly to match this
shift in scene. The lens is inside the cabin now. As the attendant ("her up-do's
swirl, a cyclone pinned in place. / How casual survival when in flight!") futilely tries
to engage the restless passengers to attend to safety instructions to be followed in
the event of an emergency, the speaker "[slouches] / against the window's plastic
curve to watch / spring-green Virginia crenellate" and the way in which the wind
makes and then erases "V's chalked white" on the Bay. The speaker seems aware
that after the privilege of so much time for musing on the wrongs of the big
national picture, she herself can't muster up the energy to care about whether or not
she knows to inhale to start the flow of oxygen in the mask that may fall from the
ceiling above in the unlikely event of a change of cabin pressure—surely a mask, as
we're often admonished in psycho-pop jargon, that we must put on ourselves before
we are capable of ever helping others.

"She just wants to show us how to save ourselves," the speaker admits, trusting
that the reader will see, as she does, that her own fretting about the state of the
nation, however complex, must come from a similar impulse. By closing the poem

with "we've been belted in for so damned long, / the lot of us just stares, too tired to look up," Key does not excuse yet makes room for understanding the ways in which a traveler, a citizen, a nation can become inured to its accountability, its responsibility to care, to look up, to pay attention.

DEBRA ALLBERY

Of Evanescence
for Agha Shahid Ali (1949-2001)

The mail from Kashmir, Amherst, Asheville: postmarks from a route of evanescence.
Emerald and cochineal the flight of days, their cardamom-infused evanescence.

The way she had in her rushes – of resonance,
you wrote. *I too so want to eat evanescence.*

Rococo grace on the dance floor, inscribing Arabic on air,
his hands scrolled sly tributes to evanescence.

Fame is a bee, said Dickinson. *It has a song and a sting
and ah, too, a wing* humming its minute evanescence.

A word is a stay against, against. Bare or brocaded, it breathes
into breath, defies what's at the root of evanescence.

What falls away is always and is near: even Roethke's weight
is light. Is that the beauty or truth of evanescence?

Whoever you are, pledge to me your undying love.
Undying: your message, Shahid, refuting evanescence.

Debra Allbery's ghazal "Of Evanescence" is dedicated to the late Kashmiri-
American poet, editor, and translator Agha Shahid Ali, who died of cancer on
December 8, 2001, at the age of 52. Admired for his own ghazals and translations
of them, and attributed with bringing the form to a wider audience through
his edited volume *Ravishing Disunities: Real Ghazals in English*, Ali is well known
among poets for encouraging everyone—students, colleagues, strangers on the
street, audience members at readings—to attempt writing ghazals of their own.
Fittingly, then, Allbery elects to cast her tribute in this ancient form and chooses
as her monorhyme a word Ali borrowed from Emily Dickinson in his own elegy
about transience, exile, poetic ambition, and untimely personal loss, "A Nostalgist's
Map of America." The Emily Dickinson Lexicon (http://edl.byu.edu)—an
invaluable resource out of Brigham Young University which maintains a dictionary
of some 9,275 words and variants in Dickinson's verse—defines "evanescence"
as dissipation, departure, graduate removal, a fleeting moment, demise, and the

transition of death, and cites two uses of the word in Dickinson's verse: the famous hummingbird poem (Franklin 1489, "A Route of Evanescence") and the lesser known "The Face in Evanescence lain" (Franklin 1521), in which Dickinson describes the visage of a dead person, transient with the "sheen" of the divine. Allbery makes use of all of these meanings of evanescent as she maps out her own path of remembrance and poetic legacy.

That we are meant to see this ghazal as a route/root is clearly implied by the palpable absence of "a route" from the Dickinson line alluded to in the title. And in fact the poem is replete with allusion in a way that honors Ali's own practice of dedicating his poems to and sampling from the work of friends and other writers. Stanza by stanza, Allbery's poem creates a chain of the poetic influences holding sway over both the poet and her subject. A strikingly peripatetic writer, whose exile and career gave him a myriad of addresses during his too-short life, Ali (like Dickinson) was self-conscious about his poems being in a very real sense letters to and from the worlds he inhabited and carried within (interestingly, Allbery herself has led something of a nomadic life, having called at least nine places home before settling in as Director of the prestigious low-residency MFA program Warren Wilson College in Asheville, North Carolina, several years ago). Allbery's opening line, in fact, is a shout-out to all of the references to the mail in Ali's work ("Postcard from Kashmir," for example, and "The Country Without a Post Office"); it also makes reference to a nod by Ali (who lived in Amherst, Massachusetts, for many years while teaching at the University of Massachusetts), in his poem "From Amherst to Kashmir," to Dickinson's "If I could bribe them by a Rose" ("If I could bribe them by a Rose / I'd bring them every flower that grows / From Amherst to Cashmere!"). In this way, Allbery conflates Dickinson's color-saturated, synaesthetic vision of a hummingbird in constant motion in "A Route of Evanescence" ("emerald" and "cochineal") with Ali's own ardent, multi-cultural, "cardamom-infused evanescence." In Allbery's ghazal, as in Ali's work, worlds are constantly and kinetically exchanging their secrets.

In seven discreet but entwined couplets, haunted by the repeated "evanescence," Allbery offers a graceful, mimetic testimony to Ali's generous spirit and work, interlacing and mingling lines from Ali's own poems, especially those in which he himself honors other poets like Dickinson (*The way she had in her rushes – of resonance,* / you wrote. *I too so want to eat evanescence*) with language from Dickinson herself (*Fame is a bee,* said Dickinson. *It has a song and a sing / and ah, too, a wing*), with references as well to Frost ("A word is a stay against, against"), Hopkins ("Bare or brocaded, it breathes / into breath"), Theodore Roethke ("*What falls away is always and is near:* even Roethke's weight / is light"), and Keats ("Is that the beauty or truth of evanescence?"). In one of the poem's most luminous passages, we see Ali in motion, honoring Arabic and its profound influence: "Rococo grace on the dance floor, inscribing Arabic on air, / his hands scrolled sly tributes to evanescence." I like imagining this scene as perhaps occurring at the Warren Wilson College low-residency MFA program, known for its excellent dance parties as well as its superb faculty, intrepid programming, and distinguished graduates, where Ali taught for many years and knew Allbery. Warren Wilson College, the first low-residency Master of Fine Arts Program in the country, originally founded by Ellen Bryant Voigt at Goddard College in 1976 and moved to Warren Wilson in 1981, celebrated its 35th anniversary in 2011; the program honored Ali and other distinguished teachers in the program at a gala held in Asheville that summer.

The final couplet, the penultimate line of which Forrest Gander, in his moving memoir of Ali, says was the last recording Ali had on his voice mail, brings into concert the long "/o͞o/" sounds (*too, tribute, minute, root, beauty, truth*) that have kept the "you" present throughout the poem, and, in a final gesture of praise, offers "Shahid"—Ali's name—in the last line, a "signature" spot usually reserved for the name of the poet making the ghazal. Even this move on Allbery's part, presenting Ali's name instead of her own, shows her profound appreciation for Ali's playfulness and largesse, evoking as it does the ending of one of Ali's most well known ghazals, "Tonight," in which Ali shape-shifts into Melville's famous protagonist:

And I, Shahid, only am escaped to tell thee –
God sobs in my arms. Call me Ishmael tonight.

Allbery's poem honors and devours the notion of evanescence, proving not only by its powerful, allusive, and *meta* tribute to Ali (that Allbery and Ali begin with the same sound, "all," is another rich layer of the poem), but also by its own spare, charged beauty, that poetry can both acknowledge and refute demise. Poets' names may be writ on water, but their poems, speaking always to one another across breaches of time, place, and space, like Ali's dance floor scrollings, can pay "sly tributes to evanescence." "Bare or brocaded, it breathes," Allbery writes of poetry's portal, defying oblivion.

POETIC BLOODLINES

POETIC BLOODLINES

April is National Poetry Month, and this has me thinking gratefully of the forces that have helped shape me as a poet in the 35 or so years that I've been apprenticing. If I were to speak honestly about my own poetic influences, I'd have to mention the fact that the room where I do most of my writing is also the family laundry room, and that for much of my adult life the best time to scribble notes for poems has been in the office lobbies of my children's music teachers and orthodontists (or on the bleachers at Little League games or in my car at stoplights or in the bathroom with my foot propped up against the door—"Mommy will be out in a minute!"). This and the reality that to avoid throwing out my back I need to carry around a notebook small and light enough to fit into an ergonomic shoulder bag have probably contributed as much as has the work of my literary tribe (Emily Dickinson, Sylvia Plath, Gerard Manley Hopkins, among others) to the dense, compressed lyric poem that tends to be my favored mode.

Yet I am, like most poets (except for the occasional scribe who proudly relays that he or she doesn't read other poets for fear of contaminating a singular vision), a reader. Poets have literary forebears. We have family trees. Geneologies. To paraphrase John Donne on the subject of bodies, our literary influences "are ours, though they are not we." As poets, our relationships with those writers who have helped to shape our work, both those among "the noble living and the noble dead," can be wildly ambivalent, ranging from obsessive, exclusionary possessiveness (*"my* Constantine Cavafy! *my* Muriel Rukeyser! *my* David Berman!) to awed feelings complicated by deep-seated worry, frustration, self-consciousness, even competition. William Blake admired the work of William Wordsworth but is said to have once been so mad at him over a theological point in a poem that he contracted a bowel complaint.

Some argue that the paradoxes of literary influence are especially difficult for American poets. Harold Bloom has written about the "anxiety of influence," remarking that "every American poet who aspires to strength knows that he arrives in the eveningland." But even those American poets who don't buy that view, or who are simply unconcerned with whether or not they are entering the arena in the twilight of a European/classical tradition, can experience something akin to what C. K. Williams, with regard to one of his chief literary influences, Walt Whitman, calls "the fear that if I give myself over too completely to [Whitman], my own poet will be annihilated, that I'll become a mere acolyte, a follower, an appendage."

Most writers seeking to make original work, to develop their own style or aesthetic, are nonetheless indebted to the work they have encountered that italicizes them as people and poets. Such influences possess a discernible and ineluctable hold or attraction, inspiring the reader/writer to envy, imitation, admiration, interpretation, resistance, anger, love, dejection, and even, sometimes, rejection. Our influences are our intimates, and we are as aware of their excesses and flaws as we are of the magnificent forms they present to the world. On the first day of class, the poet Charles Wright used to give his students a copy of Keats's "Ode on Melancholy" and dare them to find six other poems, by any poet, in any language, that were as remarkable on every register. The task always proved difficult. Complicating things for the reader who writes, then, is that when we deeply admire a writer, it is not so much that we want to write *like* them, but that we want to write *as well* as they do.

Any poet's literary legacy is likely to be a mongrel, even seemingly contradictory, pedigree. We can often learn as much from those poets who disturb or rankle us as we do from those with whom we share sympathies. One thing I like to ask students when we look at a poem or poet is this: "What poets had to be writing, innovating, in order for this poem or book to exist?"

One obvious way to consider a literary influence is to trace a poem or poet back through a kind of linear chain or constellar tree of poetic ancestors and heirs: Mary Ann Samyn back to Tom Andrews and Bruce Beasley to Charles Wright to John Ashbery to Ezra Pound and T.S. Eliot to the surrealists and the ancient Chinese poets, for example. Or, to take another tack with the same poet: Samyn to Brenda Hillman to Susan Howe to Gertrude Stein. Or Mary Ann Samyn to Laura Jensen to Sylvia Plath to Elizabeth Bishop to Moore to Dickinson to the Brontës to Shakespeare to Sappho. One might trace a lineage in the other direction, too, from Whitman to Pablo Neruda to Allen Ginsberg to Galway Kinnell to C.D. Wright to Alex Lemon and Gregory Pardlo. Consider the influences of Paul Legault, as another example, whose whimsical, smart experiments obviously hearken back to Dickinson and to Defoe, but also to Ann Lauterbach, Jack Spicer, Arthur Rimbaud, Federico Garcia Lorca, Marcel Proust, and Guillaume Apollinaire. The genealogies are mazy and mixed up and unchronological and provocative. Fittingly, one title in Legault's recent book *The Madeleine Poems* (Omnidawn, 2009) is "Madeleine as Portrait of Walt Whitman as Gertrude Stein as a Stripper."

Our influences can exist out ahead of us, too, and return to us in the present moment from a destination we've not yet reached (as Susan Howe says of Dickinson, "My precursor attracts me to my future"). I count on my students to keep me thinking and working this way. Not long ago, a former student, Willie Lin, a Kundiman Fellow and graduate of the MFA program at Washington University in St. Louis, wrote to say that her campus had recently been visited by the poet Kathleen Peirce. Did I know her work? Willie queried. I should know her.

And so in the interstices of pre-April poetry madness, I've been treating myself to the work of Kathleen Peirce, whose oneiric, haunting, linguistically vulnerable books *The Ardors* (Ausable, 2004), *The Oval Hour* (Iowa, 1999), and *Mercy* (Pittsburgh, 1991) have suddenly become very important to me ("Why shouldn't I / want to think of wine asleep in casks with my eyes closed? / Wasn't this always with me, the serene pause in things / held back from touch? How is it the weather feels / to have turned from what things want? / What should I let inscribe itself onto me as you do, / who love me all you can and not enough?" from "Jessamine," for example). One never feels entirely safe in these poems, something I once said to Willie about her own work, which I also deeply admire and would consider to be a personal poetic influence.

I can't resist closing with one of Willie's poems, from a series called *Sleeper's Almanac*. The poem opens with an overt nod to a letter from Emily Dickinson to T.W. Higginson ("I smile when you suggest that I delay 'to publish' — that being foreign to my thought, as Firmament to Fin — ") and strikes me, like the poems of Peirce, as concerned with the matter of originality and influence, a kind of ardent and skeptical petition for salvific, sacramental thaw of relationship, in language as in life:

from "Sleeper's Almanac"

As firmament to fin, as lust to luster. My non-belonging. Pet-peeve, I joke with the woman cleaning after her dog. My spine practices its weathervane-twitch. Where some find delicacy: snowdrift, crocus, gold filament, a throat. I finger the loosened thread from the seam of my coat pocket until the key falls into the lining. What emotions do you associate with white? With bister? Boughs twist and rent with ice up and down the sides of our street. Winter hustling shoulder and heft: salt lick, brine spring. When I said madstone, I meant heart, and when I said chest, I meant mine—it is not difficult to imagine the sea, the sweat-line pooled in the small of a back. Somewhere someone is washing her hands clean.

As Marcel Proust put it, "Style for the writer, no less than color for the painter, is a question not of technique but of vision: it is the revelation, which by direct and conscious means would be impossible, of the qualitative difference, the uniqueness of the fashion in which the world appears to each one of us, a difference which, if there were no art, would remain the secret of every individual." Our originality as artists depends to an extent upon our origins, those bonds of incipience and influence that are both prior and out ahead of us, directions we hope always to be deepening, challenging, extending.

DAVID WOJAHN

In the Attic

I unzip the plastic bag & they tremble
   The dust motes—three linen sport coats
      In the March wind's updraft. Two beige,

One a comic mustard yellow, the sleeves
   Rolled up—pure *Miami Vice*. He'd put on
      Some weight that year & they wouldn't button.

His living room in Dallas. Try them on, Jack said.
   They look good on you, he said.
      I carried them with me on a flight

To my parents & even wore one to the consult
   With the doctor: should they discharge my father,
      Or ratchet up the ECT? Nice linen,

Well-cut. The doctor would respect me.
   On the phone Jack laughed at this, a kind
      Of snorting *Hah!* that still said Boston:

Ya' didn't wear the yellow one, I hope.
   We'd been editing a book, for he loved
      Projects, collaboration, eight-ball he'd always

Beat me at, George Dickel neat but sometimes
   With ice--two cubes only. On the shag carpet floor,
      150 note cards for the book fanning out

In classic Jack—systematic & mysterious
   As Kabbalah. His jokes were legion, usually
      At his own expense. He wounded easily,

Though about that he'd stay quiet. He saved
   My ass on various occasions & his poems
      Were pathos, Borscht Belt, Rumi

In an accent of long vowel, dropped *r*.
   People would do well to read them.
      & the jackets: I think this is the one

I sported at the consult, saying yes
  To the shocks, duly signing forms.
    I slide it from the hanger & of course

It doesn't button. Inside the chest pocket,
  A wallet-sized black & white: Jack
    Without beard, the second wife who didn't

Stay long, his son caped in Teenage
  Mutant Ninja, the one Jack buried.
    The ghost jacket, for an instant,

Brings them both alive. Though to claim that,
  Jack would say, is a lie
    Even elegy cannot make good.

—in memory, Jack Myers

In the nearly thirty years since Richard Hugo selected his first book, *Icehouse Lights*, for the Yale Younger Poets prize in 1982, David Wojahn has contributed to American arts and letters a personally and politically intrepid body of ever-evolving poems. He is also a fearless, culturally savvy, and intelligent editor and essayist and an open-minded reviewer of original and substantial insight.

Wojahn brings to his work in the academy the same discerning conscience, conscientiousness, and consciousness he devotes to his writing, and his reputation as a generous, loyal teacher is legion among colleagues and devoted current and former students, many of whom are now well known poets in their own right. At a recent conference, I had occasion to speak for various reasons with a great many writers, and at least ten of them, ranging in age from their early twenties to their sixth decade—poets whose own work represents a wide range of styles and sensibilities— evoked, unbidden, Wojahn's name, referring either to something he'd once said in class or to a letter he'd written to them in response to a query or to a life-saving book he'd loaned them or to some prescient bit of his from a poem or book review. In an essay entitled "Ferality and Strange Good Fortune: Notes on Teaching and Writing," Wojahn has said that "the writing of poetry is not a business, an activity, or a hobby, but a calling; the teaching of the writing of poetry is, similarly, a calling." That this calling includes desolation, confusion, and grief as well as the exhilaration of creation and communion is part of Wojahn's practice and his vision.

"In the Attic," an elegy for Wojahn's friend and mentor, the late poet Jack Myers, embodies and in some ways accounts for this vision of collaboration, generosity, and legacy. It is late winter/early spring, time to get out some lighter clothes, time, perhaps, to emerge from a period of mourning, and the poem opens with the Zephyrus invocation of a "March wind's updraft" stirring the dust motes in an attic where the speaker is unzipping a garment bag containing "three linen sport coats / ... // One a comic mustard yellow, the sleeves / Rolled up---pure *Miami Vice*," all a gift from Jack back when he was still alive and the speaker a much younger man.

> . . . . He'd put on
> Some weight that year & they wouldn't button.
>
> His living room in Dallas. Try them on, Jack said.
>   They look good on you, he said.
>   I carried them with me on a flight
>
> To my parents & even wore one to the consult
>   With the doctor: should they discharge my father,
>   Or ratchet up the ECT? Nice linen,
>
> Well-cut. The doctor would respect me.
>   On the phone Jack laughed at this, a kind
>   Of snorting *Hah!* That still said Boston:
>
> *Ya' didn't wear the yellow one, I hope.*

In a contrapuntal style I associate with Wojahn, these terraced lines, which juxtapose heavy information (the speaker's father is in the hospital undergoing electric shock therapy) with seemingly light remarks ("Nice linen, // Well-cut"), convey so much with a light touch. As mnemonic sound-bites of scene, dialogue, questions, and interior thoughts exchange their insights, we appreciate at once the easy intimacy between the older and the younger man. We see how the latter feels stronger, more capable, wearing his friend's outgrown suit to the difficult consult about whether or not to discharge his father from hospital or to intensify his electroconvulsive therapy. We, like the speaker, are grateful for Jack's humor on the telephone in spite of what must been a wise and deeply felt awareness of his friend's complicated family situation.

The speaker pulls back from his own drama, however, keeping the lens focused on Myers—lover of projects, pool, George Dickel ("neat but sometimes / with ice")— an easily wounded maker of jokes at his own expense and of poems (part "pathos, Borscht Belt, Rumi // In an accent of long vowel, dropped *r*. / People would do well to read them"). I'm guessing that the collaborative project the speaker and Myers are undertaking in the poem ("150 note cards for the book fanning out // In classic Jack – systematic & mysterious / As Kabbalah") is *A Profile of 20th-Century American Poetry*, a collection of essays introduced and edited by Wojahn and Myers, which appeared in 1991. People would do well to read that, too.

In the longitudinal house of reverie and memory that Gaston Bachelard describes in *The Poetics of Space*, the attic occupies a special imaginative place as the repository of memory. If cellars are really "buried walls," with the dark of earth around them, the attic is an aerie, perched between earth and heaven, sheltering its discarded remnants of lives beneath a "rational" roof. The attic is liminal, high and piled with the old, the put-away, "keeping watch over the past." It is into such a space that the speaker's dead friend is called back, by the change in weather, perhaps, and chiefly by the uncovered jacket, the same coat the speaker once "sported at the consult, saying yes / To the shocks, duly signing forms. / I slide it from the hanger & of course / It doesn't button."

Wojahn presses here. What does it mean to have outgrown what our teachers have outgrown? What happens when those who have inspired and sheltered us and "saved / [our asses]" and helped us through life's "shocks" precede us into the beyond, and it is we who are standing alone, just under the shingles, holding not only the carapace of what was once a vital man, but, discovered within the chest pocket of that shed garment, a photograph,

. . . A wallet-sized black & white: Jack
        Without beard, the second wife who didn't

Stay long, his son caped in Teenage
        Mutant Ninja, the one Jack buried.
                The ghost jacket, for an instant,

Brings them both alive. Though to claim that,
        Jack would say, is a lie
                Even elegy cannot make good.

Jack, the poet tells us, would insist that neither poetry nor even love can "make good" the deception, however longed for, that art can return to us, as Dickinson would say, our "sundered things": our lost sons, friends, fathers, younger selves. But the reader of Wojahn's elegy might disagree; for more than a moment, Jack Myers bodies forth from the page, filling the room with a humble and irresistible largesse. What is offered in the poem is gratitude for an abundant and vital spirit, a generosity Wojahn celebrates here and extends through his own work and teaching. No wonder the jacket won't button.

AMY NEWMAN

While Sylvia Plath Studies The Joy of Cooking On Her Honeymoon In Benidorm, Spain, Delmore Schwartz Reclines In The Front Seat Of His Buick Roadmaster

While Sylvia Plath studies *The Joy of Cooking* on her honeymoon in Benidorm, Spain,
Delmore Schwartz reclines in the front seat of his Buick Roadmaster
listening to a Giants game on the car radio.
The car's parked on his farmland in Baptistown,
New Jersey, where obstinate plants attempt survival
at great odds, their vital spikes insulting and defending.
The thistle fans its prickly leaves,
the burdock hustles, miserly. Its dry-as death-seed
will outlast you, traveller, its dry-as-hope seedling will use you,
tenacious as the leftover god, the eye-of-the-needle-god,
the straggly one, the Shylock, who lent you your life,
who chose this desert wilderness for exile.
He manifests the empty field for you to wander.
He removeth your brilliance and set you in a basket
alone among the rushes. He maketh the coral of Seconal
and suffers you to recline in the evergreen Dexamyl shade,
while Ernie Harwell calls the last out
(Willie Jones popping up to Al Dark)
in the car's radium glow. Do you see it, American poetry?
The happy arc of the ball above Shibe Park—
a moment of promise falling off, coming to nothing.
Disappearing to atoms. Giants win, 4-2.

In Benidorm, Plath skins the market rabbit, hind to head.
She'll flour and sear the taut pink flesh
and scrape the carrots naked. Spain is a million things,
it's lantanas and hibiscus, it's roses that aren't ashamed
to split their skirts for love, rude flowers pushing out of their skins,
and all-new vines hugging the old walls, new ascendency,
shooting up into skies like something about to matter.
The peppercorns that season the stew grow in clusters
like glands, ripening, and within each pod is the seed,
the hard dry concentrated bitterness for which it is prized.

After Sylvia Plath Kicks Out Ted Hughes, Elizabeth Bishop Watches Idly From A Balcony In Rio As Police Chase A Thief Over Picturesque Hills

After Sylvia Plath kicks out Ted Hughes in England,
Elizabeth Bishop watches idly from a balcony in Rio
as police chase a thief over picturesque hills.
The fleeing man is effervescent in those exotic, congested glades,
but he's distinct, as a grassland sparrow's song is distinct:
if you try, you can hear the tiny voice
singing its hunger, like everything else.
You can lean into the sound over those brutal hills
where the blind roots host their parasites
and the rain serves the blind roots, and nature
ransacks everything, just to get along.
Brazil perseveres in a detailed breeze,
while the sky waits with a patience so infinite,
uninterested in the open mouths, in the cricket
or the crocodile. Bishop calls to her love through the rooms
like that bird that always sounds lost.

                In London, it's winter, and Plath
is filing down hunger to the necessary bone. His absence
is the blood gap cupped violet at the artery,
he's the death vow's strapping, gigantic ache.
The childrens' call sounds for her through the walls,
a sea tipped with tiny bells. Plath's ignited heart
is radiant as a priest's. She is absurd with flu,
the virus riding her proteins obsessive and eyeless,
master plunderer, unloading its stuff in glittery bits,
champion. It's a parasite of impressive abundance,
hungry at a cellular level, binding and shedding,
inevitable and determined, like everything else.

In a news release published when she was honored with a 2010 Presidential Research Professorship for "uncommon creativity and unquenchable curiosity" at Northern Illinois University, poet and scholar Amy Newman describes a moment in the early 1980s, recently out of college and working a lucrative job as a fashion stylist in New York City, when she came upon a poem by Stanley Plumly in a magazine while on a break from work, a discovery that would change everything for her: "I felt everything inessential in my life at that time fade away and something else beckon," she said, adding that she began investigating graduate school that very day. "Something happened that made me realize how significant it was to write."

This openness to the junctures of language, volition, and chance may account, in part, for the arresting edge, intelligent verve, and innovative range of Newman's various poetic projects, which have tended over the years to be serial, compelled by originally conceived and wielded engines of form, repetition, and juxtaposition. Her third poetry collection, *fall* (Wesleyan UP, 2004), for instance, explores the 72 definitions of the word "fall," pitching the arc of personal narrative over a subtextual foray into the archetypal, post-Lapsarian fall from grace. Her most recent collection, *Dear Editor*, offers a seasonally organized sequence of "letter-poems" to an unnamed editor, who at times seems part confessor/part remote divinity/ part the poet herself. Framing her letters with the stock phrases of publication query letters ("Thank you for considering . . ."), the richly tangential contents of the individual epistles reveal an underlying and disturbing familial drama told, among other things, through tropes of chess and Catholic martyrdom.

"While Sylvia Plath Studies *The Joy of Cooking* On Her Honeymoon In Benidorm, Spain, Delmore Schwartz Reclines In The Front Seat Of His Buick Roadmaster" and "After Sylvia Plath Kicks Out Ted Hughes, Elizabeth Bishop Watches Idly From A Balcony In Rio As Police Chase A Thief Over Picturesque Hills" are from Newman's new project-in-progress, *On This Day in Poetry History*, a series of poems mixing details from the biographies, diaries, letters, photographs, and histories of mid-twentieth-century poets in a lyric dramatization. In an interview about the project with the *The Missouri Review*, Newman asks, "What if we could see the character of American poetry coming into being? Elizabeth Bishop's biographical materials make vividly clear why her sandpiper averts it gaze from the roaring sea, turning obsessively toward those pretty, diverting grains of sand. If Robert Lowell hadn't broken Jean Stafford's nose (horrifying!), we wouldn't have her masterpiece 'The Interior Castle.' I imagine the history of American poetry as a kinetic diorama, the poets moving toward or away from epiphanies, navigating among odd, compelling moments, secret histories, unexpected correspondences."

It's clear from reading these two poems in tandem just how exciting and ambitious a project Newman has undertaken. Plath, Schwartz, Hughes, and Bishop seem, juxtaposed as they are, genetically, almost helixically inter-connected by temporal and temperamental currents. In 1956, as Schwartz, depressed and alcoholic, listens to a Giants game in his parked car in New Jersey, anxious about his waning creative force ("Do you see it, American poetry? / The happy arc of the ball above Shibe Park— / a moment of promise falling off, coming to nothing"), Plath, newly married and full of domestic and poetic ambition on her honeymoon in lush

Benidorm ("Spain is a million things, / it's lantanas and hibiscus, it's roses that aren't ashamed / to split their skirts for love"), is learning to cook. Yet it's impossible not to see in Schwartz's diminished terrain ("where obstinate plants attempt survival / at great odds, their vital spikes insulting and defending") and Plath's almost brutal move toward mastery and "new ascendency" ("Plath skins the market rabbit, hind to head. / She'll flour and sear the taut pink flesh / and scrape the carrots naked") versions of each other and each other's work: gifted, extreme, and vulnerable to the "hard dry concentrated bitterness" that can result from mental illness and crushing disappointment. Similarly, Newman shows us that Bishop, on a balcony in "exotic, congested" Rio, watching "police chase a thief over picturesque hills," is not far from Plath in her wintry, feverish London despair. Both are "hungry at a cellular level." We see that Plath's obsessive, "gigantic ache" and Bishop's voice, "singing its hunger" for love with the feel of "that bird that always sounds lost," are versions of the same "ignited heart."

At the heart of Newman's *On This Day in Poetry History* sequence are questions about origin, originality, genius, obsession, influence, ambition, and legacy that have always haunted American poets and poetry. Who had to write for certain poems to be written (who, as Harold Bloom asks, is "the poet in the poet")? What later work has depended upon or will depend on particular textual embodiments, and vice versa?

I like imagining a poem with a title something like this: "As Adrienne Rich Publishes *Sources* on the West Coast, the Young Amy Newman Reads the Poem 'In Passing' by Stanley Plumly in the 20 June 1983 issue of *The New Yorker* and Never Looks Back." Here is a passage from Plumly's "In Passing," which, in much the manner of Newman's recent poems, brings into an instant's chord a scene witnessed at Niagara Falls and a plot from a Chekhov story:

> In the Chekhov story,
> the lovers live in a cloud, above the sheer witness of a valley.

> They call it circumstance. They look up at the open wing
> of the sky, or they look down into the future.

> Death is a power like any other pull of the earth.
> The people in the raingear with the cameras want to see it

> from the inside, from behind, from the dark looking into the light.
> They want to take its picture, give it size—

> how much easier to get lost in the gradations of a large
> and yellow leaf drifting its good-bye down one side of the gorge.

There is almost nothing that does not signal loneliness,
then loveliness, then something connecting all we will become.

Reading this poem after experiencing Newman's work makes manifest an instance of "the character of American poetry coming into being." That Newman is open to and intelligently passionate about such influences and confluences, and is capable of articulating not only the "gradations" of the most minute details but also of envisioning the "something connecting all we will become," is a gift for which readers and writers of poetry have cause to be grateful.

HEATHER MCHUGH

As Authors Can't Perfect One Agent
(a transliteration of Shakespeare's Sonnet 23, "As an unperfect
actor on the stage")

First, Shakespeare's sonnet:

Shakespeare's Sonnet 23

As an unperfect actor on the stage,
Who with his fear is put beside his part,
Or some fierce thing replete with too much rage,
Whose strength's abundance weakens his own heart;
So I, for fear of trust, forget to say
The perfect ceremony of love's rite,
And in mine own love's strength seem to decay,
O'ercharg'd with burthen of mine own love's might.
O! let my books be then the eloquence
And dumb presagers of my speaking breast,
Who plead for love, and look for recompense,
More than that tongue that more hath more express'd.
O! learn to read what silent love hath writ:
To hear with eyes belongs to love's fine wit.

& now McHugh's line-by-line anagram of it:

As Authors Can't Perfect One Agent

so e-agents can't perfect an author.
His art (howbeit swapped shut) is his fire—
a high truth, gloom-free writ, or some centerpiece—
whose hint (torn watchband) reawakens hugenesses.

Stuff for oratories? Go after toys!
Refer thy competence to lovers? Fie!
I mind no neglected systems, nor wave one hat.
(Wired for e-thought, two moving hem-lines branch.)

Queen bee, yokel tool—both scent hem.
Best pass as underbred, my king of rampage.
Download Homer. Look for pen of clever apes—
(Heather-thoughts: Hot art department... No more exams...)

Twitter HELLO earthward, to vanish alone.
Fetish's vow is now to be: all heterogeneity.

The anagram—which involves rearrangement of the letters in a word, phrase, or sentence to produce another word, phrase, or sentence using the original letters only once—is a centuries-old form of language play. Anagrams are often employed to create pseudonyms (the Romanian poet Paul Celan, for example, created his surname from "Ancel," a version of his original name, Antshel). In other instances, anagrams are intended to reveal some sub-textual or intuitive truth about the original subject text. For example, Wikipedia offers as examples "George Bush" = "He bugs Gore" and "Tom Marvolo Riddle" = "I Am Lord Voldemort." *"Chronicle of Higher Education"* can be anagrammatically translated to "No Chute Cliché for Head Origin."

A host of free on-line anagram generators now makes it easy to have fun with the form, but if there is a living poet who is capable of coming up with a legion of witty, pithy anagrams without resorting to technological engines, it is the remarkable wordsmith Heather McHugh, who has been practicing what she calls extreme "language sports" for decades, in poems of formal experimentation, exultant wordplay, and inventiveness, as well as in piercingly astute essays on contemporary poetry and poetics. Attuned to etymology, measure, punning, stereoscopy, materiality, the economies of whole and part, and the mathematics of fraction and sum, McHugh's work impresses with its daring and fearless intimacy with language, our uniquely human gift.

McHugh's "As Agents Can't Perfect One Author," a line-by-line anagram of Shakespeare's Sonnet 23 ("As an unperfect actor on the stage"), "reliterates" and talks back to Shakespeare's themes with a feist to match Shakespeare's own. In sonnet 23, we see Shakespeare, himself a consummate linguistic acrobat, taking up some of the rhetorical plaints and modes we have come to expect in his love sonnets. Like an "unperfect" actor, he posits, whose fear keeps him from adequately playing his part, or a being so overcome with rage that "his own heart" is weakened and unable to perform, the speaker ("for fear of trust" and "o'ercharg'd with burthen of [his] own love's might") is guilty of neglecting to adequately pronounce, to speak aloud, his love to his lover (one senses that his lover may have whinged a bit about this). The poem is a plea for the lover to value his "books" (that is, what he, the poet, has *written*, perhaps in plays, certainly in the sonnets themselves) over his own unspoken words, perhaps his sexual performance, and, importantly, over the spoken words of any rival ("that tongue that more hath more express'd").

Shakespeare's concluding couplet commands that the lover "learn to read what silent love hath writ: / To hear with eyes belongs to love's fine wit." *My* writing, Shakespeare woos, is better than *his* talking any day.

One subtext of Shakespeare's sonnet, of course, is that the culpable, even slightly anxious or insecure speaker would like to be noticed and preferred both as speaker *and* as writer. He wants to be "seen" in and for his words; he wants to be loved for them. McHugh picks right up on this, moving her sonnet into the post-modern realm of complex, fluid agency, the elusive otherness of any notion of a fixed self, and the particular slipperiness of identity afforded by electronic media. Her anagrammatic re(l)iteration embraces and challenges Shakespeare's speaker's anxieties by questioning the significance of any one, preferred, perfectible poet or poem, lover or loved one, agent or reader.

The word "agents," of course, offers a play on agent as actor, as subject, as well as agent as purveyor of literary texts. McHugh's title and line one are both anagrams of Shakespeare's first line, and in these two lines alone McHugh manages to address several questions at the heart of the literary enterprise, especially in our time and with regard to publication: Is there such a thing as a perfect author? Or just one perfect author? Or any author at all? In the especially shifting realm of cyberspace and on-line "publication" (perhaps more like Renaissance manuscript circulation and scribal publication than the intervening decades of print and book culture), can any one author or maker or purveyor of texts be determined? Importantly, how is this all related to the matter of love and to the pitching of one's woo?

One senses that at least one intended reader for McHugh's sonnet is Shakespeare, and in a way her poem is offered as a consolation. Never mind, she intimates, that oratory and "high truth, gloom-free writ," however clever, might miss the mark or go unheard. One might as soon pursue toys as harbor that illusion. And why compare one's own "competence" to that of other lovers? "Fie!," she exclaims, moving into her manifesto: "I mind no neglected systems, nor wave one hat. / (Wired for e-thought, two moving hem-lines branch.)" I love McHugh's spin on Whitman's "I contain multitudes"—she is both "Queen bee" and "yokel tool," full of paradoxes and many selves (especially rich is her tangent into a suddenly downloaded, fourth-wall-breaking and meta "heap of / Heather-thoughts: / ("Hot art department . . . No more exams . . .)." The self is not promiscuous, but manifold and paradoxical ("Twitter HELLO earthward, to vanish alone"). Just as Shakespeare's lover-poet wants, synaesthetically, to be heard with eyes, to be both lover and rival, text and reader, McHugh eschews the idea of any fixed economy of self, of agent or author, "hetero-" or Heather: "Fess now all vows to be," she urges. "Hit hetero- / geneity."

In "What Dickinson Makes a Dash For," just one of the essays that make essential reading in McHugh's *Broken English: Poetry and Partiality*, what McHugh says of Dickinson also applies to Shakespeare's early modern speaker and to McHugh's own post-modern one: "Dickinson's poems don't *argue* the coincidence of opposites; they embody that coincidence, in acts of poised equivocation. Here equivocation is the greater truth. . . . It makes no sense to seek the *point* of such a poem; one's work as a reader is to hold the more-than-one (and often, more importantly, the more-than-two) in mind—to be of many minds." I admire how these poems of "many minds" speak to one another across the centuries. When Shakespeare implores his lover to "let my books be then the eloquence / and dumb presagers of my speaking breast, / Who plead for love, and look for recompense"—when he wants to be self *and* other—one feels the truth of McHugh when she writes, in the Dickinson essay, "these interpretive branchings (channeling for consistency), begin to resemble the alternative pathways of computer programs. What is amazing about them is both their zeroing in and their zeroing out; the readings made available tend to cancel each other, but the sum is an astonishing set of potentials." What does it mean to play in the fields of language if not to keep vital this astonishment, this susceptibility to manifold potency and promise?

PAUL LEGAULT

from The Emily Dickinson Reader

1104. It gradually became night through a process marked by crickets, hats being taken off, and the Sun descending past the visible horizon.
1105. Flirtatious Emily Dickinson is mad at austere, heartbroken Emily Dickinson.
1106. Nature is a hotel without indoor plumbing or room service.
1112. When people realize God doesn't exist, God will die.
1113. That guy has a really big face.
1114. Sometimes I stop loving people.
1115. I like Heaven. I also like it when people tip their hat to me in the street. I like that very much indeed.
1116. I prefer sunsets to the Sun.
1117. Death is over there again, petting his dead sheep. He's kind of weird but all in all a nice guy.
1123. I prefer liquor when I'm drinking it.
1124. There are two scientific extremities. The infinitely large and the infinitely small. People usually forget about the infinitely small. Don't do that.
1125. Paradise is being able to opt out of "Paradise."
1127. I am glad that days exist.
1132. I wish I were a vampire.
1136. I'd prefer to keep my soul.
1141. Sometimes I eat roses. Because I'm fabulous.
1145. When I'm dead, you'll be dead to me.
1165. I hope the last thing I say before I die isn't stupid.
1171. I like to watch people sleeping (a little too much).
1178. When it comes down to it, I prefer small, insignificant things, like humans, to God and Jesus and all those guys. They're kind of boring.

When my eldest daughter was college-hunting, I took advantage of an autumn trip with her to Amherst, Massachusetts, to fulfill what had been for me a long-held dream of visiting the Emily Dickinson Homestead. Later that afternoon—still high myself from the power of taking in Dickinson's tiny writing table and looking out the bedroom windows from which Dickinson often wrote the world—my daughter and I drove with friends out to Hampshire College and met a pleasant young student tour guide who noticed the Emily Dickinson Homestead sticker that had served as my entrance ticket to the Homestead still pressed to my jacket lapel. "Booyah!" she exclaimed in sisterly solidarity. "I take classes in Emily Dickinson Hall. I *own* Emily Dickinson!"

As Millicent Todd Bingham, daughter of one of Dickinson's first editors, once remarked, "They all think they own her." And it's true that for all of her oblique, damasked "veil"—both in her poems and in her life—Emily Dickinson often inspires a remarkably intense intimacy with her readers that can lead to a thrall of recognition and insight but also to possessiveness, a cult of sentimentality, mythic idealization, academic and poetic turf warring, and a wide range of projection and appropriation. To paraphrase Dickinson, portions of her have been assigned to (or taken up by) by feminists, Marxists, foodies, Queer theorists, agoraphobics, psychologists, the tourist trade, culture vultures, L=A=N=G=U=A=G=E poets, gardeners, and a host of others. Her work (letters, poems, letter-poems, aphorisms, fascicles, fragments) and biography are at the heart of debates about textuality, scribal practices, intention, Bowdlerization, and the character of the lyric poem itself. Recent critical readers have questioned, in fact, whether or not what Dickinson was writing in her wild scrawl—Thomas Wentworth Higginson, *Atlantic Monthly* editor and friend and correspondent of Dickinson, compared her handwriting to the "fossil bird-tracks" preserved in the Amherst College library— with its almost hypertextual use of variant readings, can even be considered lyric poetry, suggesting that the "poems" we now attribute to Dickinson are really redactions and constructions of various editorial decisions and the move from script to print culture.

At present, Dickinson seems to be enjoying a "moment," one of several the poet has experienced since her death as various versions of her poems have became available over time to a wide range of readers, beginning with the highly edited and regularized Todd and Higginson edition, *Poems by Emily Dickinson*, in 1890, four years after the poet's death. Recent interest in Dickinson must owe in significant measure to the excellent and innovative work that continues in the wake of the scrupulous reparative scholarship and re-visioning of Dickinson's manuscripts by R. W. Franklin in editions made accessible in the 1990s. The past two years alone have seen the publication of important new books about Dickinson by Helen Vendler, Aífe Murray, Alexandra Socarides, and Lyndall Gordon, texts which in turn build upon the excellent scholarship of the past decade by the likes of Sharon Cameron, Susan Howe, Jerome McGann, Martha Nell Smith, Virginia Jackson, Brenda Wineapple, and many others. A popular recreation of Dickinson's flower garden, including an exhibit of her extraordinary schoolgirl herbarium, by the New York Botanical Garden in the spring and summer of 2010 also brought Dickinson's work and "[lunacy] for bulbs" to a wider audience. Perhaps the "Twitterable" compression and intensity of Dickinson's lyrics also account in part for this renaissance.

Poets have quite naturally been influenced by Dickinson's "long shadow" (William Carlos Williams, Robert Frost, Agha Shahid Ali, Sylvia Plath, Marianne Moore,

Louise Bogan, Mary Jo Bang, Heather McHugh, Marianne Boruch, Lucie Brock-Broido, Charles Wright, Rae Armantrout, Mary Ann Samyn, Karen Volkman, Brenda Hillman, and Lynn Emanuel, to name but a few) as have a wide range of other artists, including Martha Graham, Judy Chicago, and Leslie Dill. One young American poet, Paul Legault, already the author of three innovative books of poems, has recently published *The Emily Dickinson Reader* (McSweeney's, 2013). Legault's project involves what he calls "English-to-English translations" of Dickinson's work. For the past several years, he has been involved in the endeavor—part homage, part parody, part experiment—with the intention of "translating" all 1,789 poems and fragments offered in Franklin's reading edition of *The Poems of Emily Dickinson.* Legault's translations of poems 1 – 499 were gathered in a chapbook, *The Emily Dickinson Reader: Translations, Vol. 1,* published by Try and Make Press in 2009. Iconoclastic and impudent in a way Dickinson herself can sometimes be, these poems, as Legault himself says in an interview with Julia Guez on *BOMB* magazine's blogsite, "are a joke that became serious." In the same interview, Legault goes on to say, with regard to Dickinson, "People are ready for her—for queers and vampires and the two in combination. (I would include E. D. in both camps.) People are tired of the sacred the same way Dickinson was tired of it—if still obsessed with its possibility. Of course when I say 'people,' I mean me." A sampling of Legault's translations from the book appear above, and the numbers correspond to the numbers assigned to Dickinson's poems in the Franklin reading edition.

Harold Bloom says that parody offers a "carnival sense of the world" and that "everything has its laughing aspect, for everything is reborn and renewed through death and ambivalence." Legault is often able to go straight to the "laughing aspect" even of Dickinson's most serious poems, but his translations are not merely parodic. In the spirit of Jack Spicer and Robert Creeley, other innovators unafraid to talk back to iconic poets they love, Legault is engaged in a kind of playful, funhouse "mirroring" dance with Dickinson. What Peter Gizzi has written about Spicer's Lorca project, for instance—that it "enacts a play—a drama—between materiality and invisibility, the lines and what's between them" and that "part of the absurd labor of poets is to parry with each other" as a kind of homage—might be said of Legault's project as well. (Interestingly, Legault, who works at the Academy of American Poets and is the co-founder of the translation press Telephone Books, studied screenwriting before getting his MFA in poetry.) One chief effect of Legault's talking back to Dickinson in this way is the sleight of hand and foot by which the translations bring us not only dos-à-dos, back to back, with a poet we might think we understand and own or know, but they also return us, send us back, with fresh vision to the incomparable poems of Dickinson herself, in all of their difficulty, complexity, ambiguity, and seemingly inexhaustible, regenerative power.

SOME MUSINGS ON POETIC SELF-PORTRAITURE

SOME MUSINGS ON POETIC SELF-PORTRAITURE

When a friend of mine, a painter, wants perspective on newly finished work, he walks his canvas in front of a large mirror hanging in the studio. It is only in a reversed, refracted reflection of the piece that he can locate enough distance to assess what he's accomplished. Another colleague, who prints and makes books, often takes a tome he's recently stitched and bound and buries it in his back yard for a few days. When he unearths it, he feels ready to "see" the thing he's made.

Writing itself is a kind of drawing, and for centuries writers and artists have worked in and cross-pollinated both disciplines, with poets drawing inspiration from works of art and from the techniques of their makers. Ekphrasis, which in modern times has come to refer exclusively to writing that is about art, comes from the Greek (pl. *ekphraseis*) for "description" and is an ancient mode (the *Princeton Encyclopedia of Poetry and Poetics* cites, for instance, Homer's description of Achilles's shield in the *Iliad* and the tapestries of Minerva and Arachne in Ovid). Poets working in ekphrasis might use a work of art as spark for a sustained meditation on imagined scenarios and abstractions (Keats's Ur-poem "Ode on a Grecian Urn," for example) or borrow from a visual artist certain techniques (juxtaposition of color planes, for instance, or the use of negative space or distortion of scale) they can then "translate" onto the page (in syntax, lineation, form), something Charles Wright attempts in what he calls his "failed experiment," the beautiful "Homage to Paul Cezanne."

Especially interesting in this regard is the self-portrait poem. Artists have been making self-portraits since antiquity (what model is cheaper and more readily available?), but the self-portrait *poem*, as a self-conscious literary entity, is arguably relatively new. Some might posit that the self-portrait poem, at least in the lyric tradition, is a tautology—isn't every poem a "portrayal," however disguised or indirect, of its maker, be it Sappho, Bashō, Mirabai, or Gerard Manley Hopkins? And yet, with notable exceptions, it isn't until the mid-twentieth century that we begin to see poets calling their works "self-portraits." A recent Granger's search yielded 103 results for poems with "self-portrait" in the title. Only a handful of these writers, mostly from Europe, were born before the twentieth-century. And while Emily Dickinson taunted "I'm nobody! Who are you" and Whitman claimed to celebrate and sing himself, and although it is possible to see Eliot in Prufrock or Yeats in "Among School Children," with some exceptional early to mid-twentieth century forays into the self-portrait (Williams, Creeley, Ammons, Justice, O'Hara), it is not until the appearance of John Ashbery's *Self-Portrait in a Convex Mirror* (1975) that the practice of writing self-portrait poems appears to explode.

Why? An exploration of the reasons is something I've just begun to consider and is far beyond the scope of this piece. But I've always been attracted to self-portrait poems for their compelling mix of revelation and veil, for the way they abstract their subjects and implicate my reading of them into their bodying forth. I'm intrigued by the ways in which, as poet and critic Leslie Wolf has written of Ashbery, "to reach [painting's] state of freedom in a verbal art, the poet must use the signifying quality of his medium *against itself*....The poet must arrange 'brushstrokes' of his tableau in such a way that they yield contradictory clues." One thing that seems fair to say is that early experimenters in the self-portrait poem were interested in and knowledgeable about art, and that the use of "self-portrait" in their poems is an overt nod to its long, fascinating, and complex tradition in art history.

Julian Bell, in his Introduction to *Five Hundred Self-Portraits* (a gorgeous Phaidon compilation of 500 visual and spatial self-portraits from ancient Egypt to the present) calls Ni-Ankh-Ptah [whose limestone relief carving *Self-Portrait, Kneeling in a Boat* (c. 2350 BC) adorns the Tomb of the vizier Ptah-Hotep] the earliest known self-portraitist ("enjoying a drink while his Egyptian sailors joust"). Around 1500 AD, however, with the greater availability and quality of mirrors coming out of Venice and an increased ambition on the part of artists to elevate their social status from craftspeople to the learned class (painters began to work themselves into their historical and religious paintings in a "calling card" kind of way, for example), self-portraiture moves, as Bell says, "from the margins of Western art to centre-stage." Also affecting the burgeoning of self-portraiture, of course, are Renaissance notions of individual self-fashioning and an increased awareness by artists of the techniques and philosophies of their calling. As Shearer West writes in *Portraiture*, "underlying all self-portraiture is the mystery of how an individual sees himself or herself as other. A self-portrait involves an artist objectifying their own body and creating a 'double' of themselves. Artists could use the self-portrait as a means of drawing attention to the medium and the process of production of the work, to show off their skill, or to experiment with technique or style. The viewer of a self-portrait also occupies a strange position of looking at a metaphorical mirror that reflects back not themselves but the artist who produced the portrait. Viewing a self-portrait can therefore involve the sense of stepping into the artist's shoes... [making] self-portraits both compelling and elusive."

No doubt this ability to distance (and thus to *see*, to efface and even deface) the self while engaging in a tradition that offers the expectation of portrayal may be one attraction of self-portraiture for poets. In a meditation on Velázquez's *Las Meninas* (and evoking Michel Foucault's analysis of that painting's "blind point"), Anne

Carson comments on the ways in which canvases and mirrors within that painting (which includes a portrait of the artist and positions the viewer of the painting in the shoes of the on-looking royals reflected on a far wall) allow the poet/reader to achieve what is almost impossible: to catch oneself in the act of seeing. "Artifice triangulates our perception," Carson explains, "so that we all but see ourselves looking…that point where we disappear into ourselves in order to look."

Charles Wright ("Portrait of the Artist with Hart Crane"), Jorie Graham ("Self-Portrait as Hurry and Delay"), Mary Ann Samyn ("Self-Portrait as Wall Paper with Little Stoves"), and Lucie Brock-Broido ("Self-Portrait with Her Hair on Fire") are just a few contemporary poets who have worked in a serious, serial way with self-portraiture. Of special interest to me is the self-portrait work being done by young poets, the thirty-somethings and younger, whose immersion in a culture of ubiquitous self-portrayal—in the media, technologies, social networking, even in the mirrored surfaces of our environments—furthers and alters the self-portrait conversation. In closing, I offer poems by three emerging poets, David Francis, Michael Rutherglen, and Sarah Schweig, whose pieces strike me as contributing to the notion of what constitutes a self-portrait poem in distinct and exciting ways, whether as a "declared" self-portrait, or not. Part of a generation dramatically both more claustral and more people-connected than their predecessors, these young poets are involved in creating as well as reflecting a sense of what it means to be a self in poems a decade into the current century of the era Anno Domini; they help us to see ourselves.

Quelle Night
by Sarah Schweig

She is, tonight, in spite of.
That's what she said, going out,
locking the door, closing her winter coat
against the cold. She is
in spite of it all.

To hell, she says, with the weather,
swaggering to a café on Broadway.
She needs a drink & a novel
project. But how belabored
it all is. All these people

with all their first-world problems
talking over espresso red-eyes, commending

their dead-pan deliveries of jokes
about Nietzsche & flattering
each other's dry Wittgenstein:

One of the most misleading
representational techniques
in our language is the use of
the word 'I.' (I sees that—
& yet—) "Exhausting," she says.

"Quelle night." What are you
searching for? As Miss S strays
back home, the salt trucks
salt the dirt-sick snow:
In spite of, in spite of, in spite of.

Self-Portrait as Mosquito
by David Francis

Midway through the latched room
I flew to sniff you in,

lick your blood;
rapturous hover-stud, fiber-tearing,

tooth-sinking, to drain the interstitial
vein. All I'd hoped for: a lit stove,

a taste I'd imagined: warm, a bit
of sweat mixed in, body welted

from sun, water wanting. This
is the hour you'd pulled

my sharp kiss thin and this
is the door you'd locked

with wetted key, leaving
the fan's blades to turn. Wind

on a mattress ripped at the bed's leg:
love in a cotton-field noon and forsythia's

yellow-spattered stems—
I descended in.

The Flâneur Returns
by Michael Rutherglen

from the crowds of the streets
to speak with himself
of the flow of the crowds
iterating across

to the books of his shelves
and their loose, silent sheets
their involute loops
irregular grids of

illuminated streets, their
movements inflected through
stoplights and lampposts
like lit notes arranged

intricate, minuscule
signals
that draw him onward
down axes abstracted

in a dim andante
he wanders through to
the codaless quiet
of his shelves and himself

past clusters of figures
a distant position
close of the loop
a twilit ellipsis

ERIC PANKEY

The Problem with the First Person

I confront silence as if it were a space,
A space altered by my occupying it,
A ragtag space, say, of a wilderness.

Each *I* I add to the addendum, to the slippery,
Serpentine *thens* equals, for now, the *now*.
Who am I but fragments and accretions,

A raft built from a shipwreck's scavenged timbers,
A man in the dark as he pulls his shirt over his head,
A malleable metal bent over an anvil's prow

Awaiting the hammer, awaiting the hammer's fall?
Muddled by time, my attention is drawn away,
As I aim, as I thumb the arrow's nock, and release.

An angel bends the date palm branch within Joseph's reach.
I am neither the angel nor Joseph, but am the hunger
One knows intimately and the other can only imagine.

Beneath Venus

Bled through dusk-ore—the evening star

The roads cross at an oblique angle
The way two narratives dovetail

Lit by a black and white television
A woman unbraids her hair

Each night he stops to watch
He counts the seconds of his gaze

As a boy counts the pages left
In a book he'd like never to end

As if a charm or heirloom
He carries with him daily his death

Half a world away bees
Build a hive in a lion carcass

On the sidewalk home he hears
A tapping he cannot place

Perhaps a metronome
Perhaps chalk on a blackboard

As someone stalls solving for x

In *Lyric Time: Dickinson and the Limits of Genre*, Sharon Cameron relates the project of the lyric poem to the story of the Fall from grace—to the awakening of human desire, trespass, and expulsion from symbiotic Paradise (where words were not needed, every need being already known and met) into the realm of banishment, hunger, and mortality: "To transgress the limit," she writes, "is to gain knowledge and death. Transgression displaces presence whether by knowledge or its designate language. True, Adam named the animals before the fall, but he had no real use for those names until after it. The desire for knowledge is, one might say, the desire for the possession of one's own center, the desire to know the presence around which existence circles; knowledge, in its turn, puts desire at the center of existence: death is the consequence exacted for this radical displacement….Man knows death through the primacy of language—the symbol of being's separation from itself."

One might argue that the birth of a discreet self—of an "I"—a first person— is commensurate with this "first" banishment, and that language is implicated intimately in the experience, particularly the language of the lyric poem. Critic Roman Jakobsen asserts that "lyric poetry speaks for the first person, in the present tense—a present toward which lyric always impels any past or future events." As David Baker puts it in his rich compendium of essays on the lyric, *Radiant Lyre*, "If a lyric poem is a song of oneself, what is that self?….The self exists. It is a vexed, changing, elusive, and fictive—a linguistic—construct. But linguistic constructs are real. We make the world when we say it, and it's the only world we have."

Each of us, then, has a moment, perhaps many moments, when we are "first" a person, sharing something akin to Adam and Eve's thrilling, bewildering, terrifying moments of original consciousness and separateness. We realize that we are not our mothers, that we are separate beings who must learn to use language to get what we need and to attempt to recover or rediscover some of the wholeness from which we have been banished. The homes or relationships we thought secure crumble, the touchstones of our lives disappear, a bodily illness or natural disaster or struggle with our work or ourselves forces us to confront ourselves anew. In distinct ways, Eric Pankey's "The Problem with the First Person" and "Beneath Venus" address the construct of the self in the lyric poem: its crucial paradoxes of claustral, essential solitude and implacable desire.

From line one of "The Problem with the First Person," the reader encounters a self struggling with its own invention—specifically with its invention in language. The "ragtag space" the narrator, the "I," confronts must, on the one hand, be the page, the nada altered by the word, the signifying "I"—but it's an elusive self, who, the moment it pronounces itself an "I" inhabiting and moving through time, is already changed by the loss of that prior self to the spoken "now"—the speaker is not the self he was when the poem began, or even a syllable past. This is the lyric predicament, or one of them. As Cameron writes, "In a search instigated by longing, language is by definition a back-tracking through the space left in the wake of presence, in the hopes that it might rediscover its source. ...[P]resence is a memory or a hallucination or a dream, a pure alterity....It is a memory of a past before language and before the need for language, of that flickering beginning where fulfillment seemed, illusorily, to precede desire."

Pankey means for us, I think, to feel in his lyric pronoun the specter of the banished Adam, expelled from Eden and now mortal, "muddled by time" in the wake of seductive "serpentine" powers:

Each *I* I add to the addendum, to the slippery,
Serpentine *thens* equals, for now, the *now*.
Who am I but fragments and accretions,

A raft built from a shipwreck's scavenged timbers,
A man in the dark as he pulls his shirt over his head,
A malleable metal bent over an anvil's prow

Awaiting the hammer, awaiting the hammer's fall?
Muddled by time, my attention is drawn away,
As I aim, as I thumb the arrow's nock, and release.

One consequence of freedom, then, is the burden of self-awareness, and the "howl" of this first person is the plaint of the thinking human. What or who am I? What constitutes a self? A hodge-podge of conditional, chance, and subjective shards?

A saving remnant? A tool of the Gods? Though our speaker, who now must hunt to live, tells us he has little time to ponder these existential questions, Pankey's stanzas have the feel of pensées. This is perhaps especially true in the final tercet, in which Pankey evokes the apocryphal story, told variously as occurring en route to Bethlehem or on the flight into Egypt, in which, again variously, the Christ child *in utero* or an angel divinely moves a remote date palm within reach of Joseph, so that he can pluck the fruit for the desiring Mary. This tale tropes the primal story of the Garden and allows Pankey to conflate the "first-person" (self, consciousness) with hunger, desire, something immortals can "only imagine" and which humans, because of our mortal knowledge, know all too intimately.

Like "Problem with the First Person," "Beneath Venus" pitches the language of mathematics and reason (*add, problem, equals, counts*) against the mortal, troubled "muddle" of the self in time, specifically under the spell of Venus, Eros, bodily desire. The entire poem is cast "under" the spell of Venus, what Blake in his famous blank verse sonnet called the "fair-hair'ed angel of the evening," evoking both the star and the goddess of love for which it is named. The poem concerns the "dove-tail[ing]" narratives of beauty and death—a man pausing in his evening walk to watch through a window a woman braiding her hair by the light of a television, for example, or a boy in one temporal world counting

> . . . the pages left
> In a book he'd like never to end
>
> As if a charm or heirloom
> He carries with him daily his death
>
> Half a world away bees
> Build a hive in a lion carcass
>
> On the sidewalk home he hears
> A tapping he cannot place
>
> Perhaps a metronome
> Perhaps chalk on a blackboard
>
> As someone stalls solving for x.

Especially moving in these lines is the way "He carries with him daily his death / half a world away" (the boy is young—his demise, one hopes, is far off) blurs, syntactically, into "half a world away bees / Build a hive in a lion carcass." Life is a *vanitas*, and death is the mother of beauty (or the "mother of nothing," as Charles

Wright puts it), host of new life. Surely the "tapping" the man at the crossroads, walking home, "cannot place" is not only the minutes passing, his own heartbeat, but also what must stand in for what is already lost to him: the pen sketching on paper, fingers tapping on keys, eyes transcribing the miraculous intrusion of breathtaking desire into the terminal sentence, score, and script of our lives. And what is the lyric poem, the heart's infinite capacity for exultation within the body's mortal equation, if not a stalling on the inevitable way to "solving for x"?

JOHN POCH

Echo

I couldn't understand the thing he told me.
He said he couldn't make it any clearer:
I'd rather die of thirst than have you hold me.

Hold me, I said. His elegance consoled me,
and his refusal made him all the dearer.
I couldn't understand. The thing he told me,

twice (how could anyone repeat it?), bowled me
over. I put it to myself, and queerer:
I'd rather die of thirst than have you hold me?

Give me a look at least, I wished. Behold me!
You wish, he mocked and looked toward his mirror.
I couldn't understand the thing he told me.

Perhaps our likenesses, not love, controlled me.
Then something turned and spoke in me. I hear her:
I'd rather die of thirst *then* have you hold me,

is what I should have said to draw him nearer.
We have in common our redundant error.
I couldn't understand the thing he told me:
I'd rather die of thirst than have you hold me.

Back in November 2010, the *New York Times* ran a piece about the plans of the personality disorders committee of the *Diagnostic and Statistical Manual of Mental Disorders* to eliminate "narcissism" from its fifth edition, due out in 2013. The removal of narcissism from this highly regarded list of personality disorders caused no small stir in the mental health profession, and a typical reaction among lay persons ran something like "narcissism must be so prevalent in our self-absorbed culture that it's now considered normal and not an aberration."

Whatever one thinks about whether or not narcissism should remain an acknowledged full-blown personality derangement or just one of an array of traits that might contribute one dimension to a complex "self," it's worth remembering that the mythical Narcissus, at least in Ovid's version, gets something of a bad rap in relation to the eponymous "disorder." The typical dirt on Narcissus is that he is so self-involved that he falls fatally in love with his own reflection, refusing food and punishing himself as he pines over his own unattainably gorgeous image. And in a way this is of course what happens. But Narcissus doesn't realize that he is gazing at himself, at least not initially. When Narcissus leans down to drink from that "unclouded fountain" he is "astonished" by an image of an "extraordinary boy." But he does not recognize the reflected image as himself. "Unknowingly," Ovid writes, "he desires himself…What he has seen he does not understand." Addressing his reflection as an *other*, Narcissus cries, "Whoever you are come out to me!" And when he finally acknowledges, with despair, that "I am he," Narcissus so much wishes to be *not* himself in order to know and hold his beloved that he cries "O I wish I could leave my own body!"

The villanelle seems new-minted in John Poch's revisiting of the story of Echo and Narcissus. Both of the form's requisite repeated lines end with "me," and this self-insistent pronoun fittingly stalks a poem that concerns itself with narcissism and its "echo." Cursed by jealous Juno, who robs her of normal speech and permits her only to "[repeat] the last of what is spoken and [return] the words she hears," Echo, as the narrator of Poch's poem, is allowed to generate thought, if not speech, in whole but incrementally repeated phrases, some of them her own statements and others the words of Narcissus, with whom she has fallen passionately, desperately, and unrequitedly in love. Rebuffed by Narcissus, Echo retreats, haunting caves and other recessed and secreted places, becoming all voice. But she is nonetheless present at Narcissus's endgame, helplessly witness to his demise at the pond's mirrored edge.

Formally, there is much to admire in Poch's villanelle—his use of feminine rhymes, for instance, which keep more supple and mysterious the currents of desire, refusal, and misunderstanding that course within the psyche of each of the poem's mythic players, and also between them. The plight of these two blighted figures is portrayed in moments of deft dramatic irony, as when Echo, who can only repeat what others say, says,

Hold me, I said. His elegance consoled me,
and his refusal made him all the dearer.
I couldn't understand. The thing he told me,

twice (how could anyone repeat it?), bowled me
over. I put it to myself, and queerer:
I'd rather die of thirst than have you hold me?

Perhaps the great achievement of this poem is the way it reveals the connections between Echo and Narcissus despite the self absorption that effects and affects their utter separation. In doing so the poem says something essential about Eros, as well, which Sappho and others would suggest depends upon a finally unbroachable separation or distance.

Echo's thoughts in the stanzas just above, for example, could well have been spoken by Narcissus to the beautiful boy he looks to in the water. Echo says as much: "Perhaps our likenesses, not love, controlled me. / Then something turned and spoke in me. I hear her: / I'd rather die of thirst *then* have you hold me, // is what I should have said to draw him nearer. / We have in common our redundant error." That slight but significant vowel change turning *than* into *then*, the conditional and idealized into the actual and temporal, the God-like into the mortal, is at the center of this poem. In her insights, Echo borders on empathy; by extrapolation, we feel this potential, too, in Narcissus's pledge to privilege thirst over fulfillment. Conversation is suggested over mere mimicry—a sense that before one voices, one must listen. Poch grants his Echo something like introspection, the self in metamorphic dialogue with itself.

That the predicament of each of these mythic figures—the bodiless Echo, the beautifully embodied Narcissus—corresponds to the failures of imagination, misunderstandings, and self-involvement that can emotionally stall contemporary human relationships makes Poch's redux of Ovid's "strange prayer" timeless and arresting. What lingers in the final yoking of the two repeated lines is not the onus of an entirely hopeless stalemate between two isolated individuals, but rather Echo's *transformation* of Narcissus's lines. As Gaston Bachelard says in *The Poetics of Space*, "This frail, ephemeral thing, a voice, can bear witness to the most forceful realities ....But before speaking, one must listen"...must listen: to others and to oneself. Poch's poem acknowledges the empathetic power of listening, which at times seems to be an increasingly rare and important human capacity.

WILLIAM THOMPSON

Stutterer

Trained never to forget the all
-importance of control, his face
remembers always to suppress
each unintended syllable

and can't. Hence the expressionless
expression he maintains, a dead
-pan scowl where umbrage shadows rage.
He hurts. It is his privilege,

or was: the ones who mocked or stared
grew into people of good will
who, patient, notice nothing as
the hard words flare and sting his eyes.

The Prayer Rope Knot

Each time the monk who learned this knot
had tied his own, a devil came
& loosened it. Eventually
the monk, just as the devil hoped,
got pissed; he couldn't pray at all.
That night his angel wakened him
& taught him how to interweave
double strands into a web
of 7 crosses. Pulled tight,
they closed into this perfect knot
whereby the devil's silently
upbraided, and the heart sings whole.

A friend of mine, a writer who stammers in stressful situations, often begins a
public reading from one of his books by singing, his clear, lusty baritone never
failing to call to my mind Emily Dickinson's note to her grieving Norcross cousins:
"Let Emily sing for you because she cannot pray." Surely singing/writing/prayer
all relate, in one way or another, to ways in which our tongues can slip up, betray us,

LISA RUSS SPAAR   139

become knotted—by fear, nerves, (dis)belief, psychic trauma, physical impediment, delight, or sheer astonishment.

These two poems by William Thompson concern themselves with fluency and its obstacles. "Stutterer" makes powerful use of its established formal expectations and deployment of rhythmic and syntactic surprise to enact for and in the reader a palpable sense of the tremendous strain and control the stammerer must at all times sustain. At key points, a startling enjambment revealing a hastily compounded word or the full stop of a mid-tetrameter line caesura imitates the blocks, prolongations, and other therapeutic ruses by which stutterers learn to mask if not master their unwanted repetition or curtailment of speech sounds:

Trained never to forget the all
-importance of control, his face
remembers always to suppress
each unintended syllable

and can't. Hence the expressionless
expression he maintains…

For all its undeniable physicality, the poem is also deeply psychological, presciently suggesting a double betrayal, paradoxically wrought by public kindness. As the stutterer outgrows his childhood of taunting and misunderstood otherness, he must, in adulthood, give up the compensating "privilege" of feeling righteously wronged as a consequence of his own increased "control":

He hurts. It is his privilege,

or was: the ones who mocked or stared
grew into people of good will
who, patient, notice nothing as
the hard words flare and sting his eyes.

It is interesting to consider how many stammerers were or are also writers— Virgil, Aesop, Borges, Henry James, Elizabeth Bowen, Lewis Carroll. Clearly Thompson means for us not to forget what others might take for granted: our human birthright of wielding language, and the great obstacles, often unseen and underappreciated, to articulation. "Stutterer" reminds us, as well, to recognize the ways in which our most powerful utterances, especially in poetry, are haunted and even typified by disordered speech.

"The Prayer Rope Knot" recounts the story of St. Anthony the Great, the father of

Eastern Orthodox monasticism, who, it is said, attempted to tie a simple knot into a leather rope every time he uttered a ritual prayer but was impeded in the process by the Devil, who invariably followed up behind him and undid his knots in order to sabotage his devotions.

Each time the monk who learned this knot
had tied his own, a devil came
& loosened it. Eventually
the monk, just as the devil hoped,
got pissed; he couldn't pray at all.

Inspired by a vision of the Mother of God, St. Anthony devises a means to tie the knots in a way that confounds the Devil:

That night his angel wakened him
& taught him how to interweave
double strands into a web
of 7 crosses. Pulled tight,
they closed into this perfect knot
whereby the devil's silently
upbraided, and the heart sings whole.

A genuine pleasure of this poem of forthright spiritual difficulty and unalloyed joy is, again, Thompson's intelligent and intuitive use of form. The four-stress, predominantly iambic lines convey a sense of the shuttling of weaving and unweaving, of tying and untying. Yet as the monk masters his divinely inspired complex knot, the sword of spirit by which he will defeat the Devil's trickery, the line itself pauses, and a spondee ("pulled tight") assures us of the invincibility of this "perfect knot." The Devil is outwitted, his unbraiding is "upbraided," and the monk's fulsome restoration to prayer is emphasized by the clarion call spondees that close the poem: "the heart sings whole."

In their exploration of the various and intricate ways in which acts of courage and receptivity can overcome hindrances of the voice and spirit, Thompson's poems also reveal the eloquent power of silence. When the "hard words flare and sting" within or the "heart sings whole," the hush that surrounds these experiences is as articulate as anything that might be spoken aloud. Olivier Clement, in *The Roots of Christian Mysticism*, relates the story of desert father Abba Agathon, who "carried pebbles in his mouth for three years, not to become an orator but to learn to keep silence." The impediments, the pebbles in the mouth, for Thompson's stammerer and his monk, serve to open his subjects and his readers to a receptivity that has as much or more to do with fluid attentiveness as it does with speaking aloud.

KAZIM ALI

from The River Cloud Sutra

Launch

Unmake yourself   year by year
your urge

surges in your ear
no purpose at all   but dispersal

lost in the labyrinth
desperate   to wring yourself

dry of lust
wanting exhalation

to mean   disappearance
in the space between lightning and

thunder
fling yourself skyward, son-storm

a hagiography   of feathers
glued to your   sin-singed skin

arrowing   sunward
like a son on fire   singing the whole way

I'm leaving you behind   a ghost of a prayer
leaving you behind   the shining thread—

Skyward

to Jonji and Suzanne

we met at last in a lifetime after the dry season charmed us

drawn along filaments of fire while you roar the river cloud sutra

the self disguises itself as what hovers up

over the water eternally

a body is a coalition of matter, a body that falls

in the lull between generations, mere moment, lit from the inside

hide me from myself in the prehistoric valley

glaciers themselves forming from clouds

hollow the ear a beast in its lathe dark urge

to bind in afterlife the temporal word

listen when the white-leafed arms fold up in prayer I left

father will the sun always unwing me

how else will I

Kazim Ali's impressive body of work—several books of poems, a novel, a short-story collection, a cross-genre autobiography, and a gathering of interviews, reviews, and essays—concerns the circumference of self and other, word and world. Crossing and concocting genres with agility and passion, Ali creates a complex, spiritually hybridized geography in which the self, wrapt by god-hunger and desire, transgresses various emotional, mythic, and interpersonal borderlines and check-points. Jorie Graham writes, "The world is there, but the border between the self and the world is, as I see it, a differently fluid juncture according to each person's occasion." For Ali, the *occasion*—the tensility between the embodied and the aspiring, the pilgrim/son and the ultimately unknowable parent/Beyond—is borne out in acts of imagination and language that are ever on the verge of prayer.

These paired, quietly urgent poems—pages from a kind of iconoclastic breviary—offer Ali's flood subjects in provocative diptych. The word "sutra" derives from the Sanskrit *sutra*, thread, and is akin to the Latin *suere*, to sew, to suture. In both Buddhism and Hinduism, a sutra is an embodiment in language of canonical and/or literary scripture or teaching, often mnemonic, aphoristic, and lapidary in intensity. Ali is not the first contemporary poet to borrow formally from this tradition—Brenda Hillman, Allen Ginsberg, and Gary Snyder, among others, have appealed to the sutra as a trope or structure for poetic material.

"Launch," which deals itself out in condensed, thread-like, spaced-apart phrases, opens in the imperative. A you—who appears to be deliberately courting his or her own unmaking in a diaspora of the self, a "disappearance / in the space between lightning and // thunder," but who is blocked, "lost in the labyrinth / desperate to wring yourself // dry of lust"—is admonished by the speaker to "fling yourself skyward, son-storm // a hagiography   of feathers / glued to your   sin-singed skin."   Mixed in with Zen notions of nirvana and desire for the extinction of the discreet self in a blaze of beatitude, then, are clear allusions to the well known plight of Icarus. Filial anxieties beset the text and, visually and acoustically, the poem is a maze of stops and starts, blind alleys, false beginnings, hesitancies, surges, and a visceral, mounting sense of impending action, the "launch" of the self out of stasis and into ecstasy. Stitching through the lines, a word like *urge* becomes *surge*—then *purpose*—then *dispersal*. *Son-storm* metamorphoses into *sunward*, then *son on fire*; *sin-singed* transforms into *singing*. Part charm, part pre-game pep talk, part incantatory admonishment, the poem's intensifying energies propel the you from maze to amazement, and the last italicized lines of the poem, notably, belong not to the speaker but to the launched addressee,

arrowing   sunward
like a son on fire   singing the whole way

I'm leaving you behind   a ghost of a prayer
leaving you behind   the shining thread—

The "shining thread" of "Launch" leads to a companion poem, "Skyward," in which, "drawn along filaments of fire," the *you* (who in this poem becomes more obviously both the I, and even the *we*) "[roars] the river cloud sutra / [as] the self disguises itself as what hovers up / over the water eternally." Launched into the ether between heaven and earth, the hour of tree blossom, of cloud and water, can the you (both other and self) know itself as both "lit from the inside" and at the same time hidden from itself "in the prehistoric valley / glaciers themselves forming from clouds"? Is there, finally, any way to "bind in afterlife the temporal word"— the prayer left behind—and to reconcile the life in a body ("a beast in its lathe dark urge") with the soul's desire for transcendence? Again, the poem's last lines, a query, seem to come from inside the you, the son—"father will the sun always unwing me / how else will I"—and the abrupt falling off of the last phrase enacts what is at stake in these poems. Will I...*what*? Here the reader is compelled to fall into, to re-enter, to take up again the thread of the world of "Launch," where we see that it is perhaps the *cycle* of lostness, yearning, curiosity, and epiphanic enchantment that is in itself both the spiritual/artistic practice and the lesson.

ALLISON SEAY

Town of Unspeakable Things

Then there was the time I looked directly into the face
of the life I thought I was missing,

of love. I used to think to be not alone meant
never having to walk through the high wheat

or struggle in the water. Not having to decide not
to fling from some height.

Once, the two of us rode one bicycle.
I wore a straw hat and perched on the handlebars

and beside us the sea oats swayed like skirts
and I heard a trilling in the crabgrass.

The sidewalks were bleached as grecian stone
as we rode past the fish shop smelling of morning—
salt, bread, limes, men.

Riding in front, it was such that
I could not be heard always, at least not the first time

for you pedaled into the wind
and my hair was a ribbon in your eyes.

I said I thought bougainvillea was a stoic plant
and then had to say twice, *no, stoic!* and then
no, the bougainvillea! and then you said easily

it was nothing like that at all.

But our future was clear enough when I asked if you saw
the clean aprons of those men

(how much longer you think until they clean the fish?
did you see how white those aprons were? did you see?)

To which you said
How much is it, then, you think you need?

What is a face? What does it mean to look "into the face" of someone, something? To face up. To kiss face. To save face. We "face" people and situations in order to confront, to salvage reputation, to admit, to concede. And though certain of the faithful may "seek his face continually" (1 Chronicles 16:11), God tells Moses in Exodus that "man shall not see me and live."

Clearly, faces are powerful entities. In certain cultures, contexts, ceremonies, plays, private games, crimes, and periods of mourning or carnival, the face is veiled or masked. Experts tell us that humans, even as infants, are especially wired to "see" other human faces, which we tend to take in as a Gestalt rather than by individual parts. And judging from its use on drivers' licenses, passports, lanyard cards, Facebook profiles, and other material and virtual documents, the face is still regarded as the feature that best identifies a person. Ubiquitous emoticons aside, faces are also essential to the expression and registering of human feelings. Deriving from the Latin *facies* ("appearance, form, figure), related to the Latin *facere* ("to make"), a "face"can refer physically to the sense organ complex on the front of the head (comprised of eyes, nose, mouth, chin) or figuratively to anything which is the world-directed part or aspect of a place or circumstance, such as the face of someone's love affair, which is the subject, in part, of Allison Seay's "Town of Unspeakable Things."

As though in the midst of an ongoing narrative, and with the almost offhand flippancy of an aside, Seay tells her reader in the very opening clause that "Then there was the time I looked directly into the face / of the life I thought I was missing, / of love." The reader has the sense that the speaker has, before the poem commences, been in the midst of relating some sort of meditation on the nature of life and love and has now turned her attention to one defining moment in particular. But we know from the title that something about her narration is "unspeakable," and she suggests, in fact, that the very face she is about to "look directly into" is in itself a fiction—it's not the life *she is in*, but a life she *thinks*, or once thought, she might be *missing*, a life she equates with love. So already the reader is at several veiled removes even as the speaker intimates that she's on the cusp of making a revelation.

Despite her use of temporal tags ("I used to" and "once"), however, Seay's narrative is not linear. Just when we think we're going to hear about that important time of facing up, of seeing into the truth of things, we're taken on a tangent into the speaker's notion of what she "used to think to be not alone meant"—again, the mesh of conditional tenses, infinitives, and negatives clouds the picture—life and love have been elusive and ambiguously bound up for the speaker with fantasies about fugue state bouts of perilous loneliness, including "[n]ot having to decide not / to fling from some height."

"Once," the speaker continues, shifting gears yet again, "the two of us rode one bicycle." We are several stanzas into this tale within a tale before we realize that *this* bike ride along the seashore now being recounted is, in fact, "the time" referred to in line one. Things seem idyllic, even romantic, at first—our speaker in straw hat,

> perched on the handlebars

and beside us the sea oats swayed like skirts
and I heard a trilling in the crabgrass.

The sidewalks were bleached as grecian stone
as we rode past the fishshop smelling of morning—
salt, bread, limes, men.

Yet something is not right. The narrator, "riding in front," cannot see her lover, who is behind her on the bike, pedaling "into the wind." And so when the speaker tries to point out things as she passes, her words are swallowed by gusts and misheard, if heard at all, by the pedaller of the bicycle. What might, under other circumstances, be a humorous, malapropistic vignette, however, takes a dark turn when we realize that the lover's inability to hear the speaker has less to do with the fact that she and he are not facing one another (although this is metaphorical) and that the buffeting sea breezes are garbling the sounds she makes, and has more to do, finally, with his seeming indifference, self-absorption, and even dismissive detachment ("and then you said easily // it was nothing like that at all"). By the time we reach the epiphanic moment—the truth the speaker faces down—the economy of the poem has turned from matters of time to issues of quantity, to matters of what, finally, accounts for "enough," in the relationship, in terms of what lies ahead for the narrator as she stares out ahead into a future that does not hold the full commitment of the lover at her back, who has betrayed a willingness to give only so much, and no more:

But our future was clear enough when I asked if you saw
the clean aprons of those men

(how much longer you think until they clean the fish?
did you see how white those aprons were? did you see?)

To which you said
How much is it, then, you think you need?

Those clean fishermen's aprons, destined for staining—hard not to see them as the white page of the poem, the speaker's full-frontal and difficult adjustment of the fit between her own expectations and her realization that the fulfillment she thought she was missing might not after all be any more than a solitary, one-sided, one way experience. What C. D. Wright says in an exquisite pamphlet about Jean Valentine, *writing a word / changing it*, published by Brian Teare's micropress, Albion Books (2011), might also apply to Seay's poem: "In words, narrative is ultimately inescapable, but scattered elements of it will get the job done. Rather than narrate, she is organizing her emotions." To face the truth about her truth, the narrator of Seay's poem borrows the temporal semblance of a coherent story, the account of a love affair, but with the interior acoustics of the lyric.

Looking into the "face" of this poem reminds me of the experience of seeing Richard Avedon's *In the American West* exhibit at the Amon Carter Museum in Fort Worth, Texas, in 1985. For his oversized black-and-white portraits, Avedon chose to photograph his often life-ravaged subjects in front of white sheets rather than before their actual contexts—rodeos, midways, carnivals, small towns. The subjects gaze one way, out of their frames, and the effect of removing the particulars of time and space in the backdrop is that the faces, finally, do the work of narrative, of fiction, making unspeakable but powerful testament. Interestingly, we never really look into any faces in Seay's poem. But the poem brings the speaker and her readers face-to-face with an almost untranslatable negative epiphany. Seay creates a suggestive, temporal narrative of unrequited love by confronting its ineffable paradoxes, its lyric entrapments.

ILLNESS & POETRY

ILLNESS & POETRY

When we consider the physical and mental maladies and disabilities that artists, like other humans, have borne with courage and stamina, it is tempting to contemplate the effects these afflictions may have had not only on the physical making of works of art, but on the content and form of those creations, as well. Could a seizure disorder (epilepsy?), for example, account for Van Gogh's nimbused vortexes and ferocity of light in some of his paintings? Did Beethoven's fury and frustration at his own slowly advancing deafness (otosclerosis? lead poisoning? syphilis?) contribute to the complex and dissonant "arguments" of some of his later compositions? Is it possible that the eye ailment that sent Emily Dickinson to Boston for treatments and kept her from reading for what was for her an excruciating hiatus (the first text she savored when allowed to read again was Shakespeare) explains in part the prevalence of ocular imagery in her poems and letters ("Before I got my eye put out— / I liked as well to see / As other creatures, that have eyes— / And know no other way— "). Insomnia, melancholy, bi-polarity, post-partum depression, blindness, deafness, quadriplegia, obsessive-compulsive disorder, cancer, narcolepsy, multiple sclerosis, alcoholism, anorexia, schizophrenia, post-traumatic stress syndrome—when one starts making a list of the physical and mental infirmities known to affect human beings, it seems obvious that few artists could be exempt from a periodic bout, if not a chronic struggle, with the body/ brain nexus. At times physical affliction can feel and in fact be unendurable. In "Elegy," Theodore Roethke writes, "I have myself an inner weight of woe / That God himself can scarcely bear."

One wonders what effects modern pharmaceuticals might have had on the luminous work of writers with physical and mental illnesses. Such speculations are not new. As Kay Redfield Jamison writes in *Touched With Fire: Manic-Depressive Illness and the Artistic Temperament*, "The fear that medicine and science will take away from the ineffability of it all, or detract from the mind's labyrinthian complexity, is as old as man's attempts to chart the movement of the stars. Even John Keats, who had studied to be a surgeon, felt that Newton's calculations would blanch the heavens of their glory." With anti-depressants making a halcyon field of the psyche, banishing the dark corners in which the Id might lurk and surprise, or with mood stabilizers evening out the roller coaster of emotional highs and lows, would writers like Virginia Woolf and William Blake, for example, have produced songs and texts of such prescient and haunting witness?

Perhaps, medicated, these writers might have led happier, more stable, and, in the case of Woolf and others, longer lives. At a party a few years ago, I overheard two poet colleagues arguing about which anti-anxiety medicine was better for poets to take, with a particular drug making one of the pair "just not able to come up with the right word when I need it." An interesting book that engages this topic is *Poets on Prozac*, edited by physician and poet Richard Berlin, and published by John Hopkins University Press in 2008. In sixteen essays, poets articulate their battles with a variety of psychiatric and other mental/brain disorders, provoking questions about whether or not these illnesses contribute to the success of the poems, or if the real achievement is that the poets manage to succeed as writers in spite of their affliction.

In his memoir, *My Dyslexia*, Pulitzer prize-winning poet Philip Schultz explores these and related questions as he recounts his discovery of his own dyslexia in mid-life and looks back on how his undiagnosed struggle with the disorder affected his childhood and early adult home and student life, helping to shape the writer he would become despite his long misunderstood impediment. "Dyslexia" [<Gk *dys-* (abnormal, bad, difficult) *lexis* (word)] is a term for a wide range of learning disabilities involving the decoding and processing of language, particularly in matters of writing and reading. Schultz, now in his 60s, did not discover his own dyslexia until he was 58, when his oldest son, a second-grader at the time, was diagnosed with the disorder: "I learned from his neuropsychologist's report that we shared many of the same symptoms," Schultz writes, "like delayed processing problems, terrible handwriting, misnaming items, low frustration tolerance for reading and most homework assignments involving writing, to name a few." As Schultz makes clear, dyslexia's damage reaches beyond the learning disability itself, affecting the dyslexic's self-esteem, maturity, and relationships. "I understood that I was different from other kids. I lived in a world of differences measured not by appearances, wealth, or even intelligence....My differentness felt freakish. My brain wouldn't obey me, nor my parents or my teachers. If I had trouble learning to read a clock, knowing my left from my right, hearing instructions—things everyone else seemed to do easily—how could I trust my own thoughts or anything about myself?"

Schultz is not alone in suffering from dyslexia. The Levinson Medical Center for Learning Disabilities reports that over 40 million American children and adults are or have been affected by some form of the disorder, and names Pablo Picasso, Thomas Edison, Leonardo Da Vinci, Jay Leno, and Whoopi Goldberg among the many well known dyslexics who have managed to thrive despite their difficulties. But because dyslexia involves the use and apprehension of language, its impediments are especially daunting and relevant for writers. Driving Schultz's meditation on the subject (which has the same fresh forthrightness and tensile clarity of his poems) is the question of how "someone who didn't learn to read until he was eleven years old and in the fifth grade, who was held back in third grade and asked to leave his school," found his way to poetry, to a life involving the most intimate and deeply articulate acts of communication in language, and to the making of poems whose power and craft garnered him the Pulitzer Prize for Poetry, one of the nation's most prestigious awards for poetic achievement?

Discovery of his own dyslexia, Schultz explains, was like fathoming "a mystery I'd been grappling with my entire life." Exploring his life prior to and after the revelation of his dyslexia, Schultz recounts his years-long struggle with and sanctuary in language. His book trains its unflinching, frank, and darkly humorous lens on a childhood and adolescence rife with difficulty, fear, anxiety, shame, self-doubt, behavioral problems, and anger. Chief among the memoir's insights are those Schultz makes into the role his dyslexia has played in his development as a poet. Laughed at by an early tutor to whom he confessed his desire to be a writer, Schultz nonetheless persisted in his ambition. In a way, he suggests, his sense of otherness, of exile, foregrounded for him, early-on, something essential to the processes of all writing: "the life of an artist is in many ways similar to the life of the dyslexic. Both are essentially dysfunctional systems that produce in each individual volumes of anxiety, perseverance, and rejection, as well as creative compensatory thinking. Each, by their very nature, makes a victim of its creator, turning him into an outsider and misfit. It's true of all artists, I think, at every level of success….Each must, without appeal, strive to tolerate its own forms of self-defamation, creative excitement, and lack of forgiveness."

I would urge readers of the memoir to seek out Schultz's psychologically astute and eloquently vernacular poems, as well, including those in his Pulitzer-prize-winning *Failure* (Harcourt, 2007), whose title evokes Samuel Beckett's admonition to "Fail again. Fail better," and whose pieces about the narrator's aggrieved and beset father could as well address Schultz's private travail, as in these lines from "The Magic Kingdom": "Bless the plenitude of the suffering mind…/ its endless parade of disgrace / and spider's web of fear, the hunger / of the soul that expects to be despised / and cast out, the unforgiving ghosts / I visit late at night when only God is awake…." It is a privilege to close with a poem by Schultz, "Getting Along." A love poem, it confronts what Schultz calls in *My Dyslexia* a "true and original language" and, elsewhere in the memoir, an archeology of the soul. With its kinetic pronominal exchanges ("When the I won't stay / hidden inside the we, / forgets where it ends / and the we begins / a lush / green river of intimacy / smothers it (me)" and its "hurt / buried inside the pride / hidden inside the pain"), it is as articulate an expression of marriage (and of the marriage of the "broken" mind and the "opalescent prescience" of the poetic imagination) as one might hope to encounter, both within, prior to, and beyond language.

Getting Along

My wife and I are getting along.
Right now, she's listening
to Bruce Springsteen
in her studio, making out
of copper wire and pieces
of broken jewelry (plastic rats
and wedding rings) a cloud
of opalescent prescience.
Yesterday, she loved me,
she said, even though
sometimes I'm an asshole.
Grateful for the sometimes,
I said much of the time
I feel like one. Everyone
does, she said, except
the ones who really are.
They think fate is fucking
with them. When the color
of her eyes turns dark walnut,
it means: I loved you once;
or green: always, maybe.
Marriage is the hardest thing,
she thinks, harder than God,
childhood or childbirth.
When the I won't stay
hidden inside the we,
forgets where it ends
and the we begins, a lush
green river of intimacy
smothers it (me.) Unrequited,
it's the point we're always
trying to make, the hurt
buried inside the pride
hidden inside the pain.
Love is an accident of fate,
an idea of surprising elasticity,
she thinks I think. Once,
we said nothing on the phone
for one hour. Each syllable
we didn't speak was visible,
each breath we swallowed

swallowed us, each unspoken
allegation a covenant of fidelity,
a razor our silence rubbed
us against. As if love were
a house of mirrors we can't
stop wandering inside,
viewing every intention
from every side. As if
we're stuck in hindsight,
every day an anniversary,
forever crossing a January
Monday morning to meet
for the first time, how she
wouldn't look at me, as if
everything we meant to say,
feared, and longed to be,
was there, in the stark fierce
diction of her eyes, a story
of once, maybe, and always,
waiting for us (for we) to read.

JOANNA KLINK

The Graves

Wind for your sickness.
The moon for your sickness.

A river of night-
trees. Mossy patches

where something recently slept.
A hand-drawn sketch of
fish for your sickness,

red and ghost-
loamed. From your mother,

for your sickness, a late
flock of snow-geese
swept up in a gust.

From your father, a cave
of violas in luminous
pitch. For the panic

desolation. For scratchy bed-
sheets, the gathering of tumors,
a dispensation traveling in

far-nesses across the
galaxy-quiet of what is

to come. Dark-sunned,
you are swimming in schools.

For the despairing quality of
hospital fluorescence,

the secondhand alarm—
theft of time theft of

hope. The messages
arrive like flowers.

For the common un-
contested light of dusk.
For tobacco moths

    in clouds of wings at
    the door. For the dawn-

emotion, a calm-in-vastness
that descends upon
what is. Upon the storm-

    tangle of branches, wing-
    veins and hand-veins
    shadow-shown on that pale

skin of sky. Too stone for
fear. Too brittle for

    findings. From the powers that,
    born on the site of sorrow,

fall in strands of smoke
across your sickness,
for your sickness,

    and carry and keep you.
    That would keep you here.

André Hodier once described jazz bebop saxophonist Charlie Parker's distinctive soloing, something he achieved not in the traditional way, by reconfiguring the melody, or head, of the tune, but by embroidering all around it, defining it by its absence. Joanna Klink's "The Graves," an advent poem in many ways—an incantatory, nocturnal vigil, a talismanic keeping-watch—riffs in a similar way around the unnamed center of the poem: the impending death of the ill "you" the poem addresses.

From its first note, the poem keens with the anaphoric rhythms and accrued kennings of an ancient Celtic or Gaelic blessing, and the speaker, in intimate but also all-seeing relation to the sick subject of the poem, offers a series of gifts, prescriptions, remedies, compensations extended as though in receipt for or to alleviate or even obstruct the addressee's afflictions: "Wind for your sickness. /

The moon for your sickness. // A river of night- / trees. Mossy patches // where
something recently slept. / A hand-drawn sketch of / fish for your sickness, // red
and ghost- / loamed."

One of the many things I admire about Klink's lyric gift is her ability to conjure
psychological experience through fluid shifts of perspective and point of view.
The speaker makes us privy to both the subject's domestic sphere—the sick one's
mother, for instance, sends "for your sickness, a late / flock of snow geese swept
up in a gust" and the father offers "a cave / of violas in luminous / pitch" to
ameliorate "the panic / desolation" and the "scratchy bed- / sheets, the gathering
of tumors"—and also to the things the sick one cannot possibly know, fate, for
instance, "traveling in // far-nesses across the / galaxy-quiet of what is // to
come." The reader feels, too, the "despairing quality of / hospital fluorescence,
// the secondhand alarm— / theft of time theft of / hope"—a despair no child's
drawing or CD of golden notes can, finally, keep at bay.

"The Graves" makes a charged title for the poem, evoking as it does, of course, the
destination of the body's dust, our burial, our mortality—but also suggesting weight,
gravity, seriousness. The shape of the poem—undulating couplets and tercets that
call attention to the line—signals, too, that Klink means us to think consciously of
(en)gravings: carvings, markings, text, words. In a way, "graves," in this context,
becomes akin to "psalms" or "collects" or "ghazals." Klink seems to be inventing
her own poetic form here (and in fact another poem in her most recent collection,
Raptus, is also called "The Graves"), a language act capable of confronting fate,
"that pale / skin of sky" that seems "[t]oo stone for / fear. Too brittle for //
findings."

The remedial and recompensatory *for* that propels the first part of the poem
turns into new prepositions/propositions as the poem culminates. We hear that
the "dawn- / emotion, a calm-in-vastness / …descends upon / what is." This
"upon"—somatic and burdened—moves the poem forward. This "dawn-emotion"
also descends "from" a more generative source:

> ...the powers that,
> born on the site of sorrow,

> fall in strands of smoke,
> across your sickness,
> for your sickness,

> and carry and keep you.
> That would keep you here.

Klink's "graves"—each startling image, as Robert Hass would put it, an elegy to what it signifies—bear the truth of Stevens's statement that death is the mother of beauty—as, by extension, is poetry, love, and a guarded, expectancy akin to hope.

MARK JARMAN

Oblivion

While I was under
I was oblivious. So
that is what it means.

*

Time passed for others,
but not for me. Still I was
the one changed in time.

*

A drug for dreamless
sleep and amnesia—but what
was there to forget?

*

Foretaste? Forewarning?
But nothing comes of nothing—
and this was nothing.

*

The aesthetics of
anesthesia: blankness
has its own beauty.

*

Released from the spell
of virtual death, waking, too,
feels like enchantment.

*

Ashes to ashes,
dust to dust, both the old flesh
and the new chrome joint.

*

You pass through the door
to the unknown and enter
the same room you left.

It is now understood that what we think of as haiku written in or translated into English (short poems of Japanese origin consisting of three lines of 5, 7, and 5 syllables, respectively, presented in three horizontal lines) represent a departure from the traditional haiku form (a brief poem, originally called *hokku*, often printed in a single vertical line, and consisting of 17 *on* (or *morae*) (sound units which are not the same thing as syllables), offered in phrases of 5, 7, and 5 on and characterized by "cutting" (*kiru*)—a juxtaposition of key elements—and a seasonal reference (*kigo*), which may or may not be drawn from the natural world.

Nonetheless, the haiku has persisted as a popular form since Bashō and others gave it new life in the 17th century. In the twenty-first century, haiku societies abound across cultures and throughout the cyber-community, with focuses both scholarly and playful (at one Dog Haiku site, for instance, a reader can find such haiku-inspired gems as "Love my master; / Thus I perfume myself with / This long-rotten mouse" and "Today I sniffed / Many dogs' behinds – I celebrate / By kissing your face"). Books devoted to haiku on various pop cultural themes (*Hipster Haiku*, for example) abound, and the form remains a staple in elementary schools even at a time when public school curricula, for one reason or another, are bereft of poetry in general. In one *Beavis and Butthead* episode, a frustrated English teacher goes into paroxysms of joy when the snarky duo inadvertently *heh, heh, heh* their way into an impromptu haiku.

There can be no denying, however, that a good haiku possesses an inimitable power, even in its myriad and loose adaptations, and it makes sense that Mark Jarman, perhaps the most traditionally formally adept poet writing in America since the passing of Donald Justice, would choose it for an exploration of oblivion [<L *oblivion, oblivio*, to forget, perhaps from *ob* ("the way") and *levis* ("smooth")] and in particular of the "aesthetics of / anesthesia" associated with a medical operation. While recovering from surgery to replace his right hip joint, in fact, Jarman wrote a haiku every day about the process. From the many of what he calls "hip haiku" produced during that convalescence, "Oblivion" consists of a sequence of 8 discreet haiku poems. One effect of Jarman's yoking together of these separate poetic "frames" is to mimic the flirtation with "dreamless / sleep and amnesia,"

nothingness, nada, and the Big Sleep that surgical anesthesia, with its "virtual death," suggests. Oblivion denotes both "the fact or condition of forgetting or having forgotten," but also "the condition or state of being forgotten or unknown." Both states can be terrifying, and must ultimately be confronted by the patient slipping in and out of general anesthesia:

While I was under
I was oblivious. So
that is what it means.

*

Time passed for others,
but not for me. Still I was
the one changed in time.

Jarman, the son and grandson of Christian ministers, has never been one to shy away from issues of faith and doubt in his poems. Across his long and acclaimed career, Jarman seems to believe that the path and not the destination is the way to enlightenment, a view shared by many Zen practitioners of the haiku form. In his Foreword to Stephen Berg's *Cuckoo's Blood: Versions of Zen Masters* (an anthology that includes Bashō, Issa, Ryōkan, among others), Steven Antinoff looks at what he calls Zen "art toward" in light of "Paul Tillich's famous definition of religion as 'the state of being grasped by an ultimate concern.' One's ultimate concern is that which concerns one unconditionally whatever the specific conditions of one's existence." Working in haiku allows Jarman not only to recreate a sense of the altered consciousness and heavy tides of amnesia associated with the state of being anesthetized, but also to confront what has ever been one of his "ultimate concerns": what lies on the other side of life in our bodies and minds as we inhabit and know them. Is this temporary drugged state a portent of the "beyond," of death, Jarman asks? What awaits us there? Heaven? Salvation? Oblivion?

Foretaste? Forewarning?
But nothing comes of nothing –
and this was nothing.

The vision presented here is akin to what Antinoff calls "the contradiction inherent in any true koan: absolute negation and absolute demand....The Zen quest artists, or any artist in the grip of an ultimate concern, cannot cease striving to arrive at the source, even though infinitely thwarted." Put another way in the words of Zen master Shin'ichi Hisamatsu (1889 – 1980), "In Zen art, skill means two things: through skill man is led from reality to the source of reality; art is the way by which man can enter the source. On the other hand, art is the way by which man, having entered the source, 'returns' to reality. The essence of Zen art lies in this return. This return is the activity of Zen…and in it resides the significance of Zen works of art….It is the separation from all bonds, the release from the fetters intrinsic to all form. This release is also called nothingness. All these terms mean the same thing….The essence of Zen lies not in going toward the source but returning from it."

And it is toward the *return*, the reprieve, the "recovery" from induced oblivion that Jarman's sequence moves:

Released from the spell
of virtual death, waking, too,
feels like enchantment.

And perhaps this paradox—that nothing leads to nothing (or that all leads to all)—is the gift of the sequence. The final haiku does not purport to possess or understand the "ultimate concern"; it allows it, as Antinoff would put it, to appear. Blake called death the movement from one room into another, something the reader senses as Jarman returns to the world of the conscious, the rehabilitated, both the same and yet utterly transformed:

You pass through the door
To the unknown and enter
The same room you left.

In an interview with Robert D. Wilson, Sam Hamill, poet and master translator of Bashō and others, has said that "In the best haiku, the real poetry is in the silence at the end of the seventeen (or so) syllables." Is the knowledge that eludes us as we travel, "both the old flesh / and the new chrome joint," something we carry in us always? The silence in the "room" the poem ushers us into at its close is palpable with this possibility, its "own beauty" and ultimately unknowable mystery.

ALICE FULTON

After the Angelectomy

And where my organ of veneration should be—
wormwood and gall. Grudge sliver.

Wailbone, iron, bitters. I mean to say the miniature
waterfalls have all dried up in this miniature

place where day is duty cubed, time is time on task
and every mind optimized for compliance.

Time to delint my black denim traveling stuff.
The florescent major highlighter has dimmed

to minor. I'm so dying I wrote
when I meant to write so tired.

And when I sleep I dream only that
I'm sleeping. Please see my black stuff's

dusted off. Night has no dilution anxieties,
but only the infinites are happy:

Math. Time. Everything happy goes
to many decimal places

while flesh passes through
gradations of glory. I visualized it,

the nurse said of the bedsore. Everything exists
at the courtesy of everything else.

Please see that my grave is kept clean.
Beloveds, temporal things

in which the infinite endangered itself,
excarnate to memory and the divine substance

has limited liability. You're kind,
I tell the infinite. Too kind.

What would it mean to have permanently excised from oneself the capacity to bear and receive messages? And not just any messages, either, such as "LOL!" or "R U OK" or an automated, computerized voicemail reminder of your root canal appointment, but the real *news*—terrible or amazing, of change and imagination, of redemption, of oracle and prophecy—that is so hard to get from the divine, from poems, from anywhere? How would it feel, Alice Fulton asks, in her fierce and unsettling poem, to exist "After the Angelectomy"?

The word "angel" derives from the Greek *angelos*, "messenger," and was one of the earliest Germanic adoptions from the Latin. Culturally and over time, angels have been associated with supernatural beings (for good or ill), God-sent harbingers, servants, and intermediaries, protective or guiding spirits, and the innocent and benevolent among us ("you're an angel"). Angels have been sentimentalized, militarized, and appropriated by New Age and orthodox communities, Latter Day Saints and theosophists, greeting card companies and songwriters, film-makers, and sports teams alike. Nor is belief in angels a phenomenon relegated primarily to ancient, mythical, or Biblical realms. According to a 2008 article in *TIME* magazine citing a survey conducted by the Baylor University Institute for Studies of Religion, "More than half of all Americans believe they have been helped by a guardian angel in the course of their lives....In a poll of 1700 respondents, 55% answered affirmatively to the statement, 'I was protected from harm by a guardian angel.' The responses defied standard class and denominational assumptions about religious belief; the majority held up regardless of denomination, region or education — though the figure was a little lower (37%) among respondents earning more than $150,000 a year." People who admit to having been attended by angels describe the experience, among other things, as involving a radiant light, a perfume, or a sense of being touched.

The making and reading of poems would seem almost to *require* some sort of angelic visitation or "translation," some extra-human inspiration—the muse, the sublime, the accident, the beautiful intrusion of one world into another. One thinks of Yeats's séance-fueled dictations, Merrill's Ouija board inspirations, the radio media of Jack Spicer or of Cocteau's Orphée. "Caedmon's Hymn," the first known English poem, was in part the gift to an illiterate lay brother by an oneiric angel urging him to "Sing the beginning of the creatures!"

Fulton's poem seems to imply that some angelic, gracious force, once intrinsic or accessible to the speaker, has been removed. The extraction does not seem to have been the sublime experience Michelangelo describes regarding the making of his statue of David ("I saw the angel in the marble and carved until I set him free") but

rather a procedure far more insidious, dire, and diminishing. To feel emptied of the
capacity to be more or other than oneself is cause for despair; as Fulton puts it,

And where my organ of veneration should be—

wormwood and gall. Grudge sliver.

Wailbone, iron, bitters. I mean to say the miniature
waterfalls have all dried up in this miniature

place where day is duty cubed, time is time on task
and every mind optimized for compliance.

The world Fulton describes, après angelectomy, is sterile, bereft, and characterized
by the anomie and hopelessness we associate not only with dehumanizing,
futuristic scenarios, but also with jobs, political arenas, personal relationships—
any circumstance in which life itself has gone flat and meaningless. It is a world
in which even "the florescent major highlighter has dimmed / to minor" and the
speaker is so exhausted ("I'm so dying I wrote / when I meant to write so tired")
that even when she sleeps she dreams "only that that / I am sleeping."

Fulton is an adept at tonal shifts, which is one of the ways in which she marries
lyricism with fearless social commentary in her work. In this poem, her narrator's
fragile balancing act of terror and panicked control, for example, comes through
powerfully in the asides, directed as much to the self as to some vague lackey
or listener, interjected amidst the bitterness. These phrases are part knee-jerk
imperatives that appear to belong to a lost world ("Please see my black stuff's //
dusted off") and part abject surrender and supplication ("Please see that my grave
is kept clean"). That these verbal registers—by turns rote, dissociated, catatonic,
terrified, ironic, pathetic, bitter, discerning—mix in among Fulton's Blakean vision
of a world dominated by soul-less contingencies only contributes to the poem's
power:

Night has no dilution anxieties,
but only the infinites are happy:

Math. Time. Everything happy goes
to many decimal places

while flesh passes through
gradations of glory. I visualized it,

the nurse said of the bedsore. Everything exists
at the courtesy of everything else.

In the first of his oracular Duino elegies, Rainer Maria Rilke asks, "Who, if I cried
out, would hear me among the angels' / Hierarchies?" Fulton shares Rilke's sense
that "Every angel is terrifying." "Whom can we ever turn to / in our need?" Rilke
asks, "Not angels, not humans, / and already the knowing animals are aware / that
we are not really at home in / our interpreted world." Fulton extends this vision,
which has at least one origin in Caedmon's angelic interpretation among the stabled
animals, and brings it into our post-modern, post-romantic realm (in which even a
bedsore can only be "visualized" and in which "Beloveds" are "temporal things //
in which the infinite endanger[s] itself") with fresh fear, tenderness, and scathing
irony.

In a recent seminar discussion about Emily Dickinson, my students were speculating
about faith. Its opposite, they decided, is not doubt. Doubt depends on faith,
and vice versa. The opposite of faith is indifference. "After the Angelectomy" is
testimony not only to the dangers of indifference, of failure or inability (because
of depression or other grievous circumstance) to host, nurture, and preserve our
capacity for wonder and "divine substance," our trust in the unseen, but also to
poetry, which helps us to articulate and recoup the soul's imaginative, personal,
spiritual, and social imperatives.

JILL BIALOSKY

Teaching My Son to Drive

My sixteen year old is listening to Beach 104
on the radio dial,
singing along with the rapper.
He's been waiting
for this day for a long time.
He turns up the music.
I turn it down. We drive along the road.
Horse farm on the side of the street
where we encounter a field
of young English riders with crops
preparing to mount the hurdles.
It won't be easy.
On the other side the day camp
he returned to every summer; the children
playing manhunt in the garden.
The clouds in the sky are moving too fast.
The trees berth too wide. I look at the speedometer.
I want him to slow down.
The thrashers in the branches are frantic.
There must be more to teach him.
Eyes on the road,
ready to accelerate
he glances into the rear view mirror
to see what's behind,
changes lanes and careens
gracefully into his manhood.
When I turn to look
I see the pensive boy in the back seat
strapped in his seat belt
watching two red squirrels run up a tree
and back down.

In the fall of 1968, when I was in junior high school, my sister's classmate, while
her mother was still at work, left the apartment they shared, made her way down
through the spot-lit parking lots and scrub of sumac, chain link fencing, and tree of
paradise to Rt. 287, lay down on the asphalt of the dark highway, and was killed by
a passing tractor trailer truck. For weeks afterwards, in the hallways, at our lockers,

in health class, we puzzled over what had happened. What might drive a 13-year-old girl to such a desperate and at the same time seemingly eerily premeditated self-demise? Why had we not guessed the depths of her despair? Could we have prevented her suicide? Our wild, confused, and entranced concern, of course, was nothing compared to the unspeakable and unappeasable misery we heard in the halting testimonies of the truck driver and the girl's mother. Suicide, we were learning, involved a nexus of pain, guilt, anger, shame, denial, and staggering remorse that travelled into and out of the person taking his or her own life, across a wide spectrum of intimates, strangers, generations, times, and places.

It is the rare person who has not been touched, however distantly, by suicide—its inheritances and legacies. Suicide (<L *sui* "of oneself" *-cidium* "a killing") is a mysterious, unsettling phenomenon that is probably as old as self-consciousness. Ritualized suicide has existed across cultures since antiquity, and in the early Western tradition has been the object of philosophical musings by the likes of Plato and Aristotle. St. Augustine, Thomas More, Michel de Montaigne, John Calvin, and John Locke also wrote about suicide—as, in more modern times, have David Hume, Immanuel Kant, and twentieth-century existentialists like Albert Camus and Jean-Paul Sartre. A recent e-mail from the American Foundation for Suicide Prevention tells me that "more than 36,000 people died by suicide in 2009, making it the 10th leading cause of death in the U.S. With the suicide rate in this country trending upward," the cyber-message admonishes, "there is a greater urgency to do more." As I read, I confront anew that suicide is especially disconcerting in the young.

Leaving aside the question about whether or not poets are more likely than others to commit suicide (perhaps they are just more likely to communicate their anguish), poems about suicide and suicidal tendencies have certainly brought me to a deeper understanding of the dark allure and terror of suicide's possibility. As the priest and poet John Donne once wrote in empathy, "Whenever any affliction assails me, I have the keys of my prison in mine own hand, and no remedy presents it selfe so soone to my heart, as mine own sword. Often meditation of this hath wonne me to a charitable interpretation of their action, who dy so." Among the many poets who have helped me better to comprehend (and to plumb the limits of my ability completely to fathom) the anguish of those afflicted, however fleetingly, with the desire to die—Sylvia Plath, Al Alvarez, Emily Dickinson, Deborah Digges, John Berryman, Rachel Wetzsteon, Debra Nystrom, Gerard Manley Hopkins ("Not, I'll not, carrion comfort, Despair, not feast on thee; / Not untwist—slack they may be—these last strands of man / In me ór, most weary, cry I can no more. I can; / Can something, hope, wish day come, not choose not to be"), to name but a few—is the poet, novelist, and editor Jill Bialosky, whose work I have admired for years and whose grapplings with a younger sister's suicide have been the subject of several of her poems. Bialosky's experience with her sister's death receives fuller attention in her memoir, *History of a Suicide: My Sister's Unfinished Life* (Atria, 2011).

Bialosky's memoir, which she at one point calls a "psychological autopsy," is a contrapuntal exploration of her younger sister's "suicidal map"—a threnody of excavated journal entries, poems, expert and familial testimonies, recollections, descriptions of suicide survivor group meetings, and plundered psychological and literary texts (most particularly and luminously *Moby Dick*, whose opening passage includes a phrase—the "damp, drizzly November of the soul"—that Dr. Edwin Shneidman, whose counsel Bialosky seeks during the writing of her book, equates with suicide). Bialosky brings these elements into juxtaposition in an attempt to understand why her sister Kim, a young adult struggling with substance abuse and a recent romantic break-up, made the choice to end her life. With a child of her own on the cusp of the crucible of puberty ("more concerned with the mysteries that dwell inside himself, the possibilities" than he is with the opinion and worry of his parents), Bialosky writes that she felt compelled by an urgent need, after many years of denial and grief in the wake of her sister's death, to wrestle with it full-on. As she puts it, "These pages narrate the story of what happened to Kim and my voyage to come to grips with her suicide. Since I cannot bring her back, I have struggled to make her lapse into darkness and the devastation of suicide understandable. Suicide should never happen to anyone. I want you to know as much as I know. That is the reason I am writing this book."

This is a book I'd like to put into everyone's hands. In clear, accessible, amply researched and articulated prose, animated throughout with examples from poems (her own and others), Bialosky acknowledges that each of us, overtly troubled or not, possesses the power to cease to be and also, as Hopkins puts it (in syntax so convoluted that we feel the struggle), to "not choose not to be." What is our responsibility, if we can muster it, for that volition, that possibility, in ourselves and those we love? Perhaps it is her poet's lens that lends Bialosky's exploration of young Kim's death a forthright, vivid, and resonant mix of remorse, anger, shame, empathy, and hope. "How would Kim feel about having her private life probed and reinvented through my words?" Bialosky asks. "Am I doing justice and honor to her experience? Would she be pleased?....Am I able to make her story universal? Avoid self-pity and blame? I tell myself that, if I can portray her inner world, it may offer a window for other readers to understand the fragility of the suicidal mind....
The great tragedy is that knowledge—even incomplete—comes late. I can never bring Kim back. And yet, irrationally, through writing, a part of me believes I can."

While Bialosky was writing her memoir, her son was thirteen. In Bialosky's poem featured here, the speaker is teaching her son, a sixteen-year-old, to drive. Among the many gestures to admire in this poem are the ways in which Bialosky gives the antic world agency and displaces onto the careening trees, racing squirrels, and wild thrashers all of the mother's anxiety about her son's rite of passage. Though not overtly about suicide, this poem concerns the precarious balance of living. Laura McGinnis, a spokesperson for the Trevor Project, whose mission, in part, is to operate as a kind of support network for suicidal persons under the age of 24, says that "suicide never has one cause, [which] is something important to recognize ….Parents should pay attention to what's going on in their kids' lives and what is important to them…[and] establish trust, listening, accepting everything they say and not judging them. Let them share their story." In the journey that is her memoir, Bialosky allows Kim, posthumously, to tell her story. In *History of a Suicide*, and in the thrall of this poem (image, enjambment, symbol, music), the reader shares the vertigo and symbolic grace of risk, of the lanes, safely changed for now—daringly, and with a full awareness of what the rearview holds even as parent and child move ahead.

KIKI PETROSINO

Ragweed

Neither wax, nor egg, nor honey on the knife.
In garden not, nor street nor bus nor bank—
Not sleep. Not word. Nor will-over-will
Not lung. Not hull, or sail. Just crank & tread

in place [no place] & white [not white] gets hot
& seethe & seethe—my sleep like steam
not long, but less. So less, till I am I who cracks
at last, begs *air* & says *Am I such root? Such rot*

for rage who scrapes, who darks each swatch of flesh
each branch of mesh & salt & bit? This rag—it rob
& sneak & rob & sneak, my tongue gets pins & pine & less
& less. Can run, but run gets gone. Can bellow, bellow

change. Only *most,* only *half,* & less & less get
here, get thick & stick. Not breath.

Who has not, at one time or another, felt powerless in the face of natural or bodily forces, as victim of a natural disaster, witness of a sublime sunset or of a soul-altering birth or death, or as sufferer of any physical or mental illness or other somatic transformation, including the changes wrought by pregnancy, orgasm, exercise, and…allergy? Statistics show that over half of all Americans suffer from some sort of food, plant, or other allergy. And while it would seem to be an earthling's birth-right to be able to breathe freely, according to the Asthma and Allergy Foundation of America, from a period commencing in late summer and continuing until the first hard autumn frost, some 10 – 20 percent of Americans suffer in particular from discomforts related to the late-summer and autumn pollen effusions of ragweed, also called bitterweed or bloodweed. Symptoms for those allergic to ragweed range from red eyes and stuffy noses to more severe reactions, such as full-blown and sometimes dire asthma and other breathing-related attacks. Why the human body reacts in this disordered way to ostensibly harmless environmental substances remains in large part a mystery.

Kiki Petrosino's "Ragweed," a loose sonnet, opens with a series of negations. Nothing, the speaker suggests—no remedy, no rest, no word, no place, no act of "will-over-will"—can protect the body under siege by its own immune system. The afflicted human has no choice but to "crank & tread / in place [no place] & white [not white] gets hot / & seethe & seethe." Eerily, even the descriptors "place" and "white" are immediately negated, as, with ruthless and punishing force, the allergens mount their attack, invading and robbing even sleep, until the speaker—in lines within which truncated, abrupt phrases and caesurae mimic the contraction of her breathing—cries, "I am I who cracks / at last, begs *air* & says *Am I such root? Such rot / / for rage who scrapes, who darks each swatch of flesh / each branch of mesh & salt & bit?*"

In a powerful move, Petrosino puts into italics the very "rag rage" (how provocative, these two words in juxtaposition) that her speaker has no remnant breath left to curse. Job, Patron Saint of undeserved malady, haunts the diction and the content here, but in the third quatrain, Petrosino adds her own spin to the lament, granting the ragweed a kind of antic agency: "This rag – it rob / & sneak & rob & sneak, my tongue gets pins & pine & less / & less. Can run, but run gets gone. Can bellow, bellow // change."

At the cusp of expiration, the poet, in her sonnet's couplet, suggests that when we are at the limits of our verbal and fugal capabilities ("Can run, but run gets gone"), we have as a last recourse, however halved or lessened, our primal, pre-literate ability to bellow of and for release, rescue, change. "Bellow" is animal noise, is prior to human language. Yet the anguish in that sound— that wish to live, to be heard—is one source of lyric poetry:

> Can bellow, bellow

Change. Only most, only half, & less & less get
Here, get thick & stick. Not breath.

As the poet moves in the final two lines from staccato anapests, into heartbeat iambs, into halting but insistent spondees, we see the poem distilling itself, as though to its most essential, surviving syllable. Not "not breath," but "breath," an assertion of acutely qualified life force.

DEMENTIA'S COMMONPLACE BOOK

DEMENTIA'S COMMONPLACE BOOK

Jonathan Swift, who would in late life suffer from dementia, was keen on the importance of keeping a "commonplace book" in which a person might record insights, overheard bits, observations, excerpts from reading—a personal magpie anthology of things one does not want consigned to forgetfulness or oblivion. Swift writes, "A commonplace book is what a provident poet cannot subsist without, for this proverbial reason, that 'great wits have short memories': and whereas, on the other hand, poets, being liars by profession, ought to have good memories; to reconcile these, a book of this sort, is in the nature of a supplemental memory, or a record of what occurs remarkable in every day's reading or conversation. There you enter not only your own original thoughts, (which, a hundred to one, are few and insignificant) but such of other men as you think fit to make your own, by entering them there." In his "Reading and Writing the Renaissance Commonplace Book: A Question of Authorship," Max W. Thomas says that "commonplace books are about memory, which takes both material and immaterial form; the commonplace book is like a record of what that memory might look like."

Writing, obviously, is linked inextricably with memory; after all, Mnemosyne is one of the nine muses. Alzheimer's disease and other dementias, which rob human beings of so much, including the power to recollect and, finally, to wield language, are devastating for everyone associated with them, perhaps poignantly so for writers, whose work depends upon mnemonic recall and imagining to make semiotic meaning.

Literature is full of accounts of the ravages and cruel absurdities of dementia—Anne Carson's treatment of a father with Alzheimer's in *The Glass Essay,* for instance, or Dickens's portrait of "Mr. F's Aunt" in *Little Dorrit.* Writers who are themselves afflicted with dementia (among the notable authors believed to have suffered from dementia are Iris Murdoch, Robert Graves, E. B. White, Dorothy Wordsworth, and Agatha Christie) often grapple in their texts with their diminishing faculties even before they are consciously aware of them. A case study done by Dr. Peter Garrard of Iris Murdoch's last novel, *Jackson's Dilemma,* for example, shows that the work Murdoch undertook after the onset of dementia betrays a shrinking vocabulary and simplification of diction.

It is hard not to read a portrait of his own eventual mental demise in Swift's account in *Gulliver's Travels* (written when Swift was 59) of Gulliver's encounters with the Struldbruggs, a race of immortals who, though unable to die, nonetheless suffer the insults of aging: "They have no Remembrance of any thing but what they learned and observed in their Youth and Middle Age, and even that is very imperfect....In talking they forgot the common Appellation of things, and the Names of persons, even of those who are their nearest Friends and Relations. For the same reason they never can amuse themselves with reading, because their Memory will not serve to carry them from the beginning of a Sentence to the end...neither are they able ... to hold any conversation (farther than a few general words) with their neighbors...." One of the last journal entries of Dorothy Wordsworth, penned before she slipped into a period of laudanum-aggravated dementia that lasted many years, contains a poem:

My tremulous fingers, feeble hands
Refuse to labour with the mind
And that too oft is misty dark & blind.

As Kathleen Jones describes them in *A Passionate Sisterhood: The Sisters, Wives and Daughters of the Lake Poets*, the last pages of Dorothy's final notebook "are scrawled with disconnected words. Among them 'Torments...dysmal doom...no iron hinges' are clearly discernible as tragic indicators of her agony of mind."

As I cope with my own mother's decline into dementia, I've turned in the past several years to a number of helpful studies, anthologies, and literary texts, notably Susan M. Schultz's *Dementia Blog* (Singing Horse Press, 2008), Carol Frost's *Honeycomb* (TriQuarterly Books, 2010), and Holly Hughes's edited anthology *Beyond Forgetting: Poetry and Prose about Alzheimer's Disease* (Kent State UP, 2009). Most recently I've been reading poet, editor, essayist, and professor Rachel Hadas's *Strange Relation: A Memoir of Marriage, Dementia, and Poetry* (Paul Dry Books, 2011). The book recounts the poet's experience of discovering and then coping with the early onset dementia of her husband, George Edwards, a composer and professor of music at Columbia University. "This story," Hadas writes in the introduction, "if it is a story, lacks both a clear beginning and a final resolution. Within the cloudy confines of those years when reading and writing were part of what kept me going, I tried to keep on track; I tried to tell the truth." Acknowledging that she cannot, finally, "know" what her husband's thoughts were as he declined, she nonetheless conjures a vivid sense of "the flavor of his personality before it began to vanish" even as she exposes and explores her own grapplings, loneliness, and losses.

Hadas's memoir includes a myriad of poems and passages from literature (among them Hardy, Dickinson, Hall, Cavafy, Larkin, Auden, Frost, the poet's own work, and examples from ancient myth) and offers quotations from her husband's letters, catalogs of her own recollections, as well as scenes from doctors' offices, in the couple's city apartment, at the family house in Vermont, and at a facility where George lives when he can no longer function well at home. In many respects, then, Hadas's memoir is a kind of commonplace book. Hadas explains her compulsion to write about this experience: "Some of the chapters in this book were written in response to my need to record a conversation, a dream, a walk, or yet another doctor's appointment. I rediscovered what every writing teacher knows, that writing what you remember helps you to remember more. Turning life at its bleakest or dullest into prose was absorbing and also rewarding; the more I wrote, the more I remembered and understood."

Hadas's poem "Hugger Mugger Road," below, recounts with formal dexterity the disorderly, muddled, "hugger mugger" path she traverses with her husband after his illness becomes known to them. The poem—which affects the reader with the force of Hadas's memoir, writ small—evokes with humor, dignity, despair, guilt, uncertainty, and courage the corrosive erosions of dementia. Although the disease is ubiquitous (facts support that the dementias are prevalent—5.4 million Americans are currently living with Alzheimer's, according to the Alzheimer's Association), there is absolutely nothing commonplace about the individual stories of those affected by it, as Hadas's memoir and moving poem ("So long as I am sentient—then our son— / You won't have disappeared without a trace") attest.

Hugger Mugger Road

i   On the Road

He walked into her room (she was in bed)
and tried to drape a blanket over her head.

"That's the last straw!" the Director cried.
No; one more step on Hugger Mugger Road,

not first, not last. I follow in his wake.
He strides, then slows. The final goal will take

how long to reach? Oh do not estimate.
So zigzag is the path that its few straight

stretches seem deceptive. So stand still.
The road is winding, but it's all downhill.

What's the hurry? This is not a race.
Sometimes I feel sunlight on my face

and rest a little, shift the heavy load
as he and I proceed down Hugger Mugger Road.

ii   The Thirty-Sixth July

Unlikely now, that first remote July
when we met and everything aligned
to fuse two ways to one trajectory.
It might have been sheer happenstance, the blind

bumping of spheres. We didn't need to know.
A path had opened up, so on we strode,
swathed in the safety of our ignorance.
I scrambled to keep pace on the long road.

Call us two children, each with a good mother.
Two teachers – lucky mutuality,
each of us bringing something to the other.
Fast forward to this anniversary.

The weight has shifted. Mine is to remember,
report, interpret for you, and translate;
to hold onto some sense of who you were;
to reminisce and laugh and mediate.

A heavy vessel balanced on my head,
I must walk slowly so as not to spill,
crossing each threshold at a stately pace.
It's you I carry, so I must stand tall.

So long as I am sentient—then our son—
You won't have disappeared without a trace.
This morning I climbed from the box of dream
still hearing your voice,

witty and urgent as you used to be.
Many nights lately I have heard you speak.
How natural—you have things to say to me.
Everything is fine. And then I wake.

iii The Book of Days and Nights

Look after what you wrongly think's your own.
Sad castle, no foundation, in the sky.
Hope? Patience? Flip the pages with your thumb.
Youth and beauty ride the IRT.

House in a hollow; a deep bowl of light.
Flip the pages: anger, grief, and loss.
Sleeping in a shadow bed each night,
I am dowered with a silent ghost.

One thing has changed lately: now I ride
the subway north, get out at a new station.
Gratitude, weariness, uncertainty:
the book has ample room for variation.

iv To Reconcile the Raspberries

Where this path goes I know.
How long, and winding how, there is no telling.
Nor is there ever any turning back.
The pace varies: slow to very slow.

Wait, whose path? I seem to have forgotten.
His or mine?
Can I step off to the side,
let him trudge on alone?

Can I say in tomorrow's light
yet again "This episode is over,"
this incident,
this latest misdemeanor from last night?

Garden, heat lightning, crescent moon—not mine.
Where the track's rough, I teeter to and fro.
Does he recognize you?
That question comes over and over again.

So many questions. Answers? I can say
another morning will come. That I know.
I do not know how to reconcile ripe raspberries
with this long winding way.

LISA RUSS SPAAR   181

Here is the hammock slung in its old place
between two trees. Our son hung it there
for me. Oh stillness, oh pine-scented air!
But how to reconcile a dream of rest

with the long road? The hammock in my mind
I can lie down in, I can sway and read.
The raspberries are hanging velvet ripe.
Not a breath of wind.

v   On the Beach

I and our son are bouncing up and down
in shallow surf and batting back and forth
the only topic all this gold and azure
boils down to, the old question
to which there is no answer, though we toss
the ball of speculation to and fro.
Here he is now – how could I not have seen him?

Tall sea creature, unspeaking,
smiling a little, bouncing in the waves
along with us, leaping and lithe, his silence
lost in the splash and spray
as the shriek of a child is covered by a gull's cry.
Parallel to the horizon, this strip of sand
has no beginning and no end.

George Edwards passed away in October 2011; a moving tribute to him by
Edwards and Hadas's son, Jonathan Hadas Edwards, can be found at http://www.
rachelhadas.com/Rachel_Hadas/In_Memoriam_George_Edwards.html.

CLAUDIA EMERSON

Ephemeris

The household sells in a morning, but when
they cannot let the house itself go for
the near-nothing it brings at auction,
the children, all beyond their middle years,
carry her back to it, the mortgage now
a dead pledge of patience. Almost emptied,
there is little evidence that she ever
lived in it: a rented hospital bed
in the kitchen where the breakfast table
stood, a borrowed coffee pot, chair,
a cot for the daughter she knows, and then does not.
But the world seems almost right, the near-
familiar curtainless windows, the room
neat, shadow-severed, her body's thinness,
like her gown's, a comfort now. Perhaps
she thinks it death and the place a lesser
heaven, the hereafter a bed, the night
to herself, rain percussive in the gutters—
enough. But like hers, the light sleep of spring
has worsened—forsythia blooming
in what should be deep winter outside
the window—until it resembles the shallow
sleep of a house with a newborn in it,
a middle child she never saw, a boy
who lived not one whole day (an afternoon?
an evening?) sixty years ago in late
August. And as though born without a mouth,
like a summer moth, he never suckled
and was buried without a name. She had waked to that—
that cusp of summer, crape myrtles' clotted
blooms languishing, anemic, the cicadas
exuberant as they have always been
in their clumsy dying.

               This middle-born
is now the nearer, no, the only child.
The undertaker's wife has not bathed
and dressed him; the first day's night instead
has passed, quickening into another

day, and another, and he is again awake,
his fist gripping a spindle of turned light,
and he is ravenous in his cradle of air.

Perhaps because we abide in bodies, which themselves provide a kind of ambivalent
shelter, houses make emotionally and somatically charged images. As Gaston
Bachelard puts it in *The Poetics of Space*, "Our house is our corner of the world
....it is our first universe, a real cosmos in every sense of the word." In Claudia
Emerson's "Ephemeris" (the title denotes both an accounting of astronomical
bodies and the fleeting transience of vanishing), the contents of an elderly dying
woman's house have been sold, and she has been moved out, presumably to a
nursing home or hospital. However, when the woman's grown children "cannot
let the house itself go for / the near-nothing it brings at auction," they "carry her
back to it." There, on a hospital bed in unfurnished rooms, in a "light sleep" state
between waking and sleep, ebbing life and incipient death, the old woman dredges
up from the deep well of her experience a memory of a child she once had who
died shortly after being born:

A middle child she never saw, a boy
who lived not one whole day (an afternoon?
an evening?) sixty years ago in late
August.

With her gift for uncanny image-making (as Charles Simic says, the image is the
closest thing poets have to working wordlessly, as in painting or photography or
film), Emerson creates a terrifying, even sublime sense of her subject's Dickinsonian
"nearness to her sundered things," hauntingly evoking what it might be like to be on
the cusp of being unhoused.

It is always unsettling to feel out of synchronicity with the weather or a season,
literally or figuratively. Classic examples are, of course, phenomena like holiday
depression—the grief and vexation of being sad amidst predominant festivity—or
the experience of the ecstatic, newly married couple who step beaming out into
the world despite a cold, glowering, unrelenting wedding day storm. The dying
must perforce feel dissociated from the living realm, and for Emerson's subject this
sense is certainly exacerbated by the "almost emptied" house, "where there is little
evidence that she ever / lived in it: a rented hospital bed / in the kitchen where
the breakfast table stood, a borrowed coffee pot, chair, / a cot for the daughter
she knows, and then does not." The emptied house is so surreal, in fact, that the
speaker speculates that the dying woman might think "it death and the place a lesser

/ heaven." Also disturbing is the way in which, outside, it is a restive, preternaturally early spring, rather than a season that might more closely resemble the dying woman's condition. A quenching rain is "percussive in the gutters" and "forsythia [blooms] / in what should be deep winter." And surely this edgy sense of internal and external weathers being slightly off ("until it resembles the shallow / sleep of a house with a newborn in it") contributes to the unbidden memory of the lost child:

> ...And as though born without a mouth,
> like a summer moth, he never suckled
> and was buried without a name. She had waked to that—.

Suddenly, it is no longer the early spring of the poem's "real time" or the symbolic winter of her dying, but again that late summer, that August long ago, "that cusp of summer, crape myrtles' clotted / blooms languishing, anemic, the cicadas / exuberant as they have always been / in their clumsy dying," when her own body lost irrevocably what it had for nine months housed.

With the return, the restoration, of the lost child, the narrative of the poem pivots and intensifies, and time collapses and blurs. With a clear nod to Dickinson ("the first day's night instead / has passed, quickening into another / day, and another"), a poet also capable of finding language for the ephemeral passages and wages of dying, Emerson makes the lost child, who has already crossed over into death, "the nearer, no, the only child." He is again "awake, / his fist gripping a spindle of turned light, / and he is ravenous in his cradle of air." The literal house disappears, is irrelevant, and the dying woman, about to be parted from her body, awakens at the last to its purpose. She is once again a young mother who must rise in the night and feed her voracious child. She is her own last house (Bachelard says that "all really inhabited space bears [its] essence"). She is her own final sustenance and her own hunger, and the power she must confront, unnamed but wielding its scepter/scythe of light, is ephemeral and implacable.

MEGHAN O'ROURKE

In Defense of Pain

So now the sleighs have slid away
and the ice on the trees cracks,
sharp champagne pops, toasts
silenced by the snow-bound woods.
Half asleep beneath an eiderdown
stitched with dawn-red-thread,
you are in a painting, walking the high slopes
of a mountain
above the timberline.
Even as you climb you are turning past the overlook.
None of us can see the switchbacks as we rise.
Below, the forest shudders in wind.
You have been here before,
in this painting, on this gray-green rock,
staring across the valley—
For years, you thought there was a door
on the other side, a sky scrap,
redbirds and red cedars and more—
now you see the door
is the scar of a bulldozed home:
the red earth ugly
on the mountainside, a scalp
bleeding from a sore.
Does that mean you won't
come here anymore?

A few years ago, when I was seeing a hand specialist for some temporary nerve damage, the intake nurse would point at each visit to a chart on the wall that showed a series of ten round Emoticon-type faces lined up below a numerical scale marked from one to ten. At the "one" end of the spectrum, a green orb grinned happily, but at "ten" the accompanying visage was scarlet and contorted. Even with prompting (is it throbbing? pulsing? burning? more like a stabbing?), I often found it difficult to "rank" my pain, and even harder to put a description of it into words.

I am not alone. In *The Body in Pain*, a definitive study of physical pain and its language, Harvard professor Elaine Scarry writes that "physical pain—unlike any other state of consciousness—has no referential content. It is not of or for anything. It is precisely because it takes no object that it, more than any other phenomenon, resists objectification in language." And responding to Virginia Woolf's complaint about the scarcity of literary representations of pain ("The merest schoolgirl when she falls in love has Shakespeare or Keats to speak her mind for her, but let a sufferer try to explain a pain in his head to a doctor and language at once runs dry"), Scarry goes on to say that "even the artist—whose lifework and everyday habits are to refine and extend the reflexes of speech—ordinarily falls silent before pain"—pain whose sources are somatic and emotional, even existential.

This is not the case in Meghan O'Rourke's "In Defense of Pain." Readers familiar with O'Rourke's poems, essays, and reviews, which appear regularly in places like *The New Yorker, Slate, Poetry, The New Republic*, and the *New York Times*, will already know that there would seem to be no challenging subject beyond the reach of her eloquent and questing intelligence, be it horse-racing, bullying, gender bias in literary culture, or prevailing trends in marriage and divorce. Over the past two years, O'Rourke has published a number of essays about the processes of grief and bereavement inspired by the untimely death of her mother by cancer on Christmas day 2008. A memoir, *The Long Goodbye*, recounts her experience.

"In Defense of Pain" would appear to begin in winter, at the start of a new year:

So now the sleighs have slid away
and the ice on the trees cracks,
sharp champagne pops, toasts
silenced by the snow-bound woods.

The lines that immediately follow—"Half asleep beneath an eiderdown / stitched with dawn-red thread"— at first read like a further description of those snow-bound woods, but into this quiescent scene of aftermath and hush the poet introduces a subject, a "you," who, it turns out, is asleep beneath the eiderdown and who is, surreally, also "in a painting, walking the high slopes of a mountain / above the timberline." Is this a dream?

It doesn't matter. Like Emily Dickinson, O'Rourke's sister poet of the wake of grief and the experience of pain (" 'Twas like a Maelstrom, with a notch, / That nearer, every Day, / Kept narrowing it's boiling Wheel / Until the Agony // Toyed coolly with the final inch / Of your delirious Hem"), O'Rourke is unafraid to use pronominal slippage (at one point "you" becomes "us" and "we," and of course the poem is haunted by an "I" who is clearly conflated with / disassociated from the "you") and distortions of time and place ("You have been here before" and "For years you thought there was door" and "now you see the door") to speak her truths. There are frames within frames, doors within doors of perception here, and "we" are implicated in this journey into the deepest reaches and sources of anguish.

This territory above the switchbacks and the overlook is not new ("You have been here before / in this painting"). Perhaps it is the ontological terrain of our human exile from paradise, Adam ("man of the red earth") and Eve's imagining of some sort of escape from their travail, an instinct intuited from childhood. "For years," the poet tells us, we've stared at the other side of a valley where we thought there was a door and something on the other side of it [heaven ("a sky scrap"?), the natural world going on without us ("redbirds and red cedars and more")?]. Deeply into her reverie, the difficult climb, the you has an epiphany:

now you see the door
is the scar of a bulldozed home:
the red earth ugly
on the mountainside, a scalp
bleeding from a sore.
Does that mean you won't
come here anymore?

The imagined door turns out to be a brutal wound, one embedded deeply within the dream-self, one which betrays a wrecked home and evokes disease and mortality, "a scalp bleeding from a sore." The door, it turns out, is a window into pain, the real. After the bubbly, the *auld lang syne,* the dream of a happy dream "on the other side" of what hurts, what life serves up, if we're brave enough to acknowledge it, is the truth about human mortality on this earth, where, as Keats said, "men sit and hear each other groan; / Where palsy shakes a few, sad, last grey hairs, / Where youth grows pale, and spectre-thin, and dies; / Where but to think is to be full of sorrow." O'Rourke does not flinch from this revelation. Her last question does not disclose a doubt; it is rhetorical. In defense of pain, physical and psychological, it offers its promise of attention and return. It embodies, in its imagination and linguistic fulfillments, a poetic articulation of the necessary suffering and beauty by which living is defined.

MICHAEL COLLIER

Laelaps

When it was clear I would never catch her
and that she would never escape my pursuit,
Zeus intervened and turned each of us to stone.

No longer was ardor our fate. No longer
were days marked by bramble giving way to bog,
by razory reeds that cut our swift passing.

Days when all I saw of her was airborne,
arrowy—a silvery shimmer and flash of scut.
And gone, too, the late night stillness

when I'd pause, not thinking to lose her,
but hoping, ahead of my silence,
she'd slow down and turning, see,

snout up, tongue lively, lightly panting,
undiscouraged, how at the edge of our distance
I stood, wishing she'd invite my approach.

But these are dog thoughts and I was god's
hound by way of Europa, Minos, and Procris,
so much passing on of love's troubles

I was meant to end. Who wouldn't want to die
into monumental stillness? Who wouldn't want
to be frozen in their last untaken step, translated,

like we were—my pointer's stance, her backward
glance—in the vast sky, where the gods below
had safely placed us?

Michael Collier writes a lot about dogs. In "A Real-Life Drama," for example, a
family pet who slaughters a pedigree rabbit reveals "the dark corner of his nature."
A chimerical pseudo Hillary Clinton figure "wraps his legs around Trotsky's leg and
humps like a dog" in "All Souls." Collier's elegant essay tribute to William Maxwell
(from *A William Maxwell Portrait: Memories and Appreciations,* edited by Collier along

with Charles Baxter and Edward Hirsch) is entitled "The Dog Gets to Dover: William Maxwell as Correspondent." Nor is Collier alone in penning poems about *Canis lupus familiaris*; a quick recent Google search for "dog poems" yielded 4,590,000 results in 0.11 seconds, including work by W. S. Merwin, Mark Doty, Elizabeth Barrett Browning, Stephen Dobyns, and Robert Burns. Amazon.com lists nearly 2,000 titles in the category of "dog poetry," including the popular *Unleashed: Poems by Writers' Dogs*, edited by Amy Hempel and Jim Shepard.

Collier is also a poet whose passion for and insight into classical mythology often provide a discerning and provocative context for quotidian drama in his poems (Collier has done an acclaimed translation of *Medea* for Oxford University Press, as well). It makes sense, then, given these propensities, that he should turn his imagination to mythical canines (and there are no shortage of these either—not poems about mythical dogs, but dogs in myth—with Wikipedia offering 51 pages for "mythological dogs"). The mezzo-soprano and composer Judith Cloud has, in fact, set three of Collier's mythological dog poems to music: "Argos," "Cerberus," and the poem "Laelaps," under discussion here.

One of the pleasures for lyric poets working with extant myth is that the "story" is already implied and understood, freeing the poet to work in the interstices, to delve imaginatively and musically into and beyond what the stock narrative offers, and to use the existing tale as a starting point for personal and extra-mythological meditation. And as Collier suggests from stanza one, in which he gives the gist and outcome of the Laelaps story in three deft lines, his interest is not so much in plot as in the "so what?" of what went down, the resonance and aftermath.

There are many spins on the Laelaps myth, but common to most versions is the siccing of Laelaps (whose name translates into something like "storm wind," and who was known to be the fastest of all dogs, capable of catching anything) on the Teumessian fox, a gigantic fox destined never to be caught. Zeus, perplexed and frustrated by the paradox of this perpetual chase, throws in the towel, intervening, as Collier puts it, and turning both animals "to stone."

After summarizing the myth in the first tercet, Collier, whose narrator is Laelaps, devotes four electric stanzas to what he calls "dog thoughts." Zeus may have put an end to the chase ("no longer was ardor our fate"), but it's clear that Laelaps loved the pursuit, the hope, the being *in it*, the "days marked by bramble giving way to bog, / by razory reeds that cut our swift passing." The sexual tension and anticipation (deeply human, I might add, and mortal) is unmistakable:

Days when all I saw of her was airborne,
Arrowy—a silvery shimmer and flash of scut.

190 THE HIDE-AND-SEEK MUSE

And gone, too, the late night stillness

when I'd pause, not thinking to lose her,
but hoping, ahead of my silence,
she'd slow down and turning, see,

snout up, tongue lively, lightly panting,
undiscouraged, how at the edge of our distance
I stood, wishing she'd invite my approach.

Laelaps's resigned acknowledgment that he is "god's / hound by way of Europa, Minos, and Procris, / so much passing on of love's troubles // I was meant to end" is tinged with regret (I especially admire the way Collier enjambs and breaks his stanza so that "I was meant to end" not only refers back to the chain of badly behaved gods and their consorts whose erotic problems he—passed and gifted from hand to hand—was mean to allay, but also to the fate of any plaything of the gods: we are meant to end). Resignation deepens into a kind of tender irony with the poem's concluding questions:

Who wouldn't want to die
into monumental stillness? Who wouldn't want
to be frozen in their last untaken step, translated,

like we were—my pointer's stance, her backward
glance—in the vast sky, where the gods below
had safely placed us?

Clearly Collier here is evoking Keats, who grappled in his famous "Ode on a Grecian Urn" with similar questions: which is better, to be caught up in the frustrations and enticements of the mortal coil or to be "frozen" and immortalized through death/art? But Collier has another point to make, as well. By positioning the gods below, gazing up at the stars into which Laelaps and the fox have been transformed (at least one version of the myth has Zeus turning Laelaps into the star that we know as Canis Major), he puts the immortals in the position of mortals, looking heavenward. Perhaps this suggests that the gods muck around with mortals and then end things in order to themselves feel more like them. Or, rather, Collier's Laelaps, captured forever in his "last untaken step," indicates that this is one way religion, myth, and art are perpetuated, even needed—we take what can't be understood or resolved and turn it into something monumental, sublime, and seemingly arrested so that we can ponder and petition its mystery. In Collier's poem, animal ardor—desire, velocity, instinct (the animal in us)—is the real unknowable realm, made all the more so knowing it is "meant to end."

ERIKA MEITNER

YIZKER BUKH

Memory is
flotsam (yes) just
below the surface
an eternal city
a heap of rubble
debris smaller
than your fist
an animal with-
out a leash
organized wreck-
age ghost net

or one hanging
silence on the phone—
she's gone, my sister said,
and we wept and wept
over my grandmother
while my sister sat
with her body and me
in the static and the rabbi
they sent told her to recite psalms
as comfort so we listened to each other
breathe instead and her breath was
a tunnel a handful of pebbles a knotted
Chinese jump-rope   her breath was the coiled
terrycloth turban our grandmother wore when she cooked
or walked the shallow end of her condo pool for exercise—
our grandmother still somewhere in her white turban sewing
Cornish game hens together with needle and string or
somewhere in her good wig playing poker or
somewhere in her easy chair watching CNN
while cookies shaped like our initials bake
in her oven O memory how much you
erased how many holes   we punched
in your facts since who knows the stories
she never told about the camps there are
no marked graves just too much food on
holidays diabetes my mother's fear
of ships and the motion of some

suspension bridges O memory
you've left us trauma below
the surface and some above
like the fact that I can't
shake the December
my sister's red hair
caught fire from
leaning too close
to the menorah's
candles, our
grandmother
putting her
out with a
dish towel
with her
strong
arms.

Memory is serious business. I mean that quite literally. A recent Internet search
on the topic showed an array of purchasable self-help books offering aging baby
boomers the chance to ward off dementia through an arsenal of techniques and
suggestions—Sudoku, crossword puzzles, games, physical exercise, learning foreign
languages, and, interestingly, memorizing poetry. Far more hits, too, for sites selling
RAM and other "memory suppliers" for our laptops and handheld devices than for
meditations on Mnemosyne, ancient mother of the muses. On a very basic level,
too, our ability to register, store, and recollect sensory and other information enables
us to survive. Without memory, we would be unable to use language or ponder
important abstractions like love, responsibility, God, or time. Or memory itself.
At one end of the spectrum, then, a functioning memory allows us to recall where
we parked our car in the morning; at the other end it helps to create and preserve
for us a sense of possessing a discreet identity, of being a coherent self at all, a
person with a past, a family, a job, a car, to which we must find the stowed away keys
so that we can locate that vehicle and drive it back to a recognizable home when day
is done.

It has been especially important for challenged or destroyed communities to create
written records of their histories—to preserve their character and dignity, to save
them from the ravages of cultural amnesia. Erika Meitner's "YIZKER BUKH"
("memorial book") refers to one particular genre of totemic memory-keeping.
Yizker books, collective memorials to shtetl (Jewish communities) destroyed by

the Holocaust, are usually assembled by survivors and family of survivors. Part description, part history, they often include biographies of prominent citizens and lists of those who perished in the camps, as well as photographs and other ephemera.

"Yizker" (or "Yizkor"), which means "remembrance" / "remember" in Hebrew, is also Judaism's memorial prayer for the departed, recited in synagogue four times a year. Like that prayer, Meitner's poem begins with the word "memory," and her poem, a lament for a deceased grandmother, is also a meditation on memory and what it can and cannot accomplish. In fact the poem opens with an invocatory, figurative "definition" that speaks to the obliteration and preservation that acts of remembering entail:

Memory is
flotsam (yes) just
below the surface
an eternal city
a heap of rubble
debris smaller
than your fist
an animal with-
out a leash
organized wreck-
age ghost net.

Just as the speaker's evocation of the wildness of memory, its ghosts, its "organized wreckage," intensifies—as perception and as language into disorganized syntax— we have a stanza break, and the poem moves into its emotional setting: the speaker crying on the telephone with her sister, the latter of whom is sitting with the dead grandmother's body. In their grief, the sisters listen through the phone lines to each other's breathing, and the speaker's sister's breath becomes "a tunnel a handful of pebbles a knotted / Chinese jump-rope," triggering a litany, a flood of recollected moments and details from the speaker's life with her grandmother. The poem swells with these quotidian reminiscences—the terrycloth turban she wore for cooking, the way she sewed game hens together, the wig she wore for poker games—mnemonic fragments that help to organize the "wreckage" of the speaker's grief.

But when the speaker recalls her grandmother "somewhere in her easy chair watching CNN / while cookies shaped like our initials bake / in her oven," something about the conflation of language (the letters) and the oven causes the speaker to swerve. Mid-line she abruptly apostrophizes Memory: ("...in her oven O memory how much you / erased how many holes we punched / in your facts since who knows the stories / she never told about the camps"), and we realize that this departed loved one was also a survivor of the death camps, leaving behind not only memories of an abundant spirit, but a legacy of contraction (there are "no marked graves") and trauma.

At this point, the poem funnels back toward the left margin as the speaker, momentarily disrupted within her prayer by fresh awareness of all she doesn't know, and therefore can't remember ("O memory / you've left us trauma below / the surface and some above"), takes us through a passage of seemingly random recollections ("too much food on / holidays diabetes my mother's fear / of ships and the motion of some / suspension bridges"). With its rich, longer-lined mid-section, Meitner's poem evokes the shape of the written text of the Yizker prayer (though of course the Hebrew reads from left to right from a flush right margin), and looked at from bottom to top resembles the fire image that concludes the poem. Powerfully, it is an indelible recollection that returns the narrator to herself and the occasion:

> I can't
> shake the December
> my sister's red hair
> caught fire from
> leaning too close
> to the menorah's
> candles, our
> grandmother
> putting her
> out with a
> dish towel
> with her
> strong
> arms.

Memory, Meitner shows us, *is* serious business, slurried and fictive and italicized by projection, fear, desire. It has the power to deeply console and to deeply hurt. Experts tell us that we can only store so many memories; to make room for new ones, we must sometimes let others go. As the poem closes on its knife-point of loss, its mouthful of ash (its "heap of rubble debris smaller / than your fist"), it is the grandmother's stacked "strong / arms" we most feel, allowing the speaker—who has made her memorial—to lay aside incendiary anguish even as the commemorative flame of language (the poem), history, survival, and love endures.

THE ECSTATIC
STEREOSCOPY OF SEPTEMBER

THE ECSTATIC STEREOSCOPY OF SEPTEMBER

September is one of the four months of the year that belong to two seasons. In the northern hemisphere, September's thirty days can mean a lingering torrid spell, the faded green leaves still vibrating with the last cicadas of summer, but the month can also bring sharply blue mornings rife with massive, dew-strung webs, dawns carrying with them an autumnal tinge, Robert Frost's "essence of winter sleep... on the night, / The scent of apples." For anyone bound to an academic calendar, September is often the full frontal confrontation of the conclusion of summer's sabbatical and respite (August can often feel like one long Sunday night to those anticipating the start of school) with the incipient exigencies of the classroom. A teacher friend once described to me the bittersweet and slightly embarrassing experience of pulling a large plug of sand and small pebbles out of his ear, driven there by a last tumble in the Atlantic surf just two days before he stood in front of a large group of students presenting a start-of-the-semester lecture on the Romantic poets.

Perhaps it is September's double-vision, its brackish mix of balm and brace, that has stirred so many poets to use its crucible as a stage for personal and private concerns. "September, the bed we lie in between summer and autumn," writes Charles Wright, "Sunday in all the windows, the slow snow of daylight / Flaking the holly tree and the hedge panes / As it disappears in the odd milk teeth / The grass has bared, both lips back in the cool suck of dusk" (from "A Journal of the Year of the Ox"). In *The Gardens of Emily Dickinson*, Judith Farr says that "it was not for summer's 'Consummated Bloom' but for 'the happy Sorrow of Autumn' that Dickinson reserved her most wistful yet impassioned descriptions," temperamentally suited as she was for the exquisite motions of valediction and loss. As Jane Hirshfield puts it, "The heat of autumn / is different from the heat of summer. / One ripens apples, the other turns them to cider."

Could there be something about the "two minds" of September—summer and autumn—that is intrinsically inspiring, even ecstatic, to poets? Poems come to poets in a myriad of ways, but certainly the spark of making begins when one perception or image is stirred, moved, or complicated by the float in and over it of something ...*else*—an other, another image, a memory, an ulterior place, an awakened premonition. Anne Carson refers to this "impertinence" of consciousness (with the act of poetic imagination in a sense the condition of metaphor writ large) as a "shift of distance from far to near...[a] virtuoso act of imagination [that] brings... two things together, sees their incongruence, then sees also a new congruence, meanwhile continuing to recognize the previous incongruence through the new congruence." This feat, she goes on, "demands of the mind a 'stereoscopic vision' (as Stanford 1936 puts it) or a 'split reference' (in Jakobsen's terms), an ability to hold in equipoise two perspectives at once." And if "ecstasy" is the state of being both the self and at the same time outside or beside/beyond the self (*ex stasis*, out of stasis), isn't it possible that any notion of ecstatic or stereoscopic poetry is in a sense a tautology?

In this sense, then, September provides a blue-note foundation, lending its subtext of plenitude and loss, its seasonal depth, to any subject. In these lines from Muriel Rukeyser's "Song: Love in Whose Rich Honor," for example, a deeply personal risk is compounded by its September context:

Love
in whose rich honor
I stand looking from my window
over the starved trees of a dry September
Love
deep and so far forbidden
is bringing me
a gift
to claw at my skin
to break open my eyes
the gift longed for so long
The power
to write
out of the desperate ecstasy at last
death and madness....

Denise Levertov's "September 1961," on the other hand, takes stock, in the month we associate with the return to school, of her own poetic legacy, paying homage to her great Modernist teachers ("This is the year the old ones, / the old great ones / leave us alone on the road. // The road leads to the sea. / We have the words in our pockets, / obscure directions"). In other poems, September is the setting for outpourings of public and political outrage or despair. W. H. Auden's famous "September 1, 1939," which grieves the outbreak of World War II, and W. B. Yeats's protestation of social injustice in "September 1913" are deepened by the ways in which "the unmentionable odour of death / Offends the September night."

Few reading this column will be unaware that September 11th marks the anniversary of the terrorist attacks on the Twin Towers in New York City and on the Pentagon. Particularly haunting to me, among the many powerful poems written in the wake of that assault, is a poem W. S. Merwin wrote, with characteristically capacious vision and humanity, on September 10, 2001, the day before the tragedy. "To the Light of September" begins:

When you are already here
you appear to be only
a name that tells of you
whether you are present or not

and for now it seems as though
you are still summer
still the high familiar
endless summer
yet with a glint
of bronze in the chill mornings
and the late yellow petals
of the mullein fluttering
on the stalks that lean
over their broken
shadows across the cracked ground....

It's as though the complex "light" of the month itself, both endless and finite, were offering (and Merwin channeling) a healing response, natural and redemptive, to the brokenness to come: "you / who fly with them // you who are neither / before nor after / you who arrive / with blue plums / that have fallen through the night // perfect in the dew."

John Ashbery, Raymond Carver, Robert Bly, Nina Cassian, Thomas Kinsella, Edward Hirsch, Mohammed Riza Navi, Stanley Kunitz, A. R. Ammons, Stephen Cushman, John Berryman, and Ralph Waldo Emerson are just a handful of other poets who have written poems about or set in September, but perhaps the most well known September poem is John Keats's ode "To Autumn," penned on 19 September 1819. I don't think I could live without this poem. Each fall, especially as I age, as I take up the yoke of a new school year and feel the ebb of summer, its long days, I am heartened by Keats's admonition to "think not of them." Or, rather, to recall, as poets perhaps remind us better than anyone, that maturation, harvest and fruition, even death, have their "music too." I think of this as I make my way to class through crowds of milling young people or as I trundle with my rolling backpack full of books and student papers to the place I've parked my car—as lights come on in the earlier dark, while seasons exchange their conspiracies, "while barred clouds bloom the soft-dying day."

CHARLES WRIGHT

Ancient of Days

There is a kind of sunlight, in early autumn, at sundown,
That raises cloud reflections
Inches above the pond water,
                        that sends us packing into the chill evening
To stand like Turner's blobbed figurines
In a landscape we do not understand,
                        whatever and everything
We know about it.
Unworldly and all ours,
                it glides like the Nineteenth Century
Over us, up the near hill
And into the glistening mittens of the same clouds
Now long gone from the world's pond.
                        So long.

This is an old man's poetry,
                written by someone who's spent his life
Looking for one truth.
Sorry, pal, there isn't one.
Unless, of course, the trees and their blow-down relatives
Are part of it.
                Unless the late-evening armada of clouds
Spanished along the horizon are part of it.
Unless the diminishing pinprick of light
                        stunned in the dark forest
Is part of it.
                Unless, O my, whatever the eye makes out,
And sends us, on its rough-road trace,
To the heart, is part of it,
                then maybe that bright vanishing might be.

Pack Rats

Up to the upper place to cover the bedstead against the pack rats.
The 10th of August and already they're moving in.
Industrial plastic, waste product from logging companies.
Early winter. It won't work,
                                they'll burrow in and nest,
Leaving their blood-colored urine and interminable excrement
Coming and going.
They'll leave us something shining, or bright,
In return. Bright and shining.

This grey on blue on white on grey on blue
Montana August skyscape
Has nothing to do with politics, or human relations, or people, in fact.
It has to do with fictions,
                            and where we place ourselves
Apart from the dread apart.
It has to do with what's unidentifiable,
And where our seat is in it.
It has to do with what the pack rat leaves, what's bright and shining.

Surrounded by half-forests and half-lives,
Surrounded by everything we have failed to do,
It is as though kumquats hung from the lodge pole pine trees.
Everything's doubled –
                        Once it arrives and once it fades.
Angels, God bless them rebound from the meadow, bruised gain,
I guess, from our stern world.
Back in the pittering dark of the pine trees,
                                            the rats
Are nosing for silver or gold, or whatever glints or shines.

Charles Wright is arguably the most significant, original poet writing in America.
One of a generation of luminous heavy-hitters (Gary Snyder, Mark Strand, Fanny
and Susan Howe, Mary Oliver, Jay Wright, and Charles Simic, to name just a few),
some of whom, like Sylvia Plath and Ted Berrigan, are no longer alive to grace us
with the benefit of their long apprenticeship and vision, Wright continues to create,
in a replete range of tonal, stylistic, and thematic registers, poems of prescient,
metaphysical beauty, continuously refreshing his practice with inimitable mojo and
lyricism.

Wright, a master teacher who for decades guided generations of students through the writing programs of UC Irvine and the University of Virginia, is well known for saying that each poet has just five or so poems to write and must keep finding ways to get as close as possible to telling the truth in and about them. A jones for light—for "heavenly hurt"—God hunger—what Wright has coined "negative spirituality"—is one of the "five or so" poems Wright has spent a lifetime writing. In an interview with Thomas Gardner in Gardner's *A Door Ajar: Contemporary Writers and Emily Dickinson*, Charles, speaking of his own work in relation to Dickinson's poem "There's a certain slant of light" (what Wright calls "the ur-poem in my unconscious"), says that this transumptive light "remains, as Pound said of something else, 'in the mind indestructible.' It's that moment when illumination seems possible. It never actually happens, at least not so far, but its possibility is the illumination, I guess, that one is looking for. And when one comes to terms with that, one comes to terms with everything."

Charles Wright's many books yield an abundance of light/sky imagery, both diurnal and nocturnal. This random sampling evinces both rapt perception and an immense desire for transport in and beyond language:

How the hills, for instance, at dawn in Kingsport
In late December in 1962 were black
                            against a sky
The color of pale fish blood and water that ran to white

                    (from "The Southern Cross")

Deep dusk and lightning bugs
                            alphabetize on the east wall,
The carapace of the sky blue-ribbed and buzzing
Somehow outside it all,
Trees dissolving against the night's job,
                            houses melting in air . . .

                    (from "Yard Journal")

How small the stars of tonight, bandannaed by moonlight,,
How few and far between –
Disordered and drained, like highlights in Dante's death mask.
Or a sequined dress from the forties
                            — hubba-hubba—
Some sequins missing, some sequins inalterably in place....

                    (from "Star Turn II")

There's nothing out there but light,
                              the would-be artist said,
As usual just half-right:
There's also a touch of darkness, everyone knows, on both sides
     of both horizons....

                         (from "Lives of the Artists")

Charles's "Matins" opens, "Sunlight like Vaseline in the trees, smear and shine,
smear and shine." "Why Vaseline?" a student once asked after a reading. In his
characteristically understated way (when queried by reporters how it felt to win
the Pulitzer Prize, for example, Wright quipped, "beats a poke in the eye with a
sharp stick, I guess"), Charles replied that he'd just plain run out of other ways to
describe the sky. But there's nothing tired or self-parodic about this trying to get it
right, repeatedly, moving as near as one can to what's at the abyss of articulation.
Wright has called himself a "God-fearing agnostic," and this restive going-after the
enlightenment behind the light, the dark within the light, whatever's at the edge or
prow of night, is a flood subject for him. Wright keeps looking and re-looking,
questioning intently as he goes, pulling in details from pop culture ("a turkey
buzzard logs on to the evening sky" or "We've been here for years, / Fog-rags and
rain and sun spurts, / Beforeworlds behind us, slow light spots like Jimmy Durante's
fade-out / Hopscotching across the meadow grass" from "North"), with shout-outs
and samplings from philosophy, semiotics, phenomenology, visual art, music, and
other poets (Wang Wei, Plotinus, Rothko, Cezanne, Montale, Bishop, Miles Davis,
St. Chrysostom), all the while paying a profound attention to the quotidian and the
natural world, especially his own backyard ("all landscape," Wright has written, "is
autobiographical").

Highly regarded as a poet's poet, Wright has sustenance to offer anyone looking
to believe in the salvific motions of language at its most intense and interrogated,
particularly in a world that often seems obdurate, mysterious, bereft of meaning
(one thinks of Wallace Stevens in his "Adagia"—"It is the belief and not the god
that counts.") Possibility, as Wright says, is the illumination. In "Black Zodiac,"
Wright addresses all poets, petitioners, language-wielders seeking connection:

Calligraphers of the disembodied, God's word-wards,
What letters will we illuminate?
Above us, the atmosphere,
The nothing that's nowhere, signs on, and waits for our beck and call.
Above us, the great constellations sidle and wince,
The letters undarken and come forth,
Your X and my Y.

The letters undarken and they come forth.

That Wright has offered his slant, decades-long questing after this epiphanic brilliance is a crucial, consequential gift to American letters.

"November," Charles Wright says in "A Journal of English Days," "is my favorite month, the downside of autumn // ...a pale light on the bright side of the dark, / Everything starting to glide and refract, / moving just under water...." "Ancient of Days" and "Pack Rats," two autumnal poems, reveal, among many illuminations, that Charles Wright is a religious poet, perhaps the major religious poet of the late twentieth and early twenty-first centuries. His is the way of apostasy, of the *via negativa*, of ecstatics like Juan de la Cruz and Emily Dickinson—and his project is a "negative blue" move toward defining the Divine by what it isn't available to us here on the other side, but where we can still love what Wright has called the holiness, the "beauty in the disappearance that remains." "Ancient of Days," a name for God in Aramaic, is a figure found in nearly all religions (it is also the name of an Anglican hymn and a song by Van Morrison, a famous Blakean image, and a metal band from Leeds—one senses that Wright knows all of this). Though we inhabit "a landscape we do not understand," he says in "Ancient of Days," we can, with our steadfast looking at the world, feel, however transitorily, what Wright calls in "Pack Rats" "what's unidentifiable, / And where our seat is in it." Like pack rats, humans relentlessly come and go, stalwart, seeking against all odds, "nosing for silver or gold...whatever glints or shines." In "Ancient of Days," Wright says, "This is an old man's poetry, written by someone who's spent his life / Looking for one truth. / Sorry, pal, there isn't one." But what follows these lines is a litany of signals— "the trees and their blow-down relatives," "the late-evening armada of clouds / Spanished along the horizon," "the diminishing pinprick of light / stunned in the dark forest"—culminating in a suggestion of what might stand in for the one truth: "Unless, O my, whatever the eye makes out, / And sends, on its rough-road trace, / To the heart, is part of it, then maybe that bright vanishing might be." Wright's recouping of what vanishes is a lasting vision and vital testament to the staying power of his verse.

LARISSA SZPORLUK

Vanished Harvest

They call it a lazy breeze.
Under its slow grope,
trees drop their favorite work.

And pigeons, their pigeon
droppings, and the bleach
that I drop on the porch

because my son might lick one
and die. Because autumn
is sweet on war

and winter is bitter peace,
because the river chased Achilles
for butchering too much—

breeze like a laid-back doctor,
the soul is dense
when you come so late.

Bludgeon-Man

Would that he caressed us
On the road made of feathers
of our loved ones.

Would that we could lose
all semblance of pheasant,
become Mecca in his palms

and overwhelm his senses.
Would that this were dreamy
instead of dull,

this inevitable severing
of daylight into insects
who pad the coming night

with excrement and wings—
would that it were not our life
to augur sleeveless errands.

The poems of Larissa Szporluk possess a mind of Autumn—and not the autumn
of mists and mellow fruitfulness, but of the strangely beautiful, brutal season of
fall, the Fall, of drop, of harrow, haunt, and grim reaping. They are whetted with
the scythe's edge ordure of lopped, shorn, razed things. Bespeaking a ruthless,
anarchic, fiercely intuitive somatic ethos, the menace in Szporluk's work is all
the more arresting and disturbing for its conjuring of an eerie, almost cinematic,
domestic heartland noir.

Visually—each is a columnar quintet of tercets—"Vanished Harvest" and
"Bludgeon-Man" mirror one another, like twin hay-rooks, silos, or scarecrows. They
trope one another thematically as well. Brought together, the poems present, in
distinct Szporlukian ways, the economies of "lost and won," of "come what may,"
that stalk Shakespeare's Scottish play (both of these poems appear in Szporluk's
collection *Traffic with Macbeth*). Any mythic notion of "home" or safety, as autumn
and evening and death come on, is fearlessly denied.

A reviewer once wrote that Szporluk's work is "more personal than poems that
proclaim themselves so," and also more public than its rich, solipsistic language
might suggest. "Vanished Harvest," for instance, at first seems relayed in a kind of
generic voice-over (think Mariel Hemingway narrating the opening scene of a David
Lynch film) that borrows the shape of definition ("they call it") and the architecture
of cause and effect ("because") but which, in the case of both pronominal shape-
shifting and deliberately messed dialectic, slips the noose of reason at every turn in a
syntax of mimetic dropped and vanishing clauses:

They call it a lazy breeze.
Under its slow grope,
trees drop their favorite work.

And pigeons, their pigeon
droppings, and the bleach
that I drop on the porch

because my son might lick one
and die.

If the reader misses the threat in that slow grope of the seemingly innocuous "lazy breeze," that dropping of leaves and avian excrement, we confront it in the image that the narrator, finally entering the poem in the first-person, puts before us of her child on his hands and knees lapping at toxic stone and dying. She lets the possibility of this hang a moment before seemingly extending her argument for vanishing, veering into more political and even mythic territory: "Because autumn / is sweet on war // and winter is bitter peace, / because the river chased Achilles / for butchering too much…." Again, Szporluk lets that allusion to the waters of the river god Scamander choked with bodies in the carnage wreaked by Achilles after the death of Patroclus linger before eerily returning us to the breeze that is "like a laid-back doctor," a doctor blind to our terminal condition, the doctor ignoring or oblivious to boundaries, the autumn wind suddenly transformed into the bodiless rush of the soul, all the more "dense" for being abandoned with such langorous, deceptive ease. This is not the leisure of a grape crushed against a palate fine— of the body lingering over its last oozings, hour by hour. This is negative Keats, dark Keats, Keats trafficking in the realm of Macbeth and the dark imagination of Shakespeare, the playwright he so loved. This is Szporluk.

"Bludgeon-Man" also walks a dark way, and its collective narrators are the victims of the bludgeon-wielding harvester/executioner. The speakers never question that they must travel "the road made of feathers / of our loved ones" who have gone before them to the chopping block. Their plea is rather a wish to be "caressed" by their killer, even to be cherished by him ("Would that we could lose / all semblance of pheasant, become Mecca in his palms // and overwhelm his sense") as they go. The lament, too, is that the destined passage is in no way redeemed for the speakers by thrill or even fear:

Would that this were dreamy
instead of dull,

this inevitable severing
of daylight into insects
who pad the coming night

with excrement and wings –
would that it were not our life
to augur sleeveless errands.

Although the chorus of narrators may not feel it, the reader must thrill to the ironic, gorgeous lyricism and pathos of the last two stanzas. Though their tone is more raucously punk, the Scottish trash band Nyah Fearties, underground in the eighties and nineties and known for making a wild, thrashing music by mixing traditional elements with a raving percussive use of dustbins and other machinery, comes to mind when I read these two Macbeth-ghosted poems (interestingly, the band has a song called "Bludgeon Man," which appeared on an early album).

Heaving into light the heavy, fated resignation, the "dense" soul of the harvested, the about to be vanished, is Szporluk's "errand," and it is a perspective not often risked, and risked with such darkly erotic and undeniable poetic power.

R.T. SMITH

Orchard of One

Less Eden than a starving
yard, but this half acre
of withery weeds and brush

sustains somehow the haggard
apple tree, a Spartan
undermined by woodchucks

and moles eager to lick
bark and chew the roots,
suck the broth that feeds

the fruit. How many
seasons did we pour pellets
the green of a toxic sea

into their tunnel portals,
shovel woodsdirt
and shore the trunk

with stones? We moored
our solitary with ropes
to halt its tilt and said

the bruised red yield was
less a token of the forbidden
than our survival symbol,

despite smut and bag worms,
badly sloped flood plain,
the list of the tree.

And the bran-colored animal
I surprised one morning,
tonguing salt from the handle

of a spade I'd left
leaning in the rain,
became our resident gremlin.

Now even he's forgiven,
our cellar's apple stack
crisp, sweet though meager,

and a finch chitters his
chilly anthem from the brittle
tangle of limbs

up in the snarled crown,
trembling with wind,
where winter begins.

The German poet Rainer Maria Rilke named two inexhaustible sources for poetry: childhood and dreams. To that I would add the myth of the primal Garden, which may be saying the same thing, for what is the story of paradise lost and the human fall from grace if not, in part, our dream of a lost symbiotic wholeness, a nostalgia for that realm prior to language when we felt a sense of protection, of belonging? What is it if not the story of our plummet into the remedial precincts of language?

The speaker in R. T. Smith's "Orchard of One" is a property owner trying to keep alive one apple tree, saving remnant of a phantom or long ago dismantled orchard. But paradise is on his mind from the poem's first lines:

Less Eden than a starving
yard, but this half acre
of withery weeds and brush

sustains somehow the haggard
apple tree, a Spartan
undermined by woodchucks

and moles eager to lick
bark and chew the roots,
suck the broth that feeds

the fruit...

In her study of the lyric poem, *Lyric Time: Dickinson and the Limits of Genre*, Sharon Cameron writes, "Adam named the animals before the fall, but he had no real use for those names until after it." Smith's poem is rife with naming—pellets, ropes, smut, bag worms— signifiers for the forces that threaten this old tree and for the means the speaker employs to buttress and "halt its tilt," this "solitary"

[whose] bruised red yield was
less a token of the forbidden
than our survival symbol.

Yet the "bran-colored animal / I surprised one morning, / tonguing salt from the handle // of a spade I'd left / leaning in the rain" goes unnamed. It becomes the "resident gremlin"—animus, perhaps, of what is always beyond the reach of pesticides and any scaffolding or effort in the face of what is beyond human control, beyond the reach even of language. Yet even this gremlin force is "forgiven" once "our cellar's apple stack / crisp, sweet though meager" has been once again gleaned and hoarded for the season ahead. Replacing this scant but precious harvest in the limbs of the bereft but still standing tree is a finch, "[chittering] his / chilly anthem from the brittle / tangle of limbs // up in the snarled crown, / trembling with wind, / where winter begins."

Did human song begin with winter? In *Creation and Fall: A Theological Interpretation of Genesis*, Dietrich Bonhoeffer reminds us that in Eden, the tree of the knowledge of good and evil took center stage, and that "it is characteristic of man that [although] his life is a constant circling around its middle...[he] never takes possession of it." Smith's poem confirms this obsession and reminds us, as at the hibernal solstice, that poetry—and its stand-in, birdsong— Keats's nightingale, Hardy's darkling thrush, Smith's finch—finds its voice "where winter begins"—with our inevitable ending and the music we make of the "snarled crown" of that knowledge.

GABRIEL FRIED

Ends Well

This is not the poem where the child comes back drowned.
He isn't pulled out of the pond, full of silted water
as a washday sink, lips like fish, eyes unblinking.
Nor is it the poem where the child comes back maimed.
He isn't ruined by claws or teeth, by gears or fall
the way some children are we've read about.
He wandered off while we were in a dream
or an argument. And, like something from a dream
or a retold family story, the dogs went with him,
one on either side, as if they suddenly knew to
do something other than steal roasts from the counter.
So this is a happy poem, full of relief and only a little shame.

Maybe he only went to see the cows or followed
a dragonfly, or was enthralled by the mystery
of the barn that sits like bones in the meadow.
He's been walking now for longer than he hasn't.
He walked young—nine months, ten. It has always
seemed there's somewhere he is meant to be.
We've caught up to him at the greenhouse
and across the stream, past the silo and beyond
the landing strip. He always comes back
willing, happy, even grateful; how can we scold him?
No wolf has seized him; he seems unchanged,
like nothing he has overheard has yet to matter.

"We haven't all had the good fortune to be ladies," wrote Mark Twain, "we haven't
all been generals, or poets, or statesmen, but when the toast comes down to the
babies, we all stand on common ground." Although sometimes difficult to believe
of others and of ourselves, all adults were once children. And though the child may
be father of the man, as Wordsworth exults in his *Prelude*, what becomes of that lost
child each adult once was? Where is he or she? How to believe in that alien entity,
all rootless milk teeth and ignorance and curiosity and dimples where knuckles
eventually will be? Has he or she been exiled or vanished, even banished, into willed
oblivion? Or reconstructed with an often terrible nostalgia through that supreme
fiction, memory, perhaps aided by family mythology, photographs, or video? What

LISA RUSS SPAAR   213

is the relationship between that very young person, that small body, that incipient "self"—primal, new to language, imperfectly and figuratively constructing the world—that *other*—and the discreet, coherent *adult* "self" to which we must, to keep anarchy at bay, adhere? Perhaps in contemplating our own child selves, we are, as Samuel Beckett muses in his essay on Proust, "present at [our] own absence." We *are*, and yet at the same time *are not*, both ourselves and other. Thus all of our stories about childhood must, finally, be narratives, fictions, of our becoming. And our sense of what is at stake in this recounting becomes all the more acute in the engagements between parents and their offspring.

Poet Gabriel Fried has a gift for articulating the experience of childhood with neither defensiveness nor condescension. His poems explore the ways in which children's relationships to the world—to objects, language, experience—are like those of the poet: metaphorical, fabular, primal, with a strong whiff of pre- and post-Lapsarian darkness and wonder.

"Ends Well," narrated by an adult, presumably a parent of the child in the poem, is built of two 12-line stanzas whose 5-stress lines lend a rhetorical momentum and the sturdiness of a Rorschach inkblot to this poem of almost Freudian adult yearning, childhood reverie, and culpability. We learn from line one that "[t]his is not the poem where the child comes back drowned. / He isn't pulled out of the pond, full of silted water / as a washday sink, lips like fish, eyes unblinking." He has not been maimed or ruined. He hasn't fallen or in any other way been harmed "the way some children are we've read about." Instead, the child in this poem has "wandered off" while the adults in his world were "in a dream / or an argument." The boy sets out, accompanied by the family dogs, "one on either side." Yet he *has* slipped away in a lapse of adult vigilance. While this is "a happy poem," then, it is also concerned with the response of the speaker, rendered as "full of relief and only a little shame."

That "shame," deemed diminutive, ends the first stanza but lingers, hovering over stanza two, in which the particularity fresh imagining of his child's experience,

Maybe he only went to see the cows or followed
a dragonfly, or was enthralled by the mystery
of the barn that sits like bones in the meadow,

brings the identities of our adult speaker and his boy subject very close to one another. Though the boy is clearly the offspring of the "we" who, earlier, were caught up in their self-absorbing adult dramas, and who must continuously "[catch] up to him at the green house / and across the stream, past the silo and beyond / the landing strip," it is also obvious that the speaker empathizes deeply with this little gypsy: "He's been walking now for longer than he hasn't. / He walked young—nine months, ten. It has always / seemed there's somewhere he is meant to be." Home, the body of the parent, is the place from which we commence. And commence we must. It is one thing to make those initial forays, unprepared, innocent, and, if we are lucky, protected by the felicities of fate. It's quite another to watch our younger selves, or worse, our children, start out and zag away from the zone of the familiar, having already traversed ourselves through the harrowing thresholds and gauntlet of childhood and adolescence. Yet our speaker seems seized by magical thinking with regard to his peripatetic child, a perspective perhaps brought on by the dissociation of his own adult preoccupations (fantasizing, marital argument) and symbiotic connection to the boy. "He always comes back," he says, "willing, happy, even grateful; how can we scold him?"

At this point, we realize that the parents in this poem, obviously well intentioned and clearly smitten with their progeny, might nonetheless be attempting to reassure themselves about their own parental vagrancy, distinguished from the son's innocent wanderings by the tinge of adult responsibility. "No wolf has seized him," they offer, evoking fairy tales, as though in self defense. Yet the last lines, "[H]e seems unchanged, / like nothing he has overheard has yet to matter," reveal the speaker's awareness that there may well be things that this child has heard which he does not yet comprehend but that one day may matter to him very much. What parent or guardian has not felt this wish to shield his or her charges from adult complexity, chagrin, and difficulty, especially from that vulnerability engendered by the very adults who are meant to be the protectors?

"Ends Well" insists upon the happy ending of a fairy tale. But the poem offers the darkness of tale and myth, as well. Beckett says of Proust's obliteration of Time in the service of wishing that "the experience is at once imaginative and empirical, at once an evocation and a direct perception, real without being merely actual, ideal without being merely abstract, the ideal real, the essential, the extratemporal." The boy in "Ends Well" is ecstatically out of time while at the same time already caught in its currents; the poem reveals the adults in his world to be in a parallel but not identical predicament. Fried creates for his young subject a kind of brief eternity, of which the adults may take only a conditional and culpable share, a complicity of other and self made possible inimitably through art, through poems.

JANE HIRSHFIELD

Bruises

In age, the world grows clumsy.

A heavy jar
leaps from a cupboard.
A suitcase has corners.

Others have no explanation.

Old love, old body,
do you remember—
carpet burns down the spine,
gravel bedding
the knees, hardness to hardness.

You who knew yourself
kissed by the bite of the ant,
you who were kissed by the bite of the spider.

Now kissed by this.

The Promise

Stay, I said
to the cut flowers.
They bowed
their heads lower.

Stay, I said to the spider,
who fled.

Stay, leaf.
It reddened,
embarrassed for me and itself.

Stay, I said to my body.
It sat as a dog does,
obedient for a moment,
soon starting to tremble.

Stay, to the earth
of riverine valley meadows,
of fossiled escarpments,
of limestone and sandstone.
It looked back
with a changing expression, in silence.

Stay, I said to my loves.
Each answered,
Always.

Sometimes the Heart is a Shallow Autumn River

Is rock and shadow, bird.
Is fry, as the smallest fish are called,
darting in the pan of nearness.

The frog's flawless interpretation of the music "Leaf"
is a floating black-eyed emerald
slipped between the water and its reflections.

And caution, and hope, and sorrow?
As umbrellas are, to a mountain or field of grass.

Daniel Halpern, in his introduction to *Holy Fire: Nine Visionary Poets and the Quest for Enlightenment*, offers three criteria for visionary poems: "First, they must honor their language (oral or written), whether it be English, French, German, Kashmiri, Hindi, Sanskrit, or Persian, acknowledging Santayana's observation that 'the height of poetry is to speak the language of the gods.' Second, the poems must fulfill, with unerring precision, the requirements of their form, whatever that form turns out to be. And third, the poetry must operate in a visionary realm—that is, present a view of the world that violates the superficial, reaches through the surface to touch the primal material. Wordsworth would call this act the seeing into the life of things; Ruskin wrote, 'The greatest thing a human soul ever does in this world is to see something, and tell what it saw in a plain way....To see clearly is poetry, prophecy, and religion,—all in one.'"

Poet, essayist, and translator Jane Hirshfield (whose evocative versions of the fourteenth-century Kashmiri poet Lalla and the sixteenth-century north Indian *bhakti* mendicant ecstatic Mirabai grace Halpern's anthology) is a visionary. Rarely making spirituality and her own long Zen practice her overt subject, Hirshfield nonetheless creates poems which possess a subtle lucidity that is accessible and understated on the one hand, and suffused with a resonant "beyonding" of the self and the quotidian on the other. Her poems press the experiential [an act of spiritual attention on the order of fellow visionary Gerard Manley Hopkins, who wrote in a journal (1871), "What you look hard at seems to look hard at you"] in order to transcend soma and solipsism in service of what Halpern calls a "revision[ing of] the world, perhaps even 'the creation of [a] better world.'"

Some might flinch at the notion of any ideal as unfathomable as the creation of a better world, and yet there's nothing Pollyanna-ish about Hirshfield's project. As Rosanna Warren puts it, Hirshfield's "poems appear simple, and are not. Her language, in its cleanliness and transparency, poses riddles of a quietly metaphysical nature." Yet how pull off a poetic practice visionary and optimistic over decades characterized by increasingly entrenched social, cultural, and political extremes of irony, skepticism, abstracted emotion, rampant materialism, technological cocooning and detachment, superficiality, and thoughtless, fundamentalist fear and isolationism? What accounts for the golden hold and continually refreshed staying power of this remarkable poet?

The *riddle*, the existential joke of being, of meaning, of Dickinson's "prank of the Heart / at play on the Heart," is as powerful a source as song for the lyric poem. Central to Hirshfield's vision is a kind of holy delight that is at the heart of riddles and koans—not the momentary humor of punning or mere cleverness or showing-off, but rather the deep pleasure of discovery of the word in or behind or beyond the world, and vice versa. Northrop Frye writes, "The real answer to the question implied in a riddle is not a 'thing' outside it, but that which is both word and thing, and is both inside and outside the poem. This is the universal of which the poem is the manifestation, the order of words that tells us of battles and shipwrecks, of the intimate connection of beauty and terror, of cycles of life and death, of mutability and apocalypse."

"Bruises," "The Promise, "and "Sometimes the Heart is a Shallow Autumn River," all from Hirshfield's *Come, Thief*, operate, in their various ways, as visionary riddles about the aging body, the "autumn" of life, and what abides. Interestingly, the titles provide the "answers" from the start (Frye: "it is common to give the 'solution' of riddle poems in their titles, and in such poems we move from work to title. Here is what I have to say about something; guess what it is"), allowing Hirshfield room to move into her material in a manner also essential to her poetry: it is the getting there (the Way) and not the destination, the answer, that is the source of her joy and revelation.

"Bruises" begins with a playful displacement of agency. It is the world, the speaker announces with the wry understatement of a stand-up comedian, even the world beyond our ken, that grows awkward and bruise-prone, not we:

In age, the world grows clumsy.

A heavy jar
Leaps from a cupboard.
A suitcase has corners.

Others have no explanation.

What follows, in a seamless but ecstatic turn I associate with Hirshfield, is an apostrophic call to the speaker's "Old love, old body" (here the speaker could be addressing an old lover as well as conflating, appositively, "love" and "body"— that is, her body is her old love) to recall other, prior, more erotically caused contusions ("carpet burns down the spine, / gravel bedding / the knees, hardness to hardness"). The address to the body continues in the penultimate stanza, in which Eros ("You who knew yourself kissed") is mixed with the more dangerous love-bite language of venom and stings. The punch-line, perfectly timed and granted a stanza break and the full weight of the silence of white space around it—"Now kissed by this"—is the sucker punch, returning us to the title and first line with renewed and deepened awareness: there are many kinds of bruises, and the hardest, the most painful mark we bear is the full on and in the mouth registering of our aging, our mortality.

"The Promise" (a promise is itself a kind of riddle) teases us and draws us in: what is the promise? what is being pledged? by whom? to whom? why? A surprise, then, not to be given a straight narrative, description, or definition of said promise, but rather an anaphoric catalogue of what appears to be less a promise than a command. In each stanza, the order to "stay" is pitched to an array of fauna and flora, and the response in each case is charged with a darkly whimsical humor, figurative and metaphysical:

Stay, I said
to the cut flowers.
They bowed
their heads lower.

Stay, I said to the spider,
who fled.

Stay, leaf.
It reddened,
embarrassed for me and itself.

Stay, I said to my body.
It sat as a dog does,
obedient for a moment,
soon starting to tremble.

Even the great and enduring earth, to which the speaker appeals after she feels
her own body's mutability, will not obey the speaker's command, but rather looks
back "with a changing expression, in silence." Flowers fade, spiders build transient
houses in air, leaves redden and fall, bodies, too, tremble and fail, and the cosmos
itself is in eternal and indifferent flux. It is not until the last stanza that Hirshfield,
without fanfare, reveals her answer: it is love and love alone that is capable of
making a promise to abide. This "answer" might seem simple or unearned if not
for the accrued force of the poem's incrementally repeated litany. It is the stations
of the spiritual riddle that enact Hirshfield's vision in this poem: its difficulty, its
veracity, and its worth.

Something I've admired about Hirshfield's work since I began to read it years
ago is its timeless ethos. There is nothing in any of these three poems (formally,
imagistically, in terms of diction) that would suggest they couldn't have been written
hundreds of years ago or belong to some future era. Even earlier poems like "Why
Bodhidharma Went to Howard Johnson's" strike me as timely (and wisely funny)
to all ages. I have long speculated that Hirshfield's practice of translation (she is
especially well known for her versions and translations of Japanese and Chinese
poets) has contributed to this rare quality in her work. It's as though she only uses
words she might be able to translate from a foreign tongue, and this lends the work
the shimmer of several minds at once—allowing that breaking of one world into
another, of the discovery of worlds within worlds, words within words.

I especially feel this in "Sometimes the Heart is a Shallow Autumn River," a "definition" poem of figurative dazzlement and shape-shifting. Metaphor, of course, is also riddling, tricking us into seeing the seemingly inevitable but unlikely alliances between two different entities. Even the opening stanza, with its pair of metaphorical "equations," is of at least two minds, suggesting that the heart is both what is *in the bed of* and what *is reflected* in the "shallow autumn river." In stanza two, Hirshfield offers a new metaphor, a meta-metaphor, in which the frog/leaf-music/gem/iris/poem slips "between the water and its reflections" like an angel, an entity belonging both to land and water, earth and heaven. The final note in this figurative chord cuts straight to what's at stake: "And caution, and hope, and sorrow? / As umbrellas are, to a mountain or field of grass." Such a profoundly comic vision here, of the highest order—we see those little umbrellas of our worry and our self-absorption and our cares against the vast expanse of the motions of the universe. And this returns us to the title, to our hearts, to what we can hold and refract and reflect and let go.

We see, then, how Hirshfield fulfills Halpern's notions of what makes for a visionary poetics. Hers is a poetry that honors its language, fulfills the shape of a mystery and discovery shared by the riddling koan, and pursues its ecstasy of deep seeing, something akin to Hopkins's instress. It is not new to think of all poetry as a kind of "translation" from experience to language, but in an essay about W. S. Merwin, Charles Simic writes, "Translation is one of the very few human activities where the impossible actually occurs on a fairly regular basis. Merwin once said that translation of comedy is one of the great disciplines because in translating jokes, if one gets anything wrong, nothing works. This is true of poetry too, where not only the words have to be translated but also the tone of voice, the prosody with its meaningful pauses, and various other near-intangibles that make a poem or a joke what it is." Hirshfield's poetry is serious in the most comedic sense ("comedy" <late 14c., from O.Fr. *comedie*, 14c., "a poem," not in the theatrical sense, from L. *comoedia*, from Gk. *komoidia* "a comedy, amusing spectacle," from *komodios* "singer in the revels," from *komos* "revel, carousal" + *oidos* "singer, poet," from *aeidein* "to sing"). I am grateful for the fleet travel her poems make in the mysteries of mortality, their "flawless interpretation of the music 'Leaf.'"

POETS IN THE PRINT SHOP

POETS IN THE PRINT SHOP

Several years ago a colleague in the studio art department and I team-taught a course we called The Matrix, an experiment in bringing together eight advanced printmaking students and eight advanced poets to make new work, including several high and low-end collective books. A matrix, in the printmaking lexicon, refers to the plate—zinc, copper—or other material (stone, collage) used in printing, but when we advertised the course we had a lot of interest from initially thrilled and then bitterly disappointed fans of the 1999 science fiction film of the same name, undergraduates who thought that it was high time that the cinema icon got the serious attention it deserved in the academy.

There was much enthusiasm among the young artists and poets as well, and our idea as instructors was to throw them (and ourselves) into the water, with the presumption that our disciplines—poetry writing and intaglio printmaking—were distinct enough to generate fruitful friction and close enough to allow for revelatory and empathetic artistic exchange.

This "throwing into the water" turned out to mean many things, perhaps chief among them the potentially dangerous fact that although half the class had never before set foot in a print shop (described by my art colleague as a "fifteenth-century chemistry lab without the safety features"), we were almost immediately involved in processes using acids and other toxic substances. Most fumes emitted in poetry writing workshops tend to come from the ubiquitous coffee cups and from occasional traces of cigarette smoke brought into the room after breaks; by contrast, we regularly left the print shop with filthy hands and heads high as kites from our unaccustomed breathing in of acetone, inks, resins, and other substances in a myriad of containers marked with skulls and crossbones.

Another learning curve for the poetry students was an initiation into the time commitment involved in the serious pursuit of studio art. The typical advanced poetry workshop meets for three hours once a week; print-making courses meet for 2 and a quarter hours twice a week. Our particular course was scheduled in the mornings on Tuesdays and Thursdays, commencing at 9:30 AM; allowing poetry students to explore their consciousnesses before, say, noon was another gift of the collaboration. And while it is understood that the advanced poetry student commits a lot of out-of-workshop time to musing and writing independently, this activity can be done in coffee shops, bars, subways, or in the privacy of one's bed or bathroom. Printmaking students also devote many, many hours outside of class to generating and completing projects, but this work must be done predominantly in the print shop. Another ambivalent plus, then, for the poets was the discovery of a new (and there aren't many) 24/7 venue in Charlottesville.

Despite the fact that the studio art department had been relocated for the two years that we taught The Matrix to two ventilated, corrugated metal, temporary outposts while a new, state-of-the-art facility was being built, despite the early hour of our class, despite the time commitment and the extra work (my colleague and I both taught the course as an overload to our regular departmental course commitments), the Matrix experience was intensely rewarding. I found the printmaking students, who were used to experimentation and to thinking on their feet, to be exceptionally open to the making of poems, even though most of them had never attempted poetry writing before the start of class. Perhaps because intaglio printmaking is a "negative" art (what one etches shows up in reverse on paper; what's etched away appears dark, and vice versa), "opposite" exercises (in which students "pull" new poems off of extant ones) yielded exciting new work; similarly, write-in, erasure, and strike-through exercises used techniques familiar to the printers, who were used to staining, gesso-ing, Chine collé layering, and all manner of obscuring, illumination, and multi-valence. As part of the course, all of the students were engaged in semester-long, serial, "flood-subject" projects, both individual and collaborative. As printmaking is intrinsically serial, this aspect of the course also came naturally to the print-makers.

As the poets and printmakers collaborated over time, the poets became more comfortable with a fresh range of attitudes, vocabularies, processes, and energies. We became less anxious about "ownership" (while poets are sometimes fiercely territorial and proprietary about their productions, printmakers tend to seek ways to creatively sabotage, manipulate, and in other ways sample and become involved with each other's work) and also more comfortable with foregrounding the processes of our drafts rather than privileging the final product. Often, for example, something marvelous would result from a "mistake" that a student might make along the way—an over-bitten plate, or an aberration caused by burring or over-inking. My colleague would point to the print (and here's another exciting difference between poetry and printmaking workshops: in poetry classes, the works under discussion are passed around on discreet pieces of paper or viewed on laptop screens, while in the print shop all work on paper is posted vertically, tacked to the wall, for the community to see) and say, look, that's exciting. Now figure out how to do that deliberately.

We talked a lot, as we worked together, about "the stain" and about defacement, about the line, about the bleed. All of these printmaking phenomena, new to us poets, had exciting parallels and possibilities in poems. Crucially, we learned about and made paper. We also learned to create, stitch, and bind folios. We dyed endpapers and covered and glued and pressed hardcovers. For one book project, we were privileged to work with a metal artist, who showed us how to use gilt and lapis to emboss a front cover. I doubt that any poet participating in the Matrix course now looks at or handles a book without thinking of its materiality and its making. Printmaking discourse also provided the poets with a trove of new words, all, again, with suggestive resonances in poems, as well, terms and phrases such as false bite, bon à tirer, burin, mezzotint, criblé, creeping bite, and retroussage.

Of the many gifts of the printmaking experience for poets in the Matrix class, perhaps chief among them was the reminder to writers working primarily in digital media (computer and other virtual type) that writing is, or can be, drawing. And lines drawn by hand, whether etched into a metal plate or scrawled across the blue staves of a Moleskine notebook— forays made into the matrix— possess an inimitable warmth and immediacy of expression and effect. Printmaking reminded us to attend to the ghost, to the mark, of what Keats called our "living hand" in our poetic efforts. The materiality of our techniques was revealed to us anew with each pull of a print, each dip of the plate into its acid bath, opening us up to the crucial connection, in all art, between idea and praxis, and, importantly, to the power of mistake, flaw, and the grace of a hand-made thing.

BRIAN TEARE

Hello

> But we would rather believe that music is beyond any
> analogy with word language…
> —Ives, *Essays Before a Sonata*

—interval   from felt

to string   a struck

ear's   the soul's seat

set ringing   —easy

    now   song   has a few rights   can break

    a law   if it likes   if our ear veers   hymnward

    it won't wear   no ribbon   to match its voice

—intellect is never

a whole   soul

finds things there

    —must a song   always

    be a song

    some

    in this book   can't be sung

LISA RUSS SPAAR   227

Charles Ives (1874 – 1954) was a prolific modern American composer of striking originality who, like his poetic contemporary Wallace Stevens, made a successful living as an insurance executive. Influenced by and experimenting alike with popular and sentimental parlor songs, polyrhythms, brass bands, tone clusters, and dissonance, Ives worked largely below the radar during most of his life, though his pieces garnered the respect of Aaron Copeland, Arnold Schoenberg, and others, and made possible the later experiments of artists like John Cage. Reportedly as humble and humorous as he was artistically ardent and intrepid, Ives, when he won the Pulitzer Prize for Music in 1947, gave away the award money, saying "prizes are for boys, and I'm all grown up."

Poet Brian Teare, whose evocative, playfully serious lyric and textual experiments I have followed for some years, is an innovator of this order, and his attraction to Ives, who shared Teare's interest in musical / textual sampling and quotation and his passion for the American, and particularly the "New Englandly," context (both Teare and Ives, for instance, have written about Thoreau, Emerson, and other Transcendentalists), makes sense. Ives's biographer Jan Swafford writes, "Filled with quotes of music from Beethoven to Stephen Foster and American hymnodists, Ives's mature work is music about music, or rather music as a symbol of human life and striving and spirituality." Teare's poems, whose original spin on field poetics makes startling use of the hungering page, acoustically and visually, seem to me to be poetry about poetry, about the relationship of music to song, song to text, song to song, and as work which represents, as Ives said of his own compositions in a prose piece accompanying a privately printed song collection, *114 Songs*, "marks of respect and expression."

This poem's title, "Hello," invites us, genially, generously, into the poem's field, and as the reader registers its salutation and traverses the white space drop to the poem's first "mark"—an em dash fused to the world "interval"—we already know that the poem will show us how to "read" it as we go, through its process, and that it will concern itself, among other things, with the gap between sound and meaning, music and "word language." In a humorous meta-joke, "Hello" also samples from the well-known Tin Pan Alley tune, "Hello! Ma Baby," a musical quotation Ives himself borrowed and worked into a composition, "Central Park in the Dark." What follows on the page is what Robert Duncan might call "composition by field," with the very particular effect of what Donald Wellman and others have termed "scored speech."

One thing I admire about Teare's lyricism is his rare use of the first-person pronoun. The "speaker" here has a distinct, playful, idiomatic, vernacular, intimate voice that is interior and musing,

   ... —easy

now   song   has a few rights   can break

a law   if it likes   if our ear veers   hymnward

it won't wear   no ribbon   to match its voice,

but the sensibility, the tone, is plural rather than singular. Formally, in fact, the poem comes to us on the page in "tone clusters" (Ives used his fists at times when playing the piano to achieve this effect), and it samples amply from Ives's own writings, weaving those perceptions in among Teare's own, yoking music's abstraction to the palpable veering of the ear. At play in the field of this poem are the ghosts not only of Ives, but of Dickinson, Susan Howe, Gertrude Stein (a song is a song is a song), Plath, Stevens, Yeats, Frank O'Hara, Thoreau, Pound (who was it that said that "Ezra is a crowd"?), and many others. And if this rich tapestry seems anachronistic, it is all the more true to Ives's, and Teare's, intentions. "Intellect is never / a whole," the poem tells us. "[S]oul / finds things there."

Teare's poem is replete with found and revelatory riches, among them a suggestion of what may ultimately be beyond translation: "the soul's seat / set ringing." As Ives writes of one of his "unperformable" songs, "Should it not have a chance to sing to itself, if it can sing?" The poem ends with a question that is at the heart of poetics ("—must a song   always / be a song") followed by a statement ("some / in this book   can't be sung") that is not so much an answer as an acknowledgment that each century's inherited artistic legacies and contributions, in and across genres and disciplines, don't solve anything as much as they take up and extend questions we never tire of trying to answer.

SRIKANTH REDDY

from Voyager

Is is.

There is no distinction.

One.

He records his name on a gold medallion.

Two.

The philosopher must say is.

The world is legion.

The self is a suffering form.

Is is.

Waves rise and fall, but the sea remains.

Srikanth Reddy's recent book of poems, *Voyager* (University of California Press, 2011), from which this passage is excerpted, takes its title from the Voyager spacecraft, launched in 1977, just four years after the poet's birth, which carried with it, as it explored the far reaches of the solar system and beyond, a gold-plated audio-visual disc that included— in addition to scientific data, and photographs— recordings of natural earth phenomena, and spoken greetings from world leaders like Jimmy Carter and then UN Secretary-General Kurt Waldheim.

For his *Voyager* "erasure" project, Reddy chose to engage with an extant memoir, *In the Eye of the Storm*, written and published in 1985 by Kurt Josef Waldheim, who served as Secretary-General of the United Nations from 1972-1981 and whose alleged collaborations with genocidal war crimes during the Second World War (details which Waldheim suppressed and misrepresented in his autobiography and elsewhere) have made him a controversial figure.

The formal restraint Reddy gave himself for this endeavor was to read through Waldheim's book three times, word by word, erasing language in order to unearth a poem within the original memoir. Reddy repeated the process twice more, and the resulting three "books" of *Voyager* are the fruits of this method (readers can read more about the making of Reddy's *Voyager* at http://tiny.cc/voyagermethod). Reddy was strict about resisting the temptation to add language of his own as he excavated; he wanted to see what various narratives the same text might yield.

Because Waldheim's involvement with war crimes include those of omission—that is, Waldheim failed to speak out against the atrocities in his awareness—Reddy has said that working with Waldheim's "ethical shadow" and his "autobiographical" text provided Reddy with "a way into the problem of composing a new text of our world….I have come to feel that the world enters into awareness most fully only when its existence is doubted. As a skeptical method, erasure deletes the objects blocking our horizon so that the world may reappear, or be seen once again, rising like a strange new moon beyond that horizon." Interestingly, according to Reddy, "just as Waldheim was a shadow haunting my imagination, I began to see my own silhouette embedded within Waldheim's purgatorial words. So I decided to paint my own self-portrait through erasure as well," something Reddy offers—prose meditations on autobiography, silence, and accountability—in part three of the new book.

For Reddy, as with other artists engaged in erasure work—among them Tom Phillips, Jesse Glass, and Jen Bervin—"acts of art," as Heather McHugh puts it, "are already editorial acts. We select as soon as we say or see. The holes seem as powerful as the fillings." Texts in which language is obscured or falls silent excite us with their missing testimony, the undeniable, almost erotic power of what is hidden, a space into which the reader irresistibly enters. We feel this not only in the material of poets and visual artists working self-consciously with erasure, but in ancient texts which have been fragmented by the ravages of time and weather (the rotted papyruses of Sappho and Archilochus, for instance, or the incomplete letter/ poem drafts of Emily Dickinson). Reddy's poems in *Voyager* have about them, then, not only the deliberate fragmentation of modern work, but the ancient sense of unearthing or making a fragment from a whole. A new whole from a hole, so to speak. The "new text" for a new world that Reddy speaks of earlier.

The reader is struck by the force of omission in the excerpt from Voyager given here, which seems to offer, in part, an account of the recording Waldheim makes for the Voyager golden record ("He records his name on a gold medallion"). The fragment begins with "is" in an odd phrase, "Is is," which evokes for the reader the more familiar "*It* is"—with "it," in this construction, being a pronoun with no antecedent, a move Dickinson deploys to great effect in many of her poems, a reminder that what concerns her (and Reddy) is not the cause but the effect, the aftermath, of the unnamed precipitating event. Reddy's construction creates a kind of visual static, addressing Waldheim and his own erasures of what was, what went down, what eluded and eludes testimony.

That the pronoun becomes a being verb acting as a subject is unsettling and thrilling: "Is is. / There is no distinction." No distinction between…noun and verb? antecedent and being? prior and now? Under close interrogation, "is," a verb of being signifying existence (the "I was here," of Waldheim's recording), comes under intense pressure. We learn that "The philosopher must say *is*," that "the world *is* legion," and that the "self *is* a suffering form." The movement of this small word, in Reddy's redaction of these passages, from philosopher to world to self, and from isolated word-as-word to predicate adjective ("legion") to predicate nominative ("suffering form") and then back to "Is is," highlights issues of identity that must have haunted Waldheim and that most certainly obsess Reddy as he portrays (and defaces, as Paul De Man would say) "*his* Waldheim," while at the same time revealing/concealing him*self*.

Such slippage or fracturing of identity and representation, addressed by Jerome Rothenberg in 1977 ("New Models, New Visions"), is achieved by just this kind of poetry of experimentation with "open forms": "The action hereafter is 'between' and 'among,'" the forms hybrid and vigorous and pushing always towards and actual and new completeness." One also thinks of Hopkins's notions of "inscape"—a version of Duns Scotus's belief in the unique essence of every living entity. "Is is."

Of course, there is a narrative here that reaches beyond the fictions of Waldheim and Reddy. We, all of us, despite our ambitions, our wish for distinction, to be "coined" and replicated and honored, are just alike, across time, across cultures, across inventions of identity, in our not lasting. The philosopher says so; the world is rife with this knowledge. We register its truth in our inner selves each day. Like waves, our public and private identities may "rise and fall." Like the sea (and who cannot hear the echoes of Hart Crane's "Voyages" here, with its "new thresholds, new anatomies"), however, our *self*, a suffering form, remains, abides, sustains, for better or worse. Read as a time capsule, Reddy's redacted "fragment" of our humanity gets to the gist of these paradoxes: we rise, we fall, we abide, we disappear. Through Reddy's "erasures" and the negative capabilities of his excavated text we feel, even if we cannot see, what's missing, what's gone—into outer space, into self-denial, into the ironies of history and of the role between the wielders of pens and of swords. We find ourselves—culpable, impressionable, alive—in the human space he has created.

BIN RAMKE

Cloud as an Open Set Maps onto the Hillside

under which we do and did sit
smelling the clover
then plucked
a stem which we would knot and
interlace with
another stem forming
a chain of clover in simple knots
as each cloud
of clover blossom
desiccates it loses something life
some of us grew
tired of the game arose
and returned home green stains
on our clothes
were not a problem no one's
mother noticed that night before dinner.

Were we in any way under the cloud
or under
the shadow of the cloud
the angle of sunlight against us
sharpening as
evening progressed
what is *under* is it a vision?

Hausdorff Spaces

It was like being inside a parachute
after landing—assuming survival—
the collapsing textures with light
shining through and the rotating
earth beneath you benign again.
He said. He had been loved.

A separation axiom, he said, has nothing
to do with love. Metrization, o love,
turns distance into desire, space into

place without distance. She is there
I am here but there, he explained,
being bounded but not totally bounded.
You had to be there, we said to each other.

But to be above yet falling, to be falling yet
to be unafraid, to be unafraid yet to know
reasons for fear, to be secure in knowledge
yet to respect ignorance as a kind of home:

This is not a lecture, he said, it is lunch.
He reached across her hands for wine
to pour for her, for her alone in her neighborhood.

Jokes about soft-sole shoes, thick glasses, and pocket protectors aside, anyone who has seen Max Fischer's math problem-solving fantasy scene in Wes Anderson's *Rushmore* or exulted in genius Will Hunting's stealth algebraic graph theory decoding missions while serving as a janitor at MIT in the eponymous film *Good Will Hunting* knows that mathematical ability holds a visceral appeal and powerful allure in our culture. One might also think of Roland "Prez" Pryzbylewski, Baltimore city cop turned junior high mathematics teacher, who, in season 4 of *The Wire*, teaches his ghetto students probability lessons that they then use to win craps games and score cheddar in the streets. A gift for math, it seems, is almost better than requited love. Not that the two conditions are unrelated. As my daughter once reassured me while she was still in high school, "Mom, don't worry. We all think smart is sexy."

And just as experts in STEM (science, technology, engineering, and mathematics) fields are often eager to apply their knowledge interdisciplinarily, poets, being magpies, are wont to appropriate concepts understood and even partially understood fundamentals from scientific and mathematical disciplines and discourses in service of their own work as well. For a while, in fact, it seemed impossible to pick up a current poetry quarterly or journal that did not contain at least one poem making a reference to Möbius strips or fractal geometries.

Not that poets writing about mathematics is a new phenomenon. In her article "Poetry Inspired by Mathematics," Sarah Glaz (herself a poet), suggests a common ancestry for the two disciplines. "Writing and numbers, and by extension—literature and mathematics," she writes, grew out of "a need to keep track of a growing quantity of riches, in particular grain and cattle," and the several examples she offers and to which she alludes include an ancient, anonymous Sumerian temple hymn (c. 1800 BC), Pablo Neruda's "To Numbers" (in which he writes about "the thirst to know how many"), Samuel Taylor Coleridge's "A Mathematical Problem" (Glaz says the poet is "moved into verse by a beautiful geometric proof"), and Ted Munger and Jeremy Teitelbaum's limericks inspired by Fermat's Last Theorem. In "Mathematics in Poetry," JoAnne Growney not only notes a number of poems that borrow mathematical subjects and imagery (pieces by Rita Dove, Howard Nemerov, Wisława Szymborska, and Wallace Stevens, among others) but also cites poems, pieces by Lewis Carroll, for example, that employ mathematical processes and structures as well.

Bin Ramke is a poet who does both—that is, many of his poems employ mathematical discourse and imagery, but also borrow from mathematical concepts and forms. The fact that he appears to really walk his talk in his mathematically inspired poems may owe to his early training in the subject. When he was sixteen, he attended a National Science Foundation Program at the University of Texas, where the famous topologist R. L. Moore taught him a bit about point-set topology. Ramke writes, "Many years later I realized how much his famous 'Moore method' was like a poetry writing workshop—and indeed even though I abandoned the study of mathematics for that of poetry, I have recently moved back into thinking and reading about mathematics as part of my thinking about poetry. This is due also to my reading Barry Mazur's discussions of image and mathematical objects."

As someone who never made it past Algebra III and Trigonometry in 11th grade, and who was for many years annually seized by panic at my children's Back-to-School nights whenever I'd enter the math classroom to find that the teacher had scribbled on the blackboard a problem for us parents to solve, I can't pretend to appreciate all of the registers on which these two poems by Ramke are working. But even with my rudimentary knowledge of topology (< Gk *topos*, a place and *logy*, study of, *logos*, word)—which my *Webster's* tells me is, in relation to math, the study of those properties of geometric figures that remain unchanged even when under distortion, so long as no surfaces are torn—I can intuit that "Cloud as an Open Set Maps onto the Hillside" ("under which we do and did sit") plays with notions of nostalgia, time, rupture, continuity, and connectivity in ways that are not merely theoretical but are personal as well, notions that are reinforced by musical clover "chains" of connected and eroded vowels and consonants. The geometrical figure the poem presents—the triangulation of cloud, child, and shadow—is an archetypal one over which float myths pre- and post-Lapsarian. Finally, the poem is a meditation on "under"—what does it mean to be beneath a cloud or shadow, phenomena that are themselves conjured out of ephemeral conspiracies of elements? Does it mean to be within? And within what? Is childhood, memory, the past measurable, substantial? or is it a dream? "What is *under*," Ramke asks at the poem's conclusion, evoking proofs as well as intuitions, "is it a vision?"

"Hausdorff Spaces" strikes me as an even more deeply personal poem than "Cloud as an Open Set Maps onto the Hillside." According to Wikipedia, a Hausdorff space (named for Felix Hausdorff, a founder of topology), "is a topological space in which distinct points have disjoint neighbourhoods….It implies the uniqueness of limits of sequences, nets, and filters. Intuitively, the condition is illustrated by the pun that a space is Hausdorff if any two points can be 'housed off' from each other by open sets." Hausdorff spaces sound a lot to me like instances of Keatsian negative capability. They also sound a lot like the condition of being in human relationships.

Ramke's poem opens with a description so ecstatic that the unnamed antecedent for "it" begs to be *love*: the experience of falling into it ("assuming survival"), of being in it, of being distinct within it. The poem itself becomes, in such a reading, both a description of that experience—to find oneself "in" love, "to be above yet falling, to be falling yet / to be unafraid, to be unafraid yet to know / reasons for fear, to be secure in knowledge / yet to respect ignorance as a kind of home"—and a kind of wooing through the tropes of topology, a wooing that is both self-conscious and even deeply humorous:

A separation axiom, he said, has nothing
to do with love. Metrization, o love,
turns distance into desire, space into
place without distance. She is there
I am here but there, he explained,
being bounded but not totally bounded.
You had to be there, we said to each other.

Love, after all, made apposite to "metrization" by our narrator, is what "turns distance into desire, space into / place without distance. She is there / I am here but there, he explained, / being bounded but not totally bounded." Anne Carson, in *Eros the Bittersweet*, writes about love and math, as well, saying that "the ruse of the triangle is not a trivial mental maneuver. We see in it the radical constitution of desire….Triangulation makes both [lovers] present at once by a shift of distance, replacing erotic action with a ruse of heart and language." The final triangular figure and gesture of Ramke's poem—

This is not a lecture, he said, it is lunch.
He reached across her hands for wine
to pour for her, for her alone in her neighborhood.

—strikes me as a deeply realized dramatization of the human, poetic dimension of mathematics and of the related, figurative "reach" of Eros.

LISA RUSS SPAAR   237

HANK LAZER

Two Poems

N18P60

Transcription
(notebook page size: 5 ¼ " X 8")

we will speak to each other reporting
what we think story of our wandering
as written in the books
speaking to each other
listening so as to arrive at
a few sustaining questions
these the simple
furnishings in the house of the voice

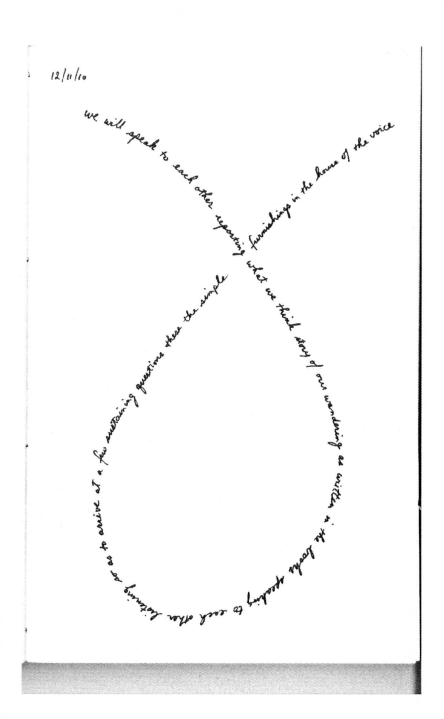

N18P64

Transcription
(notebook page size: 5 ¼ " X 8")

only to the high tower climb mistaken story of the young
when the sought for vision comes from a quiet settled moment of being here

keeper of the basic
words of their circling
keeper of their steady circulation basic words such simple
things from time to time return us to
the saying & the singing give voice to the basis of our
being here simple enigma whispering is whispering this

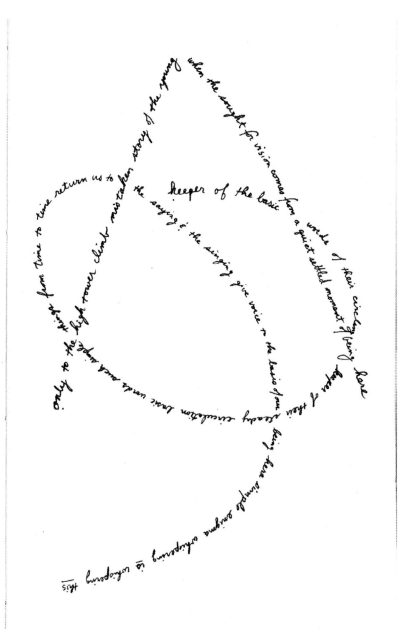

Always interested in giving himself creative, often cross-disciplinary challenges, critic, essayist, and poet Hank Lazer set out on October 8, 2006, to fill as many notebooks as could be completed during the time it took him to read Heidegger's *Being & Time*, with Heidegger's two titular themes presiding at the heart of Lazer's project. The first phase of the Notebook project took two and a half years and led him through ten notebooks of varying sizes and materiality. Working by hand in what might be called a "concrete" mode, Lazer says that he allowed the dimensions of each new "space" to suggest "a relationship of black and white on the page— and then [I would] write words to actualize the shape as envisioned. The shape of the notebook itself is always a crucial factor in the composition. I never work from drafts. I see the page and its shaped writing, and I begin writing; I think of these compositions as improvisations. I immediately write the words to the specifications of the envisioned page." After completing Heidegger's book, Lazer didn't feel ready to abandon his own "shape-writing" project, and so he embarked on phase two, linked to a reading of works by Heidegger's student Emmanuel Levinas. The two poems presented here are from this second phase of the project. An interview with Lazer about the project may be found at Charles Bernstein's Jacket 2: http://jacket2.org/commentary/furnishings-house-voice-interview-hank-lazer

Reading the autograph notebook pages of these two poems (which strike me very much as companion pieces, drawn from the same emotional, linguistic, and spiritual matrix) is a bit like walking a labyrinth—an experience both solitary and communal. The "voice" in each is plural, peripatetic, almost choral. Vatic and human. Urgent yet also calm. And concerned with the crucial relationship between story and voice. In particular, I'm drawn to their preoccupations with wandering/seeking and the simple/basic notions of *is*-ness and *this*-ness and their relationship to myth. In an essay "Poetry & Myth," Lazer writes, with regard to Robert Duncan, "I recognize a general uneasiness of many contemporary innovative poets (particularly Language poets) with myth. Within current experimental poetries, Duncan, somewhat like Charles Olson, is a difficult figure. Often, contemporary innovative poetries exhibit a textualized coolness, an ironized distance instead of the intense emotional directness of Duncan's poetry….[T]he reception and continuation of Duncan's writing is often accompanied by an evasion of his active emphasis on spirit, myth, emotional intensity, his affirmation of the heart and of love, and his generally romantic version of the artist/poet." I'd like to suggest that something similar is also happening in these poems, which frankly address somatic ardor and appetite as well as a keen interest in "the quest" or the Way. Unless I'm mistaken, I sense a spiritual joy, a spiritual "play" in the Notebook project that affects me as part of a devotional if not a religious practice or sojourning.

N18P60 ("we will speak to each other reporting"), for example, looks to me a bit like the Icthus and Darwin (or my favorite, the Gefilte) symbols that grace the backs of automobiles—and certainly there is a sense of primordial origin about the poem's shape. One can imagine speakers starting from each of the two "ends"— one at "we" and the other at "voice"—two principle sources of identity and being that cross paths at the junctures of "reporting / what" and "simple / furnishing"— recounting as they travel the "story of our wandering / as written in the books / speaking to each other / listening so as to arrive at / a few sustaining questions / these the simple / furnishings in the house of the voice." Lazer's poem, in which one can feel the engine of the pen on paper just as one feels the humble authority and inevitability of the brush in the strokes of Zen calligraphy, is almost magically of two minds, its threading making a tongue, ending and beginning its conflated origins in white space, at the brink or edge of the "listening" that "furnish[es]" the voice of our living and that will lead us to the essential questions that sustain.

Lazer takes up similar material in N18P64 ("only to the high tower climb mistaken story of the young"). Visually, this poem could be an ideogram for "life," showing us the idealistic climbing of the "mistaken story of the young," followed by the truth of descent, the coming down on the other side of the mountain (again, a nod to Zen thinking) toward "a quiet settled moment of being here." But there is nothing entirely settled about this gently shimmering poem, which evokes molecular kinesis and tethering, turns and returning. It is "here" that is the "keeper" of words, the simple things that "from time to time return us to / the saying and the singing" and which "give voice to the basis of our / being here." And the "here" is also very much the poem itself, the making of the poem, its trajectory and its crossings. Just as "simple" tropes "enigma," acoustically, "this" contains "is"— being, Lazer says, is intrinsic and it is mysterious. His visible language furnishes the house of the voice by arriving always at questions that leave his big themes—being, time, existence, infinity, language, duration, "beyonding"— more deeply felt by their absence, a palpability made possible by Lazer's material scorings.

YE CHUN

from Map

2. Gushui, Luoyang

Green tea for night, red for day.
The sun presses my temples as my father's high bike
draws another street to the east.
The sparrow I caught with a basket, twig, rope and wheat
shoots arrows at me with a slant eye.
A tadpole between my sole and sandal.
I've learned to hold a brush tight
so the teacher behind my back can't snatch it.
The ink splashes on my stiff white shirt.

> White goat's hair
> black rabbit's hair
> yellow weasel's hair
> Master Fu Shan
> says: *better ugly*
> *than charming*
> *better broken*
> *than sleek*
> *better natural*
> *than arranged*
> This is a brush
> or a cut-off finger
> That is a character
> or a pried-out eye

8. Aransas Pass, Texas

Your hair veins the setting sun. Love slashes
in my body. If the world is a crystal glass
and the dolphin its humming, why so much red?
Shall we close our eyes and walk
into the water of red swords? Shall we hold
a green flame between our eyes to see,
burn our hands into each other's back

to push, to reach? Shall we say
loneliness as the dolphin curves its echo
above the water and the water drinks us?

> This mantle
> dazzles the eye
> with train tracks
> water wakes
> game boards
> letters
> numbers
> tortoise shells
> and men in hunting
> sports
> business
> war
> A shaman's cloth
> priest's vest
> royal garment
> an offering
> Such warmth
> inside the body

9. Guangzhou

In the bus jam, you lean against a smog-dyed building,
your body shrunk, bare gums grinding, eyes darting as people
in their own restlessness float by. If only I could lead you,
hold onto the next morning and hold you
with the other hand, if only I knew the safe land—
the world terrifies me too, the world that is no
stranger than before. Tonight my nine-year-old niece wonders
if the sun will eat the earth. Will the moon
shake off the dust and shine for us.

> the bud
> and its masks—
> Typhoon, bug
> mushroom bark…
> How many
> shades of black
> can you see
> How many

mildew lines
used to be rain
The cat
they are eating
has one big eye
one small
A heart waits
on a doorway
and expands

In Bento's Sketchbook: (How does the impulse to draw something begin?), English art critic, author, and artist John Berger writes that "[w]e who draw do so not only to make something visible to others, but also to accompany something invisible to its incalculable destination." He goes on to point out drawing's shared impulses with map-making: "Drawing is a form of proving. And the first generic impulse to draw derives from the human need to search, to plot points, to place things and to place oneself."

The three lyrics by visual artist, poet, translator, and novelist Ye Chun featured here come from a nine-part series called "Map." In an interview with *Cerise Press,* Ye explains that the sequence was inspired by an assignment in an art class for which students were asked to draw a map of their hometown: "After I finished the assignment, I thought of other places I'd lived. What if I made a map for each of them, with words instead of pencil and paint? I started to write a poem sequence titled 'Map,' in which each poem is a place and consists of two stanzas—the one on the left pockets traces of experience; the one on the right serves as notes on the experience. Together they work like lines of latitude and longitude to locate the experience."

Studded with precise, sensory detail, leavened by wunderkammer cataloguing, and animated by subtle syntactic shuttling and haunted, moving shifts in scale and perspective, Ye's ideogrammatic "maps" render their various places in a way that, as Berger suggests, not only evokes literal, remembered locations but also partakes in the mysteries of habitation, of what shelters, moors, and moves us to our "incalculable destination." These are landscapes of the heart and mind, akin to W. G. Sebald's dérive psycho-geographical forays in works like *The Emigrants.* In "Gushui, Luoyang," an early poem in the sequence, for example, Ye's child-speaker, like the "tadpole between my sole and sandal," is caught between worlds, part natal water, part terra firm—the territory between early childhood and an incipient awareness of the speaker's life as a calligrapher ("beautiful writer"):

I've learned to hold a brush tight
so the teacher behind my back can't snatch it.
The ink splashes on my stiff white shirt.

As Ye gently shakes the gold-pan of memory, luminous relics flicker, each
establishing emotional terrain through the diction of situation and the coordinates
of time and space—the diurnal/nocturnal evocations of "Green tea for night, red
for day," for instance, and the compass points suggested by "The sun presses my
temples as my father's high bike / draws another street to the east." A sparrow the
speaker has captured "with a basket, twig, rope and wheat" sends out centrifugal
"arrows at me with a slant eye." Significant is the way Ye makes the *drawing out*
of these recollections inseparable from literal drawing/writing. Moving fluidly
between panoramic and close-up, unfettered and claustral imagery, Ye registers the
world in her body, the "stiff white shirt" of the page. The longitudinal "notes" that
accompany the rhapsodic latitudinal reverie of this poem follow a catalog of the
speaker's calligraphy brush hair types with an ars poetica:

> Master Fu Shan
> says: *better ugly*
> *than charming*
> *better broken*
> *than sleek*
> *better natural*
> *than arranged*
> This is a brush
> or a cut-off finger
> That is a character
> or a pried-out eye,

By this verbal, imaginative magic, Ye inhabits other touchstone places, unfurling
clews and webs and mazes to conjure landscapes that are lost and found, bodily
and mysterious. The ecstasies of a devotional Eros enter the sequence in part
8, "Aransas Pass, Texas": "Your hair veins the setting sun. Love slashes / in my
body." In the poem's gorgeous latitudinal invitation,

Shall we close our eyes and walk
into the water of red swords? Shall we hold
a green flame between our eyes to see,
burn our hands into each other's back
to push, to reach?,

Ye makes the reader feel the "word" embedded in her "sword." "Guangzhou," which closes Ye's nine-part "Map," takes up the rhetorical invocations and pantheistic bliss of "Aransas Pass" ("the dolphin curves its echo / above the water and the water drinks us") and extends them into a post-Lapsarian realm, an urban world tempered by awarenesses of terrors and "shades of black," but one Ye finds beautiful, nonetheless:

If only I could lead you,
hold onto the next morning and hold you
with the other hand, if only I knew the safe land—
the world terrifies me too, the world that is no
stranger than before. Tonight my nine-year-old niece wonders
if the sun will eat the earth. Will the moon
shake off the dust and shine for us.

In *Bento's Sketchbook*, Berger writes: "When I'm drawing I feel a little closer to the way birds navigate when flying, or to hares finding shelter if pursued, or to fish knowing where to spawn, or trees finding a way to the light, or bees constructing their cells….[Drawing is the] disturbance of distances. A disturbance that can only be accommodated if one takes an 'aerial' view in which kilometers become millimeters, yet in which the size of our human hearts is not reduced." Through the drift of her imagination,

> The cat
> they are eating
> has one big eye
> one small
> A heart waits
> on a doorway
> and expands,

Ye draws her protean map, whose interior delvings are as rich as her perceptions of the physical world, a realm whose immensities and minutiae, terrors and beauties, intensifications and dilations make their incalculable, wondrous, and destined way.

CABIN FEVER:
WINTER THOUGHTS
ON THE
PLACE OF POETRY

CABIN FEVER:
WINTER THOUGHTS ON THE PLACE OF POETRY

Anticipating winter, Rainer Maria Rilke begins the last stanza of his autumn poem "Herbstag" this way:

Wer jetzt kein Haus hat, baut sich keines mehr.
Wer jetzt allein ist, wird es lange bleiben,
wird wachen, lessen, lange Briefe schrieben . . . .

(Whoever now has no house, will build no more.
Whoever is alone now will stay alone,
will wait up, read, write long letters . . . .)

Gaston Bachelard, who calls winter the "oldest of the seasons," writes in *The Poetics of Space*: "Although at heart a city man, Baudelaire sensed the increased intimacy of a house when it is besieged by winter. In *Les paradis artificiels* he speaks of Thomas de Quincey's joy when, a prisoner of winter, he read Kant, with the help of the idealism furnished by opium. The scene takes place in a cottage in Wales. 'Isn't it true that a pleasant house makes winter more poetic, and doesn't winter add to the poetry of a house? The white cottage sat at the end of a *little* valley, *shut* in by *rather high* mountains; and it seemed to be *swathed* in shrubs'...And we feel warm because it is cold out-of-doors...Behind dark curtains, snow seems to be whiter. Indeed, everything comes alive when contradictions accumulate."

The way that some people browse seed catalogues or surf the Internet for good deals on February-doldrums trips to tropical locales, I find myself daydreaming in the winter months about sanctuary, houses, and in particular, lately, about images of writing huts depicted in an article, with photographs, entitled "Famous Writers' Small Writing Sheds and Off-the-Grid Huts," sent to me by a friend: http://www.re-nest.com/re-nest/email/famous-writers-small-writing-sheds-and-offthegrid-huts-140587.

From my own desk, pushed up against a window in the family laundry room that also serves as my study, grateful to be warmly sheltered, especially when so many are not, I pore with voyeuristic pleasure over the text and captioned pictures of Henry David Thoreau's famous, Spartan shack, George Bernard Shaw's well outfitted, passively solar-heated hut on his property in Hertfordshire (he called it "London" so his assistants wouldn't be lying when they reported he was away in the city), Virginia

Woolf's unheated, apple-lofted cabin-of-one's-own ("In winter it was often so bitterly cold and damp that she couldn't hold her pen and had to retreat indoors").

It goes without saying that to possess any sort of privacy for writing—to have the time and space to write poems and novels and stories at all—is a privilege and a luxury. But in my spell of winter reverie, I find myself particularly drawn to the images (and my concurrent conjuring) of the *interiors* of these writers' huts, and in particular to the objects (or lack thereof)—talismans, photographs, stones, wall art, souvenirs, tools of the trade?—with which the writers "furnished" and cluttered their intimate work sites. A punctum for me in the photograph of Dahl's cottage, "Gipsy House," for instance, is the electronic pencil sharpener, poised and ready as a small cannon on the table, within arm's reach of the wing-back writing chair beside it. In the shot of "London," a pair of large metal shears and wicker waste basket seem alive with waiting; Dylan Thomas's desk chair, with its missing back-slats, invites the Modigliani torso hung on the wall to take a seat.

Museums, libraries, private collections, and on-line websites are replete with the ephemera of famous writers, and the allure of these quotidian relics—charged as they seem to be with something of the mystique, presence, and creative force of the lives with which they are associated— is undeniable. At the Free Library in Philadelphia, for example, one can find Charles Dickens's pocket compass and bedside candlestick; in Amherst, Massachusetts, a visitor to the Emily Dickinson Museum can view one of Dickinson's famous white dresses, and the Amherst College library holds a lock of Emily Dickinson's hair, still auburn when she died in her mid-fifties. Once some years ago I stood before a glass case at the Pierpont Morgan Library, gazing in awe at Charlotte Brontë's tiny gloves ("less than half as broad as a modern female hand, and their fingers are scarcely thicker than a pencil," wrote Michael Frank in a review of the exhibit for *The New York Times*). One on-line collector catalogues, among other "Stuff I stole from Allen Ginsberg's Apartment," "one flesh-colored bandage, one prescription bottle of Prednisone ('when needed for severe gout', 9 tablets still remaining in bottle), and one 9" long, 1 ½" thick slightly curved and somewhat abraded candle." And at our own Special Collections Library here at the University of Virginia, one can view, in addition to Queen Victoria's cat's hairs, Sylvia Plath's Rinehart edition of Whitman's *Leaves of Grass* (1953) in which, beside his suicide passage in *Song of Myself,*

The suicide sprawls on the bloody floor of the bedroom,
I witness the corpse with its dabbled hair. I note where the pistol has fallen,

she has underlined "witness" and "note" and below this writes "but doesn't understand." Plath underlines the word "understand."

The ephemera of literary lives don't always have anything directly to tell us about literature, although sometimes they do. As Michael Frank says in his piece on the Brontë exhibit at the Morgan Library, "Charlotte Brontë's hands, which the gloves convey by proxy, hold a special place in her psychology. They were the one physical feature the writer exempted from what she described to her friend and future biographer, Elizabeth Gaskell, as her 'almost repulsive' plainness....These hands were the instrument, fed by her vigorous imagination, that produced the famous juvenilia that enlivened the unusual Yorkshire childhood Charlotte shared with her siblings....These hands also, of course, fashioned the fiction that defined Charlotte in her maturity, and they were responsible for the correspondence that connected her to worlds beyond her father's parsonage at Haworth, where she lived her whole life. Charlotte's hands were her liberators; they lifted her to fame and a measure of happiness."

Bachelard writes, "Great images have both a history and a prehistory; they are always a blend of memory and legend....Indeed, every great image has an unfathomable oneiric depth to which the personal past adds special color....Primal images....give us back areas of being, houses in which the human being's certainty of being is concentrated, and we have the impression that, by living in such images as these, in images that are as stabilizing as these are, we could start a new life, a life that would be our own, that would belong to us in our very depths." Perhaps we are attracted, if we are, to the writing spaces and everyday objects connected with writers we admire because they "give us back areas of being" and create a space, a sanctuary, within us that is newly spacious and inspired.

And so, in my winter, cabin fever-dream state, I find myself conjuring some imaginary ephemera, images I associate with poets I love, objects real and imagined. Things I would like to see: William Blake's last pencil (the one he sent for on his death-bed so that he could draw his beloved Catherine before he died, singing). Frank O'Hara's copy of Pierre Reverdy (the book the speaker of "A Step Away from Them" tucks into his pocket—"My heart is in my / pocket, it is Poems by Pierre Reverdy"). Elizabeth Bishop's tin shampoo basin. Whitman's sprig of live oak with moss. A feather from the golden-crested wren that got into Hopkins's room at St. Mary's Hall, Stonyhurst College, "at night and circled round dazzled by the gaslight on the white ceiling" before Hopkins caught it in his hands and set it free. Emily Brontë running.

CARL PHILLIPS

My Meadow, My Twilight

> Sure, there's a spell the leaves can make, shuddering,
> and in their lying suddenly still again – flat, and still,
> like time itself when it seems unexpectedly more
> available, more to lose therefore, more to love, or
> try to...
>   But to look up from the leaves, remember,
> is a choice also, as if up from the shame of it all,
> the promiscuity, the seeing-how-nothing-now-will-
> save-you, up to the wind-stripped branches shadow-
> signing the ground before you the way, lately, all
> the branches seem to, or you like to say they do,
> which is at least half of the way, isn't it, toward
> belief – whatever, in the end, belief
>   is...You can
> look up, or you can close the eyes entirely, making
> some of the world, for a moment, go away, but only
> some of it, not the part about hurting others as the one
> good answer to being hurt, and not the part that can
> at first seem, understandably, a life in ruins, even if –
> refusing ruin, because you
>   can refuse – you look
> again, down the steep corridor of what's just another
> late winter afternoon, dark as night already, dark
> the leaves and, darker still, the door that, each night,
> you keep meaning to find again, having lost it, you had
> only to touch it, just once, and it bloomed wide open...

The gorgeous, syntactically intricate poems of Carl Phillips strike me as always haunted to some extent by an autumnal, adumbrated sensibility, a subtlety of consciousness in intimate argument with its own tangential forays and asides into volition, rhetoric, and refusal. His is a "knowing" poised on the glinting knife-edge verge of disclosure, of revelation. "My Meadow, My Twilight" is a stately, elegant poem, whose nuanced, deftly fulfilled, roughly six-stress lines evoke the hexameter of the Sibylline Oracles, fitting for this fresh take on an ancient subject: the extent to which divination and oracle, or a belief in signs, can or should govern a life. The reader is almost compelled to *sing* Phillips's poem, nodding as it does, as well, to Gerard Manley Hopkins's own enormous sonnet on a similar theme, "Spelt From

Sibyl's Leaves," about which Hopkins wrote: "It is, as living art should be, made for performance and that…performance is not reading with the eye but loud, leisurely, poetical (not rhetorical) recitation, with long rests, long dwells on the rhyme and other marked syllables, and so on. This sonnet should be almost sung: it is most carefully timed in tempo rubato."

Yet Phillips begins in a responsive rather than a vatic mode, as though acknowledging a theory or statement, uttered off-stage, and then countering it with that wonderfully colloquial first word, "sure," the deceptively off-hand vernacular of which urges us to lean in and attend to the "spell the leaves can make, shuddering, / and in their lying suddenly still again." By line two we're already deeply into the magic Phillips makes out of figuration and the inverted trellis of his sentences— okay, the poet says, sure, sometimes there can be a mysterious motion in the world that, when it stops, suddenly makes us believe that something profound has occurred, that time itself is "unexpectedly more / available [to us], more therefore to love, or / try to…." This in itself is a stunning metaphysical perception, but Phillips presses further, reminding the reader that "to look up *from* the leaves …[emphasis mine] / is a choice also, as if up from the shame of it all, / the promiscuity, the seeing-how-nothing-now-will / save-you, up to the wind-stripped branches shadow— / signing the ground before you." With leaves strewn below us, and bare branches rather than leaves in frenzied theatrics above, the winter world, the poet posits, with its shadow-language, has its lessons to impart, as well. Or at least we "like to say [it does], / which is at least half of the way, isn't it, toward / belief – whatever, in the end, belief is."

Again, to articulate in just twelve lines several intuitions about the pitch between fate and human volition, fiction and belief, is a philosophical as well as a poetic achievement. Thrillingly, Phillips offers yet a third option for the seeker/listener, and that is to "close the eyes entirely." But even this tack, the speaker notes, will not take away those portions of ourselves, our lives, for which *we*, finally, and not some zodiacal inkling or quirk of the chthonic universe, are accountable—"the part about hurting others as the one / good answer to being hurt," for example. The poem concludes with a conflation of that inward gazing with what one presumes is the present tense setting and site of the poem's meditation—a meadow at twilight, "the steep corridor of what's just another / late winter afternoon, dark as night already, dark / the leaves and, darker still, the door that, each night, / you keep meaning to find again, having lost it, you had / only to touch it, just once, and it bloomed wide open…." That lost door—love, belonging, the womb/tomb—is something to which we have access, however elliptically, perhaps best in poems. Despite our ultimate culpability, shame, and responsibility, Phillips's speaker tells us, we can choose, we can "[refuse] ruin." We can believe in belief, those sudden moments of the world's language that amplify the self into meaning.

RAVI SHANKAR

Breast Feeding at the Blue Mosque

> Hidden from a queue to bag shoes a woman nurses a child
> under a wool scarf in the shadow two fluted minarets cast
> pitched towards incessant sun, a necessity somehow an insult
> to sharia law, no matter what sustenance a lemonwedge
> of breast, God's own, yields, puckering a tiny mouth
> until bright eyes glaze to doll loll. Fairly alien to ponder
> raw biology of milk conveyed by ducts lined with capillaries,
> made from pouring stuff of stars: nourishment that manifests
> minerals for bone from pulsing light.
>   Too close to the slickheat pushing out
> between the legs of nearly every woman not your wife
> but her as well? How could it be that her very being derives
> solely from her relation to you, that she could have no value
> in the calculus but to function as temptation, or its dome-
> blue corollary, disappointment? No cover covers up
> those integers holding the place of zeroes, Iznik tiles or after-
> life virgins. Ostrich eggs on chandeliers don't dissuade spiders.
> If the fear of the Lord is not the beginning of our wisdom,
> then *La ilah ha il Allah* is a breast in a mouth, else nothing is.

Milk may arguably be our first language and the mouth our primal mind. Women have been breast-feeding their own and others' infants presumably since the dawn of humankind, and while this act of sustenance and nurturing should seem the most natural of activities ("mammal" < L. *mamma*, breast), controversies abound across time, place, and cultures regarding who, when, where, and why women should breast-feed, particularly in public spaces.

The subject of Ravi Shankar's "Breast Feeding at the Blue Mosque" is a woman nursing her child "in the shadow two fluted minarets cast / pitched towards incessant sun" at the Sultan Ahmed Mosque (also known as the Blue Mosque because of the blue tiles and paint that embellish its interior) in Istanbul, Turkey. Out of modesty, and because she is in a public place, a site of worship and tourism, she is "hidden" out of sight of visitors lined up to bag their shoes before entering the mosque; she further conceals her suckling baby beneath a "wool scarf."

Though the poem begins descriptively, it quickly takes the shape of an argument.

By the end of line three the speaker asks how such a "necessity" could possibly be construed as an "insult / to sharia law, no matter what sustenance a lemonwedge / of breast, God's own, yields, puckering a tiny mouth / until bright eyes glaze to doll loll." *Sharia*, which means "way" or "path"—"path to the waterhole"—refers to the code of religious law or conduct in Islam. Although Muslims disagree about how to interpret the tenets of sharia, those guidelines related to breastfeeding seem especially complex, with the relationship between a woman and any child she nurses, her own or someone else's, for example, codified to the extent that any infants suckled by the same woman are considered blood relatives and cannot later marry. A fairly recent and highly controversial "adult-suckling" fatwa that encouraged women to feed their breast milk (in a glass) to unrelated adult males in order to allow them to be in one another's company received no small bit of notoriety.

After putting before the reader the dreamy, sated image of the woman's nursing child, the speaker, almost as though addressing a court of law, asks the reader to ponder, however "alien," the "raw biology of milk conveyed by ducts lined with capillaries, / made from pouring stuff of stars: nourishment that manifests / whiteness from pulsing light." The conflation of anatomical language and rapturous lyricism here is a keen move; our speaker insists not only upon the natural necessity of breastfeeding but also suggests that physical and spiritual sustenance are one. That Shankar's ecstatic, sidereal imagery could as well be describing the lustrous conical chandeliers inside the mosque, and the breast-like dome of the mosque itself, is surely no accident.

In fact breast imagery and tropes abound in the poem—those "two fluted minarets," of course, but also the shape of Shankar's poem itself: two fully lineated 9-line stanzas separated by an indented line, the volta at which Shankar's case intensifies, directing its ire to those who would find even this modest and necessary public "display" of flesh offensive and indicting larger societal gender issues as it does so: "Too close to the slickheat pushing out / between the legs of nearly every woman not your wife / but her as well? How could it be that her very being derives / solely from her relation to you, that she could have no value / in the calculus but to function as temptation, or its dome- / blue corollary, disappointment?" Shankar presses further, saying that there is no "cover" large enough to conceal the spiritual impoverishment of any system that would so utterly devalue his subject's personhood.

Shankar makes sure we're back at the mosque, with its ancient Iznik tiles and legendary, talismanic ostrich eggs put up on the chandeliers to keep away the spiders whose webs are common in mosques, to make his final point. His language of argument and proofs—*derives, value, calculus, corollary, integers, zeros*—culminates in a conditional syllogism that is also about the language of devotion: "If the fear of the Lord is not the beginning of our wisdom, / then *La ilah ha il Allah* is a breast in a mouth, else nothing is." The richly ululating texture of the Arabic in this Muslim proclamation of faith—"There is no deity except God"— is evocative of the sounds of suckling and meant to remind us that we all, men and women, are equally children of the universe, deserving of respect, dignity, the right to praise, to nurture and protect, and to be protected and nurtured, especially in our most holy places.

TALVIKKI ANSEL

Glaze

White putty under finger nails,
milky on fingerprints and the back of your t-shirt,
pushed between mullion and glass
it curls away when I press
and pull back my hand, putting the glass in
to glaze.

A pane in the bedroom
fallen onto the porch, three jagged
pieces and a handful of splinters
on grainy shingles. Sash too soaked
to set the new glass.
                    Outside in the dark,
sloppy wet lilacs. The dog restless,
cold pressing at the curtain of yellow in cloth
I sewed, too yellow, it suffuses the room.
One window with a pie-piece, broken corner
the squirrel stuck its head through
before it leaped to the apple's trunk,

the road, gallery with its paintings,
landscapes and glazed pots.
To not keep it at bay: the glaze of frost on shingles,
grass blades tipped in minty relief,
the infinite angles of trunk and leaf
and the white lilacs, Lincoln's coffin, the broken window
the wind comes through from that teeming world,
carrying the mud and salt.

I have followed with admiration the work of Talvikki Ansel ever since James
Dickey chose her first book, *My Shining Archipelago*, as the 1996 winner of the Yale
Series of Younger Poets Prize. Like other writers who hail from northern climes
(Elizabeth Bishop, Alice Munro, Edna O'Brien), Ansel marries a Dickinsonian
"New Englandly" restraint (and its attendant romance with ice, snow smoke, rocky
blue-rimed jetties) with a sensuously rendered alertness to the heated ordure of
tropical jungles, Mediterranean mythic scapes, and the mysteries of the most minute
domestic and exotic phenomena of the natural world and of the language we use

to collect and capture it. In a masterful sonnet sequence in *My Shining Archipelago*, "Afterwards: Caliban," for example, Ansel imagines Shakespeare's Caliban returned from his native paradisiacal island to the "Unclean city" streets of Elizabethan London. Worlds collide and exchange their confidences: "My island grows smaller, not Fixed / In Rhumb-lines on any Map. The Reare-mice / On leather wings, the Hedges, dissolve into / Night. My cane-taps sound far away. / What I tell you, what I tell you— / It is so much smaller than what I can not tell you."

Ansel's "Glaze," like the *glass* the title evokes ("glaze" <ME *glasen*, from glas, glass), belongs both to the world of tensile clarity and to the realm of fragility, of brokenness. The poem opens with an act of mending; the speaker is repairing a broken window. Tactile and erotic from line one ("White putty under finger nails, / milky on fingerprints and the back of your t-shirt / pushed between mullion and glass"), hers is not an easy task, but rather an endeavor involving "press / and pull"—even as the speaker pushes her material, "it curls away."

The second stanza flashes back to a time before the present-tense scene of reparation, and the "pain" implied by "[a] pane in the bedroom / fallen onto the porch, three jagged / pieces and a handful of splinters / on grainy shingles" confirms the hints offered in stanza one that more than a window has been broken and that more than a sheet of glass is being restored through the act of glazing. The sash, we learn, is at first "too soaked / to set the new glass," and thus, through an adroitly dropped line, Ansel shows how the outside can now seep in, unsettling the restive dog and pressing coldly at yellow curtains that the speaker, in yet a further past, once sewed and hung there, curtains whose new suffusion is "[t]oo yellow," the speaker says, as though (to paraphrase Dickinson) its plenty, its swollen evocation of sun, of warmth, hurts her.

It is spring in New England when the bedroom window-pane of the speaker and the "you" falls—"Outside in the dark, / [are] sloppy wet lilacs"—and the natural world is stirring again, restless, too. At the "broken corner" of the end of stanza two, even a squirrel pokes its head through the "pie-piece" opening before "[leaping] to the apple's trunk" and on into the last stanza, which floods suddenly with the "teeming world" beyond the temporarily ruptured domestic space. The eye travels from body to house to window to road to an art gallery (with its own glazed pots evoking landscapes within landscapes) to the vistas offered by the natural cycles of life and death:

…the road, gallery with its paintings,
landscapes and glazed pots.
To not keep it at bay: the glaze of frost on shingles,

grass blades tipped in minty relief,
the infinite angles of trunk and leaf
and the white lilacs, Lincoln's coffin, the broken window
the wind comes through from that teeming world,
carrying the mud and salt.

As the poem culminates, Ansel conflates Walt Whitman's famous elegy for Abraham Lincoln, "When Lilacs Last in the Dooryard Bloom'd," written shortly after the president's assassination in late April 1865 ("old farm-house near the white-wash'd palings, / . . . [and] lilac-bush tall-growing with heart-shaped leaves of rich green / / . . . A spring with its flower I break"), with her own grief, her wish to repair what has been broken in her world—some lost faith, perhaps, in wholeness, in love—in spring, in repair itself. In his poem, Whitman writes:

Ever-returning spring, trinity sure to me you bring,
Lilac blooming perennial and drooping star in the west,
And thought of him I love.

Ansel's last stanza casts the restoration of the first stanza (and of the poem itself) in a new light. We apprehend "glaze" in its various meanings—to furnish or fit with glass, to coat clearly (as with potting glaze or ice), to become glazed over—to be numb, to dream. The poem is the act of reparation, and the speaker is replacing the fallen pane with a whole one not in order to keep pain, the world, "at bay," but rather to acknowledge that what is broken and unsettled must always now be part of what she allows into her vision, her own trinity, the wind with its old news of "mud and salt": of love, of grief, of repair.

MARY ANN SAMYN

My Life in Heaven

This is a true account beginning now.

Here's a birch basket, tens of feathers, none of which will ever belong again.

This is like that, only more so.

Once I was a little girl who tried to write it.

Now I do twenty years' worth of looking every afternoon.

Like the insect that shed its *before* on the sand, and unstuck its wings, two pair.

Time can't be wasted; some changes are forever.

The lake's three greens know, and its darker churning, and its eyelet edge.

Given the chance, I'd wear that to meet you.

Mary Ann Samyn has always understood that the tongues of religious devotion and of erotic desire, at their most intense, are interchangeable. How to put into language a truth prior to or beyond human telling? "My Life in Heaven" yearns to relate a notion of paradise; whether this state is longed for or once experienced, however transiently, is moot. Almost breathlessly, rushed, the speaker attempts to convince the reader of the veracity of her rapture—"This is a true account beginning now"—yet immediately must resort to metaphor and simile, to figurative ruses, to express the ineffable. Could heaven be mere bark and feathers, she wonders, detritus of what once bloomed and flew on earth, "only more so"?

Trying again, the speaker admits that even as a girl she tried to imagine this celestial place, this ulterior prospect, and confesses that adulthood has only made her a more avid watcher for the truth of heaven's promise. Another way of reading these lines is Samyn's implication that writing is a little girl's prerogative; the older, mature (desiring?) woman does not write but rather does "twenty years' worth of looking every afternoon." Or maybe this is what the *kairos* time of paradise not only makes possible, but demands. Privileged to be caught up in a moment outside of chronological time, the speaker knows she can't waste time. How adequately to respond to such an ecstasy? Is seeing enough?

Perhaps, the poem suggests, the answer lies in transformation, in the stepping outside (ecstasy < *ex stasis*, out of stasis) of the discreet self, the shedding of our "before," and becoming something exponentially other, "two pair." From worm to wing. The poem, an ars poetica, concludes with a striking reminder that it may be only in the donning of the garment of this mystery (with its ambiguous deeps— "three greens…its darker churning, and its eyelet edge") that we can approach the "place" of the beloved, the Beloved, the Beyond.

MAURICE MANNING

Provincial Thought

We get things in our head, a sort
of wonder I suppose, a notion,
about where to stand on the hill to see
the white blur of a steeple eight
or maybe ten miles away
at the center of a country town
whose school has been consolidated,
and the little country store, where news
and gossip spread around and maybe
a local discovery was claimed
by one of the loafers there, is closed.
Going to find that spot on the hill
in order to see from a certain prospect
a world far enough away it seems
a symbol is a walk that brings
an important silence down on us.
You could say, I guess, it makes us think—
just walking up a hill to find
a part in the distance that looks familiar.
It makes me think that walking in silence
and going up to where the woods
have made an agreement to leave
an opening—that walk has become
a plain responsibility.
Yet it seems to be a kind of freedom.
One time, a pretty good while back,
I was walking up the little hill
early in the spring before
the leaves had laced the trees together,
and I looked down the hollow and saw
a solitary splay of white,
an early patch of dogwood blossom.
It looked farther away than it was;
it struck me as a symbol inside
another symbol, a silence inside
a silence, and another silence fell
on me. The blossom patch was strange,
but it reminded me of something—

an old woman's puff of breath,
or a white shadow, or maybe both.
It has seemed too much to think about,
an abundance too great for words
or the slower motions of my mind,
and that itself is now a thought,
lodged in a place of its own across
from a hill and in between a distance
of other hills and things unseen—
I've kept it there, and I will keep it,
from loyalty or sentiment
it doesn't matter, I'm keeping it.

In his essay "Tales Within Tales Within Tales" (1981), novelist John Barth writes that "we tell stories and listen to them because we live stories and live in them," and that "to cease to narrate, as the capital example of Scheherazade reminds us, is to die." Luckily most of us don't have to spin tales with the life-or-death urgency of Scheherazade, but it is true that some people are better at telling stories than the rest of us. Why do we heed certain voices, hanging on every breath, while the logorrhea of others makes us want to put the phone down on the desk and do our taxes, or suddenly remember a pressing reason—a shrink appointment, an elapsed parking meter—to absent the premises?

"Don't sit at the piano," Charles Wright has been known to say, "unless you can play." Maurice Manning, Wright's fellow Appalachian poet and kindred pilgrim spirit in the realms of faith and doubt, can play. By this, I mean that he can write. And he can tell a story. In the decade-plus-change since W. S. Merwin selected his *Lawrence Booth's Book of Visions* (2001) for the Yale Younger Poets Prize, Manning, a native Kentuckian, has, with a rare and credible humility, humor, and enviable formal mojo, authored three subsequent collections, each arrestingly fresh in its tellings. *A Companion for Owls: Being the Commonplace Book of D. Boone, Lone Hunter, Back Woodsman, &c.*, for instance, is a series of persona poems in the voice of the eponymous figure—as myth, as man, as "ground"; *Bucolics* is a kind of vernacular breviary of untitled psalm/poems addressed to someone the narrator calls "Boss." *The Common Man* is full of the stories that we house and that house us.

Taking a close look at the tune and lyrics, so to speak, of Manning's "Provincial Thought" may help account for the intimate hold his poems—seemingly simple and seemingly simply told, but concerned with complex spiritual and emotional wonderings—have over his many devoted readers. From the very start are three engaging factors—understatement, beginning with the title's "provincial" (and its implication of something local and, if not naïve, then unpretentious) and reinforced by plain speech diction and colloquial qualifiers like "sort of" and "maybe" and "seems," "I guess," and "you could say"; the patient, peripatetic pacing of the four-stress lines; and a rich mix of pronouns (we, I, you—we're all close, invested, and involved).

The story (the "thought") Manning articulates is not driven by plot; not a lot happens, at least not in any sort of real-time present, active way. A speaker (and the reader, who is invited along) climbs a hill and stands in a place that allows him to see a steeple, "maybe ten miles away," that is "at the center of a country town / whose school has been consolidated, / and the little country store, where news / and gossip spread around and maybe / a local discovery was claimed / by one of the loafers there, is closed." Like Emily Dickinson's certain slant of light, Manning's steeple is a signal of "internal difference— / Where the Meanings, are—," and these meanings, in the case of "Provincial Thought," deepen into all that the steeple signifies: the town around it ("unseen" from this distance, but nonetheless understood), the losses, closings, and changes that irrevocably alter a place and whose passing in actual time and enduring in imagination define who we are. The libretto of this song, then, is an ostinato (< Italian, "stubborn") re-turning to and exploration into the significance of

Going to find that spot on the hill
in order to see from a certain prospect
a world far enough away it seems
a symbol... ,

a recurring walk that, finally comes to feel for the speaker both like a "plain responsibility" and a "kind of freedom." It is the tune, the music, of Manning's lines, though, that lends the poem its subtle but primal magnetism, its aura of devotion. As the speaker unfolds his tale within his tale within his tale,

I looked down the hollow and saw
a solitary splay of white,
an early patch of dogwood blossom.
It looked farther away than it was;
it struck me as a symbol inside
another symbol, a silence inside
a silence, and another silence fell
on me,

it is the closely keyed modulations of the vowels that hold and patiently mold the meditation, the long "o"s in particular—*suppose, notion, loafers, closed, going, hollow, slower, own, motions*—so that the word "symbol," finally, seems itself to be a blossom patch, a puff of breath, or a white shadow, whatever it is that is "too much to think about, / an abundance too great for words / or the slower motions of my mind," an entity that "is now a thought, / lodged in a place of its own" and that, whether "from loyalty or sentiment/ it doesn't matter" (and that "from" is so accordantly placed—are we keeping the symbol *away* from loyalty or sentiment or *out* of loyalty or sentiment, or both?) is now made manifest and in safe "keeping" by the poem.

Reading the work of Maurice Manning affects me with the mysterious force I feel reading Robert Penn Warren's "Tell Me a Story": "Long ago, in Kentucky, I, a boy, stood / By a dirt road, in first dark, and heard / The great geese hoot northward...// I did not know what was happening in my heart." Penn Warren's poem ends this way:

Tell me a story.

In this century, and moment, of mania,
Tell me story.

Make it a story of great distances, and starlight.

The name of the story will be Time,
But you must not pronounce its name.

Tell me a story of deep delight.

That in our century, our moment of mania, the "provincial thought" of Maurice Manning heeds this call is ample cause for attending to Manning's poetic voice, for heeding poetry at all.

Biographical Notes

Debra Allbery (1957) is the author of several books, including *Walking Distance*, which won the Agnes Lynch Starrett Prize of the University of Pittsburgh Press. Her most recent collection, *Fimbul-Winter* (Four Way, 2010), won the Grub Street National Book Prize in poetry. She directs the Warren Wilson MFA Program for Writers near Asheville, North Carolina.

Kazim Ali (1971), born in the United Kingdom and raised in India, Canada, and the United States, is the author of several books of poetry, essays, fiction and cross-genre work, including most recently *Sky Ward* (poems) and *Fasting for Ramadan* (essay/diary), as well as a translation of Iranian poet Sohrab Sepehri. He is Associate Professor of Creative Writing and Comparative Literature at Oberlin College.

Talvikki Ansel (1962) is the author of *My Shining Archipelago* (1997), winner of the Yale Series of Younger Poets Prize, and *Jetty & other poems* (2003). Her poems have appeared in *Orion, Poetry,* and *The Yale Review.*

Jennifer Atkinson (1955) is the author of four collections of poetry, most recently *Canticle of the Night Path*, which was selected by Susan Stewart for the 2012 New Measure Poetry Prize. She teaches in the MFA program at George Mason University in Virginia.

David Baker (1954) is author or editor of fourteen books, including *Never-Ending Birds*, winner of the 2011 Theodore Roethke Memorial Poetry Prize, and *Radiant Lyre: Essays on Lyric Poetry.* He is Poetry Editor of *The Kenyon Review* and teaches at Denison University and in the MFA program at Warren Wilson College.

Jill Bialosky (1957) is the author of three books of poems and two novels. A memoir, *A History of a Suicide: My Sister's Unfinished Life*, appeared in 2011. She is a book editor at W. W. Norton and lives in New York City.

Suzanne Buffam (1972) is the author of two collections of poetry, *Past Imperfect* (House of Anansi, 2005) and *The Irrationalist* (Canarium, 2010). Born and raised in Canada, she lives in Chicago.

Jennifer Chang (1976) is the author of *The History of Anonymity.* She co-chairs the advisory board of Kundiman and is an Assistant Professor in Creative Writing and Literature at Bowling Green State University.

Allyson Clay, cover photograph. Allyson Clay lives and works in Vancouver, B.C. Canada. Her works are in public collections across Canada including the Vancouver Art Gallery and the Art Gallery of Ontario. She has been the beneficiary of many awards including Senior Artist Grants from the Canada Council, the Mexico/Canada/USA artist exchange residency, and the Rockefeller Foundation Bellagio Residency Program. She is represented by the Katzman Kamen Gallery, Toronto, Ontario.

Michael Collier (1953) teaches in the Creative Writing program at the University of Maryland. His sixth book of poems, *An Individual History*, was published in 2012 by W. W. Norton. He is director of the Bread Loaf Writers' Conference.

Randall Couch (1954) edited and translated *Madwomen: The Locas mujeres Poems of Gabriela Mistral*, winner of the Poetry Society (UK) biennial Popescu Prize and one of two finalists for the PEN Award for Poetry in Translation. An administrator at the University of Pennsylvania, he teaches poetry writing and poetics at Arcadia University.

Stephen Cushman (1956) is the author of four books of poems, most recently *Riffraff* and the forthcoming *The Red List* (both with LSU). He is also the author of two works of literary criticism and a book about the civil war, and he is General Editor of the newly released fourth edition of *The Princeton Encyclopedia of Poetry and Poetics* (2012). He is Robert C. Taylor Professor of English at the University of Virginia.

Kate Daniels (1953) lives in Nashville, Tennessee, where she is Professor of English and Director of Creative Writing at Vanderbilt University. She is the author of four books of poetry, and of numerous essays and articles on contemporary poetry. She also teaches writing at the Washington D.C. Center for Psychoanalysis.

Kyle Dargan (1980) is the author of three collections of poetry, *The Listening, Bouquet of Hungers*, and *Logorrhea Dementia*. He lives in Washington, D.C., where he teaches Creative Writing and actively participates in the local writing community.

Claudia Emerson (1957) is the author of five books including *Late Wife*, winner of the Pulitzer Prize and, most recently, *Secure the Shadow*. Emerson has been awarded fellowships from the National Endowment for the Arts, the Library of Congress, and the Guggenheim Foundation. Former Poet Laureate of Virginia, she teaches at the University of Mary Washington in Fredericksburg, Virginia.

Monica Ferrell (1975) is the author of *Beasts for the Chase* (Sarabande), winner of the Kathryn A. Morton Prize in Poetry, and a novel, *The Answer Is Always Yes* (Random House), named one of Booklist's Top Ten Debut Novels of 2008. A former Wallace Stegner Fellow and Discovery/*The Nation* prizewinner, she directs the Creative Writing program at Purchase College.

David Francis (1982) is a Ph.D. candidate in Romance Languages and Literatures at Harvard University. He was a Fulbright Fellow in Colombia, and has recent translations in *Guernica: A Journal of Art and Politics, Inventory,* and *The FSG Book of Twentieth-Century Latin American Poetry.*

Gabriel Fried (1974) is the author of *Making the New Lamb Take,* named a top ten poetry collection of 2007 by *Foreword* magazine and the *St. Louis Post-Dispatch.* He is Poetry Editor at Persea Books.

Alice Fulton (1952) received a 2011 Award in Literature, "to honor exceptional accomplishment," from the American Academy of Arts and Letters. Her books include *The Nightingales of Troy: Connected Stories, Cascade Experiment: Selected Poems,* and *Felt,* which received the Bobbitt Prize for Poetry from the Library of Congress.

Rachel Hadas (1948) is Board of Governors Professor of English at the Newark campus of Rutgers University. Her new book of poems is *The Golden Road* (Northwestern University Press, 2012). Her book about her husband's illness, *Strange Relation: A Memoir of Marriage, Dementia, and Poetry,* was published in 2011 (Paul Dry Books).

Brenda Hillman (1951) is the author of eight collections of poetry, the most recent of which are *Pieces of Air in the Epic* (2005) and *Practical Water* (2009). She is Olivia Filippi Professor of Poetry at St. Mary's College of California. She lives in the San Francisco Bay Area. She maintains a web presence at www.blueflowerarts.com/brenda-hillman

Edward Hirsch (1950) is the author of eight poetry books, including *The Living Fire: New and Selected Poems* (2010), and four prose books, among them *How to Read a Poem and Fall in Love with Poetry* (1999), a national bestseller, and *Poet's Choice* (2006).

Jane Hirshfield (1953), a Chancellor of the Academy of American Poets, is the author of seven books of poetry, most recently *Come, Thief* (Knopf, 2011), four books collecting the work of poets from the past, and a now-classic book of essays, *Nine Gates: Entering the Mind of Poetry.*

Mark Jarman (1952) is the author of *Bone Fires: New and Selected Poems.* He has also published two books of essays about poetry, *The Secret of Poetry* and *Body and Soul: Essays on Poetry.* He is Centennial Professor of English at Vanderbilt University.

Laura Kasischke (1961) was born in Lake Charles, Louisiana, and raised in Grand Rapids, Michigan. She has published eight collections of poetry and eight novels. She received the National Book Critics Circle award for her collection, *Space, In Chains.* She lives in Chelsea, Michigan, with her husband and son, and she teaches at the University of Michigan.

Jennifer Key (1974) is author of *The Old Dominion,* winner of the 2012 Tampa Review Prize for Poetry. Her prizes include a Henry Hoyns Fellowship at the University of Virginia and a Diane Middlebrook Fellowship at the University of Wisconsin. She teaches at the University of North Carolina-Pembroke and edits *Pembroke Magazine.*

L.S. Klatt (1962) has published work in *The Believer, Boston Review, Colorado Review, FIELD, Columbia Poetry Review, The Cincinnati Review, New Orleans Review, Best American Poetry*, and elsewhere. His second collection, *Cloud of Ink*, won the Iowa Poetry Prize and was published by the University of Iowa Press in 2011.

Joanna Klink (1969) is the author of three books of poetry, *They Are Sleeping, Circadian*, and *Raptus*. Her works-in-progress include a fourth book of poems and a lyric meditation on Paul Celan, called *Strangeness*. She is a recipient of a Rona Jaffe Writer's Award and the Jeannette Haien Ballard Writer's Prize.

Hank Lazer (1950) has published seventeen books of poetry, including *Portions, The New Spirit*, and *Days*. Lazer's seventeenth book of poetry *N18 (complete)*, a handwritten book, is available from Singing Horse Press (http://singinghorsepress.com/titles/n18). Audio and video recordings of Lazer's poetry can be found at http://writing.upenn.edu/pennsound/x/Lazer.html

Paul Legault (1985) is the co-founder of the translation press Telephone Books and the author of three books of poetry: *The Madeleine Poems* (Omnidawn, 2010), *The Other Poems* (Fence, 2011), and *The Emily Dickinson Reader* (McSweeney's, 2012).

Bailey Lewis, interior book design. Bailey Lewis is a fiction writer and graphic designer. She is finishing her MFA in fiction at the University of South Carolina.

Willie Lin (1987), who received her MFA from Washington University in St. Louis, works as a writer and editor in Madison, Wisconsin.

Maurice Manning (1966) was a Guggenheim fellow for 2011-2012. His fourth book of poetry, *The Common Man*, was a finalist for the Pulitzer Prize in 2011. Manning teaches in the MFA Program for Writers at Warren Wilson College and at Transylvania University in Lexington. He lives in Kentucky.

Cate Marvin (1969) is the author of two books of poems, *World's Tallest Disaster* (2001) and *Fragment of the Head of a Queen* (2007). Her third book of poems, *A Trembling*, is forthcoming from Norton in 2013. A Whiting Award recipient, Marvin is an Associate Professor in Creative Writing at the College of Staten Island, CUNY.

Heather McHugh (1948), a 2009 MacArthur Fellow, teaches intermittently at the University of Washington in Seattle and at the MFA Program at Warren Wilson College. She founded and administers a non-profit, CAREGIFTED (http://caregifted.org/), to give away to full-time caregivers of disabled family members week-long vacations in spectacular settings in Washington state and Downeast Maine.

Erika Meitner (1975) is the author of three books of poems, including *Ideal Cities* (HarperCollins, 2010), a 2009 National Poetry Series winner. Her poems have appeared in *The New Republic, VQR, Tin House, The Best American Poetry 2011*, and elsewhere. She is currently an Associate Professor of English at Virginia Tech.

Carol Muske-Dukes (1945), poet, novelist, essayist, and literary critic, is the author and editor of nearly twenty books, most recently *Twin Cities: Poems* (Penguin, 2011), now in its second printing. Her novel *Channeling Mark Twain* has been optioned for film, and she is currently finishing a play. Among her many awards and honors was the Poet Laureateship of California.

Amy Newman (1957) is the author of four books, most recently *fall* (Wesleyan) and *Dear Editor* (Persea). She is Presidential Research Professor at Northern Illinois University, where she teaches poetry writing, and modern and contemporary literature.

Meghan O'Rourke (1976), poet, editor, and critic, is the author of two books of poems, *Halflife* (2007) and *Once* (2011). *The Long Goodbye: A Year of Grieving*, a memoir, appeared to wide acclaim in 2011.

Eric Pankey (1959) is the author of nine collections of poetry, the most recent of which is *Trace* (Milkweed Editions, 2013). He is Heritage Chair in Writing and Professor of English at George Mason University. A new collection of poems, *Crow-Work*, is due from Milkweed Editions in 2015.

Kiki Petrosino (1979) is the author of *Fort Red Border* (Sarabande, 2009). An Assistant Professor at the University of Louisville, Petrosino teaches Creative Writing and co-edits *Transom*, an independent on-line poetry journal. Her latest collection, *Hymn for the Black Terrific*, will be published by Sarabande in 2013.

Carl Phillips (1959) has written twelve books of poetry, most recently *Silverchest* (FSG, 2013) and *Double Shadow* (FSG, 2012), winner of the Los Angeles Times Book Prize. He teaches at Washington University in St. Louis.

John Poch (1966) is Professor of English at Texas Tech University and has published three poetry collections, most recently *Dolls* (Orchises Press, 2009). For ten years he was the editor of *32 Poems Magazine*. His poems have appeared in *Paris Review, The Nation, Poetry, Agni, Yale Review* and other journals.

Bin Ramke (1947) has published eleven books of poems, most recently *Tendril* (Omnidawn, 2012). He teaches on occasion at the School of the Art Institute of Chicago, and holds the Phipps Chair at the University of Denver, where he was for seventeen years editor of the *Denver Quarterly*.

Srikanth Reddy (1973) is the author of two books of poetry—*Facts for Visitors* and *Voyager*—and a scholarly study, *Changing Subjects: Digressions in Modern American Poetry*. A graduate of the Iowa Writers' Workshop and Harvard University's doctoral program in English, Reddy currently teaches at the University of Chicago.

Michael Rutherglen (1983) is the 2012–2013 Amy Clampitt Resident and a founding editor the *Winter Anthology* (winteranthology.com). His poems have appeared in *Poetry* and *The Southern Review*.

Mary Ann Samyn (1970) is the author of five collections of poetry, including, most recently *Beauty Breaks In* (New Issues, 2009) and *My Life in Heaven*, winner of the 2012 FIELD Poetry Prize (Oberlin College Press, 2013). She teaches in the MFA program at West Virginia University.

Philip Schultz (1945) is the author of a memoir, *My Dyslexia* (Norton, 2012), and seven poetry collections, most recently *The God of Loneliness, Selected and New Poems* (Houghton Mifflin Harcourt, 2010) and *Failure* (HMH, 2007), for which he won the 2008 Pulitzer Prize. He founded and directs The Writers Studio, a private school for fiction and poetry, with branches in Manhattan, Tucson, San Francisco, Amsterdam, and online, now in its 25th year.

Sarah Schweig (1984) is the author of *S*. Her poems have appeared in *BOMB Magazine*, *Black Warrior Review, Boston Review, Painted Bride Quarterly, Western Humanities Review,* and *Verse Daily*, among others. She received Columbia University's David Craig Austen Memorial Award for poetry. She lives in Brooklyn.

Allison Seay (1980) is the author of a collection of poems, *To See the Queen*, and recipient of a 2011 Ruth Lilly Poetry Fellowship. She has served as the Arrington Poet-in-Residence at the University of Mary Washington in Fredericksburg, Virginia."

Ravi Shankar (1975) is the Pushcart Prize-winning author/editor of seven books, chapbooks and anthologies of poetry, including W.W. Norton's *Language for a New Century: Contemporary Poetry from Asia, the Middle East & Beyond*. He founded and edits *Drunken Boat*, teaches in Hong Kong & Connecticut, and is working on a memoir.

Ron Slate (1950) is author of *The Incentive of the Maggot* (Houghton Mifflin, 2005), which was nominated for the National Book Critics Circle Prize and the Lenore Marshall award. His most recent book of poems is *The Great Wave* (Houghton Mifflin Harcourt, 2009).

R. T. Smith (1947) is Writer-in-Residence at Washington and Lee University, where he edits *Shenandoah* and teaches in the English Department. His books of poetry include *Messenger* and *Outlaw Style*, both recipients of the Library of Virginia Award in Poetry, and *The Red Wolf*, just released by Louisiana Literature Press. He lives in Rockbridge County, Virginia.

Mary Szybist (1970) is the author of two books: *Granted* (Alice James Books, 2003), which was a finalist for the National Book Critics Circle Award, and *Incarnadine* (Graywolf Press, 2013). She lives in Portland, Oregon, and teaches at Lewis & Clark College and the Warren Wilson MFA program.

Larissa Szporluk (1967) is the author of five books of poetry. Her new book, *Traffic with Macbeth*, was published in 2011 by Tupelo Press, and her poem "Sunflower" appeared in *Best American Poetry 2012*. The recipient of a 2009 Guggenheim Fellowship in poetry, she teaches Creative Writing at Bowling Green State University in Bowling Green, Ohio.

Brian Teare (1974), a former NEA fellow, is the author of *The Room Where I Was Born, Sight Map,* the Lambda Award-winning *Pleasure,* and *Companion Grasses,* forthcoming from Omnidawn in 2013. An Assistant Professor at Temple University, he lives in Philadelphia, where he makes books by hand for his micropress, Albion Books.

William Thompson (1956) was born in Jackson, Mississippi. He attended Millsaps College and completed his graduate studies at the University of Virginia. He teaches at Troy University, where he edits the *Alabama Literary Review.*

David Wojahn (1953) was born in St. Paul, Minnesota. His eighth collection of poetry, *World Tree,* appeared from the University of Pittsburgh Press in 2011 and received both the Library of Virginia Award for Poetry and the Lenore Marshall Prize of the Academy of American Poets.

Charles Wright (1935) is the recipient of a number of literary prizes, including the Pulitzer Prize and the National Book Award. Wright lives in Charlottesville, Virginia, where he recently retired from the English Department of the University of Virginia. His most recent book is *Bye-and-Bye, Selected Late Poems.*

Ye Chun (1973) is the author of two books of poetry, *Lantern Puzzle* (Tupelo Press, 2013) and *Travel Over Water* (Bitter Oleander Press, 2005), as well as a novel in Chinese. Her translation of Hai Zi's poetry, *Wheat Has Ripened,* is forthcoming from Tupelo in 2013.

Claire Zoghb, cover design. Claire Zoghb's first collection, *Small House Breathing,* won the 2008 Quercus Review Poetry Series Annual Book Award. Her chapbook, *Dispatches from Everest,* is forthcoming. A graphic artist and book designer, she is Graphics Director at Long Wharf Theatre.

Copyright Acknowledgments

Index

A

Abba Agathon 141
The Academy of American Poets 123
Adorno, Theodor 68
Aesop 140
Afghanistan 33
AGNI 83
Ai 83
Albion Books 57, 149
Ali, Agha Shahid 12, 84, 100, 122
Ali, Kazim 9, 12, 19, 142
Allbery, Debra 12, 100
Alvarez, Al 170
Amazon.com 190
The American Foundation for Suicide Prevention 170
Amherst College 122, 252
Amherst, Massachusetts 101, 121, 252
Ammons, A.R. 14, 126, 200
Anagram 118
Anderson, Rob 82
Anderson, Wes 235
Andrews, Tom 106
Ansel, Talvikki 259
Antinoff, Steven 163
Apollinaire, Guillaume 106
Archilochus 231
Arigo, Christopher 33
Aristotle 170
Armantrout, Rae 84, 123
Arts & Academe 11, 14
Ashbery, John 65, 106, 126, 127, 200
Asheville, North Carolina 100, 101, 102
The Asthma and Allergy Foundation of America 173
Atkinson, Jennifer 56
Atlantic Monthly 122
Atria 171
Auden, W. H. 47, 65, 178, 199
Ausable 107
Australia 46
Avedon, Richard 149

B

Bachelard, Gaston 45, 111, 138, 184, 185, 251, 253
Baker, David 29, 132
Bang, Mary Jo 123
Barnes, Djuna 77
Barth, John 265
Barthes, Roland 13, 62, 68
Bashō 126, 162, 163, 164
Baudelaire, Charles 251
Bauhaus 67

Carter, Jimmy 230
Carver, Raymond 200
Cassian, Nina 200
Cavafy, Constantine 62, 76, 105, 179
Celan, Paul 23, 58, 118
Cezanne, Paul 126, 204
Chang, Jennifer 19, 63
Char, René 58
Chave, Anna C. 57
Checkhov, Anton 115
The Chester Beatty Library 61
Chicago, Judy 123
Christie, Agatha 177
The Chronicle of Higher Education Review 11-15, 118
Chu Yün-ming 26
Clement, Olivier 141
Clinton, Bill 61, 97
Clinton, Hillary 61, 189
Cloud, Judith 190
Cocteau, Jean 73, 166
Coleridge, Samuel Taylor 12, 22, 236
Collier, Michael 189
Columbia University 178
Commonplace book 177
Copeland, Aaron 228
Couch, Randall 67
Crane, Hart 19, 128, 232
Creech Airforce Base 33
Creeley, Robert 123, 126
Cushman, Stephen 15, 35, 200
Cyclone Yasi 46

D

Da Corregio, Antonio 56
Dahl, Roald 252
Daniels, Kate 92
Dargan, Kyle 90
Davis, Miles 204
Da Vinci, Leonardo 153
Defoe, Daniel 106
De la Cruz, Juan 205
Deleuze, Gilles 65
De Man, Paul 232
De Quincy, Thomas 251
Dickel, George 110
Dickens, Charles 177, 252
Dickey, James 259
Dickinson, Emily 12, 13, 18, 19, 24, 44, 50, 54, 62, 76, 84, 100, 101, 105, 106, 107, 111, 120, 121, 122, 123, 126, 132, 139, 152, 168, 170, 178, 184, 185, 187, 198, 203, 205, 211, 218, 228, 229, 231, 232, 252, 259, 260, 266
The Emily Dickinson Homestead 121
The Emily Dickinson Lexicon 100
The Emily Dickinson Museum 252
Digges, Deborah 170

LISA RUSS SPAAR   283

S

W

Y

Z